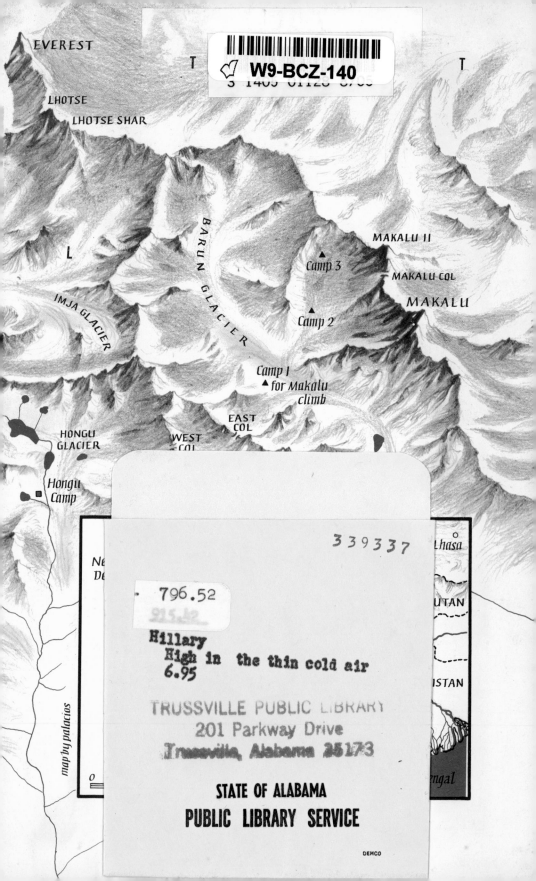

EVEREST

LHOTSE

LHOTSE SHAR

T   T

L

BARUN GLACIER

MAKALU II

Camp 3

MAKALU COL

MAKALU

IMJA GLACIER

Camp 2

Camp 1
▲ for Makalu
climb

EAST
COL

HONGU
GLACIER

WEST
COL

Hongu
Camp

Ne
De

map by palacios

O

Lhasa

UTAN

ISTAN

engal

HIGH
IN THE THIN COLD AIR

HIGH
IN THE
THIN COLD AIR

The Story of the Himalayan Expedition,
led by Sir Edmund Hillary, sponsored
by World Book Encyclopedia

SIR EDMUND HILLARY
and DESMOND DOIG

DOUBLEDAY & COMPANY, INC., GARDEN CITY, N.Y., 1962

Library of Congress Catalog Card Number 62–15860
© 1962 by Field Enterprises Educational Corporation
publishers of WORLD BOOK ENCYCLOPEDIA
All Rights Reserved
Printed in the United States of America
First Edition

PREVIOUS BOOKS BY
EDMUND HILLARY

HIGH ADVENTURE

EAST OF EVEREST
*an Account of the New Zealand Alpine Club
Himalayan Expedition to the Barun Valley in 1954*
[*With George Lowe*]

BOYS' BOOK OF EXPLORATION [*Editor*]

CHALLENGE OF THE UNKNOWN [*Editor*]

CROSSING OF ANTARCTICA
[*With Sir Vivian Fuchs*]

NO LATITUDE FOR ERROR

PREFACE

This is the story of the Himalayan Scientific and Mountaineering Expedition 1960–61. Desmond Doig, our press correspondent, expert linguist, and lover of the Himalayan peoples, tells of the search for the elusive Yeti and of all we learned of the lives, customs, and mythology of the Sherpa people. I, in turn, relate how we built the "Silver Hut" at 19,000 feet and wintered a group of scientists in it, how we reached the summit of the "unclimbable" Amadablam, came to grips with the rock and ice precipices of Mount Makalu's 27,790 feet, and gave a school to Khumjung.

In the compiling of this story we have used material from the accounts of expedition members directly involved in each phase —in particular Michael Gill, Norman Hardie, Leigh Ortenburger, Tom Nevison, and Peter Mulgrew.

The expedition could not have been undertaken without the full and generous financial support of Field Enterprises Educational Corporation, publishers of World Book Encyclopedia, whose interest in our scientific work and the Yeti legend showed a spirit of adventure worthy of such an undertaking.

Our primary objective, the physiological program, was developed under the guidance of the British Medical Research Council who gave considerable aid with equipment and personnel. Dr. L. G. C. E. Pugh, a senior physiologist on their staff, was director of our physiological program and leader of the wintering party. The U. S. Air Force and the Wellcome Trust also supported the physiological research.

Many organizations and individuals helped us to mount the expedition and for this we are grateful. I feel I should mention the following for substantial aid and for special equipment to be tested under the severe conditions of the Himalayan winter:

The National Geographic Society, for financing the expedition's glaciological program; the Building Research Station, Garston, nr. Watford, England, the Timber Development Association Limited, London, and J. M. Jones and Sons Ltd., Maidenhead, England, all of whom were concerned with the design and construction of our hut; Armour & Co. of Chicago, and the Food Research Establishment of the British Ministry of Agriculture, Fisheries and Food, Aberdeen, for freeze-dried foods; the British Petroleum Company for all fuels and for developing and supplying our cooking and heating equipment; Head Ski Co., Inc., for skis; Evans Medical Ltd. for medical supplies; and the Indian Aluminium Co. for donating the building we carried to Khumjung for the school.

SIR EDMUND HILLARY
Expedition Leader

CONTENTS

Part II OUR LIFE IN THE CLOUDS
by Sir Edmund Hillary

ILLUSTRATIONS

PART I

IN SEARCH
OF SNOWMEN

1

KATHMANDU

The festival carts roll through Kathmandu. September the ninth, the procession of Indrayatra, of virgin gods and goddesses. An auspicious time to begin anything.

It rains, intermittently, so that half the valley glows jewellike in sunshine and the other is dark below bruise-blue clouds and veils of rain. The distant snow peaks, "our mountains," are revealed in bright flashes like tilted mirrors. "That's Gauri Shankar, and that Numbur, Ganesh Himal, Himal Chuli, Langtang"—we follow pointing fingers and thrill to the knowledge that soon we will be among those distant towers of snow, mountains already so familiar they insinuate themselves into our dreams and our thinking. We smile condescendingly when a tourist points out the 22,000-foot summit of Chobutse and, told it is Everest, goes crazy with cameras and telephoto lenses. We even encourage the untruth. "Yes, that's Everest all right," we say and feel cosy because of our superior knowledge and the sudden doglike gratitude on a millionaire tourist's face.

Kathmandu, when we arrive, is feverish with festival. In the vast holiday confusion our untanned legs, weird outfits, and embryo beards, all hallmarks of the about-to-be adventurous, are happily blurred and unaggressive. Even Ed Hillary goes occasionally unrecognized. There is the morning when a tourist in a climbing outfit comes up to the table where Sir Edmund and I breakfast.

"Say, would you guys like to drive out toward Everest?" he asks, talking directly to Ed.

Thinking we have a brash multimillionaire on our hands who wants nothing less than Sir Edmund as companion for his first glimpse of Everest, I concentrate on my toast and leave policy to Ed. Ed, busying himself with an omelet, leaves policy to me.

The tourist tries again.

"Do you know you can see Everest from just six miles out of Kathmandu? I'm taking a taxi and thought you guys would like to share it with me. Have either of you seen Everest?"

Ed begins choking on a wedge of toast. I choke in sympathy.

An old Nepali professor met within moments of arrival assures me. "You will have good luck—you will probably meet the Yeti. Certainly you must meet my friend, Major Punya Bikram Rana." I do, and Major Rana tells me of a friend of his who is quite a Yeti expert, having seen a Snowman. This friend would like to help us with our plans to capture one, but alas, he's two hundred miles to the northwest at the moment and, "That is quite a formidable distance in this unhurried land."

So the major writes the name of his friend in my notebook and also a short introductory note. "You must please help Mr. Doig; he is an old and true friend." I have known the major for only ten minutes, if that, but such is Nepal. Friendliness is second nature to its people; time is often measured by warmth of feeling.

Ours was not the first expedition concerned with the Abominable Snowman. Others have devoted their entire energies to try to prove or demolish one of the world's most popular and likely legends, a legend that has the remote, high reaches of the Himalayas inhabited by giant anthropoids with human faces, man's cunning, and often man's sense of humor.

Our expedition's interest in the Snowman was secondary to high-altitude physiological research and meteorological, radiation, and glaciological studies. On the other hand, we did carry out an extensive search in areas associated with the Snowman legend and over a much longer period of time than any previous expedition had been able to devote to the purpose—and probably, I believe, with more impartiality.

OBJECTIVE

Our objective in the first part of the expedition was to establish or disprove the existence of Yetis. To do this we would examine every available clue: legends, accounts of Yeti sightings, Snowman relics, Snowman tracks in the snow. We would try to photograph Yetis, using powerful camera lenses and self-operating cameras activated by trip wires. If possible we could record the Yetis' commonly heard call: the high, whistling noise that our expedition Sherpas had apparently heard. Certainly we could observe them through our extremely powerful viewing glasses. Our ambition, of course, was to capture a live Snowman, though I am certain that none of us knew quite what we would do with the beast if we succeeded in making one prisoner. Hillary had more than once expressed himself opposed to keeping Yetis in captivity.

"I would be inclined to let the creatures go after thorough examination. I think there is precious little in civilization to appeal to a Yeti," he once said.

Our Paraphernalia

"Capchur" guns were our heavy artillery, sporting rifles and shotguns our light arms.

Capchur guns are powerful air rifles that fire drug-filled hypodermic syringes over fair distances. They can knock out a muskrat as easily as they can a mule, a squirrel as effectively as a Snowman. But it takes an experienced operator to know exactly what quantity of the drug is required per pound weight of animal.

Once anesthetized by a capchur gun syringe, animals, however ferocious, allow themselves to be captured, examined, medically treated, and generally tampered with.

The government of Nepal has a law forbidding the killing of Snowmen. None of us particularly wanted to shoot one. But we carried conventional rifles in self-defense as most accounts of the Yeti describe it as being savage in the extreme. Also in our armory were tear-gas pistols the size of fountain pens, calculated to repulse sudden animal attack. I was interested to discover that these were originally designed to protect women in the two-legged-wolf-infested jungles of civilization.

Self-operating tripwire cameras must be included among our weapons. If the shy Yeti would not allow us the opportunity to use our Capchur guns on him, we hoped he would at least stumble over our trip lines and photograph himself.

I was disappointed to find no nets, traps, or folding cages among our Yeti hunting equipment. Marlin Perkins, our zoologist, had deliberately excluded these from our essential requirements because he was aware that Sherpas are excellent trappers and was prepared to rely on their methods. On an expedition such as ours, where everything had to be carried on the backs of porters, bulk and weight are enormously important considerations. As things turned out, we never felt the need for traps and cages. Wire netting and packing cases made excellent cages for the red pandas, a langur, and a Tibetan fox cub we acquired. If we had captured a Yeti, Sherpa ingenuity would have soon contrived an adequate cage.

We took along some assorted animal calls that sounded for all the world like children's trumpets at a Christmas party. Our Sherpas could do a much better job of imitating local animals.

AREA OF OPERATIONS

In 1951 the famous mountaineer-explorer, Mr. Eric Shipton, saw and photographed Yeti tracks in the Menlung glacier in northeastern Nepal. The Sherpas of Solu Khumbu, the area directly south of Mount Everest and not far removed from the Menlung, have told of seeing and hearing Yetis ever since they began accompanying Western climbers on expeditions to their own mountains. As a result, the Sherpa country in high northeast Nepal can be considered the most likely Snowman country, and three exclusively Snowman expeditions had explored it before we did.

Our expedition, as already explained, had interests other than Yetis to consider. Any area of operation decided upon must be suitable for high-altitude physiological research, have a great mountain (preferably one already climbed with the aid of oxygen) on which to test the effectiveness of long acclimatization, as well as promising a prevalence of Snowmen.

Ed Hillary wisely chose the Rolwaling and Solu Khumbu areas of Nepal. Mount Makalu, 27,790 feet, the world's fifth highest mountain, climbed brilliantly by the 1955 French expedition, using oxygen, provided the culminating test of our physiological research. The research itself was carried out in specially designed huts on a glacier south of Mount Everest at

15,000, 17,500, and 19,000 feet, and up to 26,000 feet on Makalu itself.

In convenient proximity to our selected mountain and glacier were the wild, unfrequented valleys of the Rolwaling and Solu Khumbu areas in which the Yeti probably lived and the high snow-covered peaks and passes on which it left its footprints.

FANCY EASILY BELIEVED

So here we are in Kathmandu. Outside the hotel musicians are being propelled through the street by the blast of their own music. Drum and cymbal, horn and drum, drum and flute, and discordant bells. Nepali drums are provocative, compelling things, and it is easy to imagine the hotel servants shedding their discipline with their laundered white to whirl like dervishes between the tables and tourists as the drums thud by.

Why not? Half of the valley population is being dragged through the streets by the Pied Piper music, willy-nilly, flowers behind their ears, giggling, clapping their hands, and singing. A youth tells me that angels crowd the air, and gods, too, because even gods love a down-to-earth good time. It is fancy easily believed. Magic is always around the corner in the old wooden city of Kathmandu. The gods in a million sculptures do understandably human things. They are everywhere, on temples and palaces, above doors and windows, and holding up unholy balconies. Painted all-seeing eyes watch every street; every square and fountain has its host of deities and legendary creatures, winged lions guarding temple precincts, angels in attitudes of praise and prayer, ram-headed eagles and dragons with elephants' trunks. Nowhere in the city is one removed from the presence of gods or religious fancy. So when festivals weave their powerful spell, the gods live and gilded lions stretch and breathe flame. Garudas soar on vermilion wings. And golden serpents adorning temple roofs flick jeweled tongues.

The chariots roll, and in them are virgin children representing deities, children recognized as reincarnates and brought up to believe that they are gods. At puberty they are turned out into the world of ordinary men. Others take their place. What, one wonders, happens to a retired god?

They are beautiful children, petal-fresh with youth and dignified beyond their years with their unnatural upbringing. Tradition paints them like ballerinas, their almond eyes so exaggerated with finely drawn mascara that they appear perpetually surprised. Vermilion and sandalwood paste plastered on their foreheads imparts to them a look of unreality so they may be butterflies or exotic birds enmeshed in the golden finery of their clothes and tremulous headdresses.

All the year round they are confined in a temple in the heart of Kathmandu, close by the ancient palace of the first Gurkha kings. Very occasionally it is possible to catch a glimpse of one peeping from a carved and gilded window, no more.

But today they are carried, like the children they are, through the streets and they sat with great pomp and ceremony on the decorated chariots. To the thousands who throng the lanes of Kathmandu and crowd the multi-tiered plinths of the city's numerous temples, these children are gods. As they are drawn through the streets money and rice are showered upon them in offering. Bands play again—did they ever cease? And masked dancers in grotesque wigs of scarlet yak hair prance through the streets like agitated feather dusters.

CYPRUS BRANCH ONLY

The expedition fills five rooms of the Royal Hotel. Our mountainous paraphernalia is heaped on the hotel tennis courts; our Sherpas are in boardinghouses in the bazaar. Housed in a whitewashed Rana palace, the hotel has been a temporary home to almost every expedition to the Nepal Himalayas since it went into business.

Once there were only a dozen palatial suites with three bathrooms so large one felt lonely in the bathtubs. When I first visited Kathmandu in 1956 I occupied a room in the hotel that had attached to it the most popular of the three bathrooms. I retired early the first night but hardly slept. Every now and again there would be a tap on the door and someone would clump or tiptoe through the room to my bathroom. One intruder was a heavenly blonde with a foreign accent. I thought to be friendly; after all, it was my room. But she was in a hurry. "No, no," she whispered. "I need zi bog, I need zi bog." She dashed on through.

Now there are forty-four rooms of more prosaic proportions, and rumor (never to be discredited in Kathmandu) has one of the old bathrooms a modern honeymoon suite. The hotel gives climbers a generous reduction on stiff tourist rates and only recently began charging people seriously for their stay. Its founder-owner, Boris Lissenovitch, and his beautiful Danish wife, Inger, launch every willing expedition in bouts of alcohol, good wine, and excellent music. Boris not only is a great character but one of Nepal's greatest monuments. Everyone knows him; he knows everybody, and there is nothing he can't arrange or advise on. A white Russian, he has been artist, ballet dancer, night-club owner, hotel chef, circus hand, soldier, adventurer, in fact, just about everything that sounds glamorous.

He has a mother-in-law who is all romance and effervescent good humor, five foot in her heels and permed hair, as voluptuous as a temple carving. "Why do you want to go up those cold mountains, darling?" she asks Hillary. "Doesn't your poor wife feel lonely?"

Exposed to each other for the first time, with few exceptions, members of the expedition are reputation-conscious. If any of us want to chase helter-skelter after drums and be enchanted by the magic of Kathmandu *en fête* we resist temptation. Ed Hillary announces he has seen it all before and there is work to be done. We take the hint.

But we find time to join knots of people outside the hotel that became swarms in the city streets and multitudes in the principal square, and since conscience demands a good excuse, we take our cameras along and begin threatening the stock of expedition film. Two larger-than-life figures adorn a city temple during the days of festival. Made of bamboo and wool, one depicts a wild man of the forest and the other his amply bosomed mate. To the Nepalese they are "Ban Manchhuru." To our Sherpas and to us, for by now we're subscribing to Sherpa mystique, the figures represent Abominable Snowpeople. We photograph them *ad nauseam*.

But mostly we take pictures of the curious who stand endlessly in front of our cameras. A film is to be made of the expedition's activities, and Fred Niles, of Fred A. Niles, Inc., Chicago and Hollywood, has flown into Kathmandu to direct early operations and give advice. Fred, one suspects, is of the urgent breed that have telephones by their bathtubs and are

constantly wired for useful sound. He cuts through the multicolored confusion of festive Kathmandu like an icebreaker
through a lily pond in full bloom and somehow shoots film without a single intruding head, hand, or bicycle. He holds confer-
ences around dining tables when the hotel bar is closed and in
the bar when it is open to business—Cyprus brandy only. He has
a secretary. She is beautiful.

OBESITY AND SPORTS CLOTHES

I had met Sir Edmund Hillary in the Royal Geographic Society in London a couple of months before. The occasion had
hardly appeared auspicious for an interview which would decide whether or not I would accompany the expedition. I had
come straight off an Air France Caravelle from a Parisian holiday, full of free champagne and in French sports clothes completely inadequate for the English weather and the occasion. I
weighed something near 220 pounds and found talking and at
the same time holding my breath to keep a sagging stomach in
reasonable shape difficult. Sir Edmund was magnificent. He
ignored alcoholic fumes and obesity in what may have been a
personal save-a-soul-through-mountaineering campaign. After a
brief fifteen minutes in the presence and another fifteen waiting in the tearoom while Sir Edmund thought me over, I was on.
The good woman serving tea noticed my state of nerves and
offered me a cup with the assurance that it would be all right.
I am certain she did not know what I was there for. Perhaps
there was a vacancy for some obscure job in the building and
she considered me a candidate.

SIR EDMUND

Hillary in Kathmandu is a robot with an unruly mane but
still one of the most casual, immediately likable persons I have
met. He knows character instinctively and is never in a hurry
to impose the force of his own, which is considerable. On the
contrary, he is sympathetic in the extreme to other people's
foibles and peccadilloes in the way Orientals are, so that I believe his Himalayan adventures have collected the dust of the

acceptance and understanding that are the substance of Sherpa Nepal. Or perhaps I'm being too romantically Oriental myself and the secret of Hillary's rugged good nature is that he's an incurable individualist so certain of himself that he can afford to be sure of others. Because of its nature and its objectives this is the first Himalayan expedition with which Ed has been concerned that includes "arty types" (a Hillary definition) among its serious mountaineers. If Ed despairs at this evil necessity, he does not show it. He leaves our overfed frames and decadent minds to the 120-mile walk from Kathmandu to our 12,000-foot base camp in the Rolwaling Valley. He even pampers us in Kathmandu so that the mountaineers among us help him with the gigantic task of sorting through the thirty tons of expedition stores and equipment while the rest of us, the uninitiated, sort out our own difficult affairs—whether to sacrifice foot sprays and bath salts for cans of beer, and custom-built boots for the expedition clodhoppers, for example, or take the lot and die under the load. Does one ever know what a load is like until one is under it? And has walked with it a mile, five miles, eight, fifteen? Does one suspect that elegant hiking shorts bought with a wife or girl friend in a moment of distant and deep-freeze heroism are not quite designed with an Eastern sun and Nepalese leeches in mind? But a well-filled rucksack and highly colored shorts look good at the start of adventure and the tourists and one's ego, at least, are taken in.

"ARTY TYPES" AND MOUNTAINEERS

My immediate companion in innocence is John Dienhart. Thirty-eight, crew-cut and glib, and representing our sponsors, the World Book Encyclopedia, Chicago, John had shopped in New York and gone skiing in the Argentine in preparation for the expedition. His personal kit could equip a small expedition, and it looks as colorful as a Fifth Avenue shop window. He has pep pills and tranquilizers, foot freezers and foot warmers, dental floss and perfumed face cleaners, tissues, ointments, aids for the fainthearted, Bermuda shorts, the lot. He had reluctantly left his gay social whirl behind in Chicago but soon discovered party-giving U. S. Government workers in Kathmandu. One insisted on giving us a send-off celebration the night before the great trek, and John and I had reason to remember Gloria's friends and their excessive hospitality during the heavy-headed, foot-blistering miles of the next day's march.

"Oh hell, Des. This is the *first* day of a *nine*-month expedition. I don't dig this jazz," John kept saying, as we dragged our-selves up hills and skidded painfully down others. "Why, oh, why did I get involved in all this?" He knew well enough, of course. It had been partly his idea.

As the Public Relations Director of the World Book Encyclo-pedia, his over-all publicity objective was to make it clear that his encyclopedia was a participant in history-making events of current interest. He felt that the other reference works were merely reporters of events after the fact, and "pretty dull" ones at that.

After meeting Hillary in Chicago he sold his management on sponsoring the expedition, and he was along on the Yeti hunt to handle radio and press communications. John felt he was in pretty good shape after winters skiing and summers spent racing star-class sailboats. He repeatedly cussed this rash decision dur-ing the first few tortuous days of the trek.

In the arty group with John and myself are Marlin Perkins, director of the Lincoln Park Zoo, Chicago, TV personality, au-thor of animal books, over fifty, suave and with the kind of gray-haired good looks that sells expensive shirts in advertising, and Dr. Larry Swan and Bhanu Bannerjee. Marlin has left a bride of a few days behind him and appears to be keeping his mind off romance by studiously photographing anything and everything of interest and nosing out local animals. Dr. Larry Swan, who describes himself as a "Himalayanist," interested in everything from gnats to giant pandas and the threatened disappearance of the true Nepalese lizard, was born in India and schooled in Darjeeling. He speaks Hindustani well and has that plump cheerfulness and breezy manner that makes friends of anyone and everyone, instantly. Larry has discovered creatures where hoteliers swear they don't exist and has us all insect conscious before we set foot in the wilds. His idea of the Yeti is decidedly apelike. In fact, Larry is all set to capture a rare mountain gorilla provided, of course, that our luck holds and Yetis have not become extinct during the last few years.

Bhanu Bannerjee, a Bengali and the only Indian member of our Yeti hunting team, joined the expedition at the last min-

ute as a general aide largely to supervise the business of communication. A distinctly low-altitude type (his home town in
Bengal is thirty feet above sea level), Bhanu had some Himalayan experience when he accompanied me on a trek through
Bhutan in 1959. His family were understandably apprehensive
when Bhanu, whose initial job with the expedition required him
to go as far only as Kathmandu, wrote and informed his parents
that he was off to climb to at least 19,000 feet and hunt Yetis at
that. Few Bengali youths of twenty-three get involved in adventure of this kind, so Bhanu's father can be sympathized
with when he writes and begs me to keep an eye on his son who
"as a Bengali is unaccustomed to such high regions and beasts
like the Snowman."

As I've confessed, John, Larry, Marlin, Bhanu, and I are the
arty types whose endurance and capabilities will be judged
somewhere along the tortuous trail ahead of us. The strong back-
bone of the expedition is made up of old Hillary associates like
the bearded George Lowe and Norman Hardie, conqueror of
Kanchenjunga; Peter Mulgrew and Wally Romanes, who have
been with Sir Edmund in the Antarctic; Mike Gill and Pat
Barcham, successful young New Zealand climbers; Dr. Tom
Nevison, an American space physiologist who has been on a
Karakoram expedition; Barry Bishop, American glaciologist and
climber; the "doctors" (our scientists); and the high-altitude
Sherpas, by no means least.

Norman Hardie is something of a legend, having just emerged
as the author of a book on Sherpas; besides, it is no mean person
who battles up a peak like Kanchenjunga, the world's third
highest mountain and long considered impossible, and then in
respect of local sentiment leaves the last few tantalizing feet
unscaled. Norman and his companion did, and the gods of
Sikkim remain appeased as a result. To Norman has fallen the
task of recruiting our Sherpas and our army of Nepali coolies,
and it is to his credit that we leave Kathmandu with "the
strongest team of Sherpas ever"—Ed Hillary's estimation.

George Lowe has accompanied Hillary on numerous expeditions, to Makalu and Cho Oyu, and to the Antarctic, and his
contribution to Sir Edmund's success on Everest has been ac-
knowledged as indispensable. I believe George's strength as a
mountaineer is in his sparse frame—he could pass as an aesthetic
or a famine victim—his clockwork stride, abundant good humor,

and his capability of going to sleep anywhere, anytime, anyhow. Hardly would we come to rest during a day's scrambling before George would disappear under an umbrella and set his beard twitching in sleep. This feat he could accomplish standing up, sitting, or lying down, and as a result his nervous system was at peace with the world while the rest of ours shredded and twanged. George is a schoolmaster—almost perpetually on long leave for adventure—in Repton Public School, England.

My first impression of Peter Mulgrew is of a Disney character, a rejuvenated Father Christmas sans beard and belly. This may have to do with the scarlet cap he seems always to wear and the fact that as keeper of the stores he is perpetually dispensing largesse. Brimful of natural good humor, Peter has the polish of quarterdeck wit, being a sublieutenant in the Royal New Zealand Navy, "a dirty British sailor, that's me."

Peter was later to pay a high price for his courage and determination on Makalu, a price I have heard many people question or dismiss as unnecessary. If ever I needed to understand what causes men to climb high mountains, Peter Mulgrew's gallant struggle below the summit of Makalu is half the answer. The other is the experience of walking behind Hillary, watching his huge feet in relation to the distant wedge of Mount Everest, and trying to insinuate myself into his thinking as he looked upon "his" mountain, the peak so utterly remote and unassailable, that once was under his size 12 boots.

RADIATION AND SPIRITUAL HARMONY

On the hotel tennis court and in two of the hotel rooms preparation keeps long hours. Crates of stores and equipment are being sorted and reduced to sixty-pound loads, the weight, no matter in what shape it comes, a Nepali porter can conveniently carry. There are the gleaming sections of the Silver Hut, like anti-tank devices, curved and metallic, each designed as a porter load. I find it impossible to believe that these will be forged into a gale-proof, electrically lit, snugly warm laboratory on some 20,000-foot spur in which our scientists will brave out a Himalayan winter.

We are fitted for boots and crampons and overboots like punctured elephant's feet. We try to scrounge the extra woolen

2. Some of our 500 porters and 500 loads at the end of the road at Banepa. From here on, all transport is on foot.

3. A monsoon strikes a camp at 7000 feet, on the way to the Rolwaling Valley.

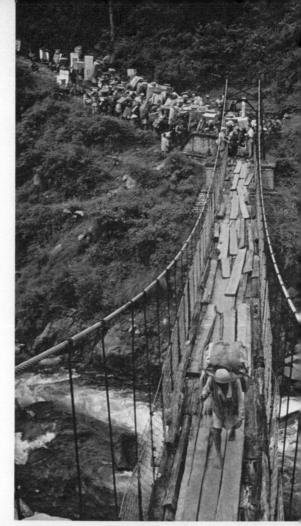

4. (RIGHT) *One of the more substantial bridges within four days' march of Kathmandu.* 5. (BELOW) *After heavy rain this stream became a turbulent flood. We heavy Westerners established ourselves in midstream and helped our lighter porters to cross.*

6. *A typical Sherpa house. The mountain in background is Khumbila, the sacred peak of Khumjung.*

7. (TOP) *A Mane wall (prayer wall) inscribed with the Buddhist prayer Om Mane Padme Hum.* 8. (BOTTOM) *Nepalese houses of the better type—these are at 5000 feet.*

shirt, wriggle into full-length underwear, make airy—we hope professional—passes with new ice axes, and pore over maps.

There are parties. At the British Embassy, where we leave our names in a visitors' book that reads like a guide to mountaineering in the central Himalayas; in the home of the American ambassador, where I sit next to a woman who has spiritual experiences. "You must try to believe, going barefooted helps, the earth's radiation, you know. Have you ever felt you are experiencing something familiar, as for the second time? That has to do with radiation and spiritual harmony. . . ." And at the Indian ambassador's residence, where we eat off silver plates and by candlelight and discover our hosts to be the most delightful of people. Mr. and Mrs. Hariswar Dayal have spent many years in the Himalayas and have journeyed to Lhasa where they met the Dalai Lama. Their official residence is hung with a set of beautiful Tibetan scroll paintings, and Mrs. Dayal explains that there is only one other set like it in existence. She promises to visit us at our Base Camp. "I want to go high, really high. I love high mountains."

We have our blood taken for examination; we are given little containers of multicolored vitamin pills for the long trek in, and we have briefings.

There will be two parties, one to hunt the Yeti in the Rolwaling Valley and the other to find a site for and erect the winter laboratories at 18,000 feet and 20,000 feet on the Everest region. Hillary will lead the Yeti hunters, Norman Hardie the hut builders. I will go Yeti hunting, and I note with some satisfaction that our party will reach Base Camp in twelve days. Norman Hardie's will stagger along for eighteen, maybe more, before settling somewhere near Thyangboche, the monastery village within ten miles of Everest. The few of our scientists already arrived will accompany Hardie. Others still in England will join us when the Yeti hunt is done and the unpredictable Himalayan winter begins to lay siege to our laboratory huts.

Slowly we get to know each other. I want to know about the huts and Ed sends me to Wally, who apparently is the expert. Wally Romanes is a professional housebuilder when not being a fine mountaineer. He has the enviable quality for remaining unruffled under the most trying conditions, a quality that was to be fully appreciated on Makalu when everything seemed to be going wrong all at once. Such men as Wally, Mike Gill, and Pat

Barcham are among life's unsung heroes who work a great deal
and say little. If Ed Hillary did not assure one that they were all
brilliant climbers they were apt to pass quietly as expedition
mules who worked like frenzy and never complained. In our
first Base Camp Mike Gill almost died of pneumonia, in our
mess tent, with all of us sitting about and jabbering. But apart
from thinking that he looked pretty spent, none of us knew how
seriously ill Mike was. Certainly he never fussed. On the contrary, only a fortnight after recovering he was climbing strongly
and had his eyes firmly on an impossible 19,000-foot rock tower
above the camp.

It was Tom Nevison's association with rockets and flying
chimpanzees that captured the imagination so that the press
and merely curious attached to him like sucker fish to a whale
and left the rest of us alone. Tom, who was a captain in the
United States Air Force, had brought an American flag along
with him and he unfurled it with ceremony above his tent every
night. Dienhart and I appeared regularly at the tent, peered
through the flap, and inquired whether this was the place to
vote. In time the flag disappeared.

Turquoise Earrings and Climbing Boots

Earlier than usual one morning we are pried from our beds
to meet our Sherpas. They are lined up on the hotel tennis court,
a gay, ragged lot who look anything but the tough and heroic
characters they have become known to be. Most of them wear
the clothing of previous expeditions: scarlet Japanese silk, saf-
fron cotton, turquoise blue English nylon, multicolored wool.
Gold pendant earrings and occasional plaits of well-greased hair
look incongruous among heavily padded jackets, woolen trousers, and boots. There are even a few striped pajama suits that
are startling. And necklaces. But the smiles are uniform, spontaneous, infectious.

We are introduced first to Dawa Tenzing, our sirdar, a patri-
archal figure of indeterminate age who exudes personality and
alcoholic fumes. This obviously is an occasion, and we make
ourselves equal to it by remembering the discarded niceties of
Victorian good manners. We are to learn that every occasion

with old D.T. is a special one, even when excessive drinking has
temporarily unseated his enormous reserve. Dawa Tenzing is
old-school Sherpa, with plaited hair and attempting mandarin
whiskers. With a fine record of mountaineering—he was with
General Bruce on Everest and has been on some great mountain
every year since 1952—Dawa is on the verge of retirement, possibly into a lamasery. The old man is deeply devout and has already given two of his daughters to a nunnery and most of his
property to the great monastery at Thyangboche. Described by
the 1952 Swiss Everest Expedition as the "King of Sherpas,"
Dawa Tenzing would do better as a dictator. As benign as he is
wise, he can be something of a terror when his authority is even
remotely questioned, and I have seen many a hard-boiled
Sherpa become jelly before the wrath of the old sirdar. Dawa
has known tragedy. In 1958 when he and his eldest son were
with separate expeditions, he on Everest, his son on Jugal Himal,
rumor had his wife believe that both husband and son had
been killed in an avalanche. Quite overcome with grief, she
walked down to the river below her village and hurled herself
in. It was Dawa who had to bear with double tragedy. When
he returned to Khumjung he heard that his son had in truth
perished in an avalanche. And his wife was dead.

Dawa Tenzing's deputy and stepson and leader of our Yeti-
hunting Sherpas is Urkien, who has an engaging habit of wid-
ening his eyes when he laughs, and he laughs often. Urkien is
tougher than the proverbial horse and a very experienced
climber. But he has one unfortunate failing, an incapacitating
temper that almost got the expedition into serious trouble before
it was properly launched. The fiery local brew called chang is
generally fuel to his rage. But Urkien is a lovable, intelligent
person when he's sober, and I've enjoyed his company, discussing things like religion and reincarnation and the need for
Sherpa education, by the hour.

Three other Sherpas imprint themselves on my memory:
Pasang Tenzing, my personal Sherpa, who has a toothy smile
and the figure and agility of a ballet dancer; Aila, a lanky long-
haired individual with protruding teeth detailed to John Dienhart, and Nima Dorje, our cook, who looks as young and as smart
as an army recruit. Nima apparently is alive by sheer good
chance. On expedition with the Swiss to Dhaulagiri, he had

plummeted three thousand feet down an ice slope when he and four others on the one rope had been caught in an avalanche. In his own words, "The snow came boom, boom, boom, like a herd of yaks stampeding. We went down head over heels, sideways, spinning, rolling, and the snow was exploding and showering all about us. I was quite blind with the snow in my eyes and so dazed I thought I was dead. Then we stopped. Our rope had got wedged over a rock. Four of us, all Sherpas, were partly buried in snow; one was hanging over a precipice, but all seemed unhurt. There was a sahib and he was deeply buried but alive; he kept shouting. Slowly we freed ourselves from the snow, but the sahib could not move. He was next on the rope to me, and I was fearful because he did not move and delayed us. Snow kept avalanching onto us and there was danger of a large slide sweeping us away again over the precipice. Should I cut the rope?" Fortunately both sahib and Sherpas survived the ordeal, and Nima went on to reach the summit of Dhaulagiri. He was then nineteen.

John Dienhart is rather horrified by Aila's looks. "Oh hell, Ed, must I have him? I mean, he looks kinda savage, and those teeth: get a load of those ivories." Unable to remember Aila's name, John has hit upon a musical gimmick, "Aila Paris in the Springtime." I would have given a great deal to know what Aila had to say about John and the jazzy dispensary he had to carry for his sahib when the trek began.

2

TREK

Peter Mulgrew was in hospital with dysentery; half a dozen others were not feeling too good. Bhanu Bannerjee was chasing packing material in Patna. He and Peter would follow us later. Something was discovered wrong with the cameras, and it was feared that they might have to be rushed back to the States. Essential stores were in the coldhearted grip of the Indian Customs in Calcutta. I personally found reducing my needs for ten months to two loads of sixty pounds each impossible.

But we moved. Somehow the days of confused activity in Kathmandu blossomed into a mobile, even efficient, machine.

There came a dawn when uniformed hotel servants called us early with the last tray of morning tea we were to see. Our Sherpas took our packs even as we packed them. Some of us managed breakfast—others spent their time being photographed, heroically, adventurously, and saying good-by, innocent of the blood, blisters, and tears ahead, in a uniform better than anything since one's days with Boy Scouts and buoyed up with that most inflatable of all personal elations, self-importance. Someone had brought beer along; the cans were stood like skittles on a jeep hood, and we swigged it down with mist still lying on the lawns and day still behind the eastern wall of the valley.

Transport took us through the streets of Kathmandu, gaping, bemused, vaguely interested, along a rough but beautiful track to Bhatgaon, one of Kathmandu Valley's ancient capitals. In a square piously looked down upon by several temples some people were beating a dog to death. Apparently it was mad.

At Bhatgaon we met our porters, a uniform gray of unrecognizable people, saw our baggage shouldered, felt good, were rephotographed, and took transport again, for Banepa, our first day's halt. In fairness let me say that some expedition members walked to Banepa, a hot, dusty eight miles. We who rode got there faster and with less effort, but the deeply gouged road, if such it can be called, gave our jeep and we who rode it such hell about our livers, knees, and wrists that we suffered no pangs of conscience.

Banepa is the last big village in the Kathmandu Valley. It is a typical Nepali town: ancient, rusty-brown, tiled, and punctuated with gilt-roofed temples. Its unexpected Seventh-day Adventist hospital, raised and cared for by Dr. Stanley Sturges of Santa Rosa, California, delayed our break with civilization for a few hours. We spent the evening with Dr. and Mrs. Sturges, sitting on settees, our feet on a carpet, and munching chilled fruit from our last refrigerator.

First Day Out

We walked out of Banepa with a swing. The morning was perfect, full of cool shadows and racing sunlight after rain. We had eaten well and the country was only gently undulating. John and I were behind the porters so our pace was slow, almost negligible. If this was to be the extent of our daily exertion the months ahead would be a picnic. How quickly were we disillusioned. After climbing to a low pass we found ourselves above a valley that was miles across—the far side so far that villages were like clusters of sequins in the fabric of forests and fields. We were to make our camp that night by a river, and obviously it was the one below us and far enough at that.

"No," said Urkien, who was now driving the porters to greater speed, "tonight's camp is beyond that ridge there, in the clouds." He pointed into the distance. "We may have our tea break by this river." Murder. This was impossible. It was unjust. And of course it was a joke. But Urkien had hurried on, driving the porters before him, and John, Marlin, Larry, and I were left on the pass, wondering why the hell we were there at all.

"Hope to hell we get back," said Larry, making a swipe at a yellow butterfly with one of his nets. "Here, would you like to catch things for me, bugs, beetles, spiders, butterflies, anything interesting?" I accepted a net from Larry and we stumbled on down the track. Fortunately the mist closed in and we couldn't see our distant goal any longer. Psychologically it helped; our feet were now our pedometers, and mine registered capacity long before we reached the river and our lunch. I was so weary I sat on a nest of red ants and didn't budge until they swarmed all over me. George, lucky fellow, was asleep.

The rest of that first day was agony. It never seemed to end; the track would go on forever, always around one more bend, and another and another, and the sun burst on us when we were at our most weary, so that we sweated and got miserably thirsty and there was no water to drink. We somehow survived the afternoon and were still walking in the evening. A waterfall saved us. We stripped and stood under it until energy returned to our bodies. Then we staggered on until there at last was the river and our camping site, our tents already up and the smoke from our campfires trapped in a grove of trees. It was late and suddenly dark. "Not a bad day," said Ed when he came in—he had started hours after us. "Tomorrow is a real bugger."

UNSHAVED AND BLISTERED

No other day was quite like that memorable first. We grew blisters and we got bored. We let the stubble develop on our chins and became blasé about our appearances. Even though we subconsciously resisted it—cursing the sun, the rain, the ups, the downs—we fell for the magic of Nepal, on the second, and the third, and the umpteenth day. The vastness: looking suddenly for miles through windows in the mist. The silence: hearing a jackal cry on another mountain, and in the night waking to feel the vibration of the stars. And beauty: of terraced fields on the limbs of mountains, trees wearing orchids, flowers, and prayer flags beside cairns of stones.

In a hilltop village a marriage party straddled the track, men on one side, women on the other. They engaged in a sort of singing duel, as if the success of the marriage depended on it. Our passing did not interrupt the ceremony, rather added to it. A few verses of song were hastily ad-libbed: "The bottom of the horse and he who rides it are the same size. Tonight the sahib will have blisters on his seat. The horse will have a broken back, Aiii, Aiii." John Dienhart and Marlin Perkins had taken to horses for a day (picked up at a nearby village and sent back at the first river), John suffering a wrenched knee and Marlin painful blisters.

On and on through forests and across bare wind-swept ridges, through lush rice fields and surprised villages, across torrents spanned by a single log and across rivers on chain bridges fashioned by local blacksmiths and chance. We toiled up slopes we normally would ignore, lungs bursting and souls despairing, and down slopes we normally would leave to avalanches and the insane. Always there was beauty to take our flagging minds off the weary business of endlessly walking, and the pains and frustrations of endless walking to take our minds off the beauty of our surroundings.

We probably smelled, by accepted standards of hygiene.

Days began early, and our umbilical cord with everyday luxury was slashed when we dispensed with the ritual of tea in bed, newspapers, a leisurely bath, and clean clothes on the very first day out of Kathmandu. If water was handy and we hadn't packed the soap and towel in some depthless sack at that very moment being spirited away by a porter eager to get on with the day's heavy grind, we washed. Toothbrush and tooth paste were carried with immediate necessities like pen, water-purifying tablets, toilet paper, and chocolate. There were complaints, growing daily more faint, that time and conditions did not even allow a quick swill of the mouth. But that, probably, was an exaggeration.

Trekking as one treks on an expedition is a selfish affair. It's your feet that matter, your weary shoulders, your ability to keep up with the rest—and damn the others. If the popular image is a happy serpent of talking people winding away into a rose-tinted distance, it's hideously distorted. After the first hour of march every man is as self-contained as a snail, occupied and bounded with his own thoughts, his own distress, his own preoccupations.

Only our baths and meals were communal. Since the porters thought us mad anyway, our nude floundering in icy streams caused no surprise and only a little embarrassment.

I wait for the day when a Sherpa turns his camera on a wallowing of naked sahibs and a Sherpa anthropologist tries to explain the phenomenon.

We began to suffer visions: of chilled beer, feather beds, and warm baths, and the silly visions of easily carried dehydrated ice, of effortless levitation, and oxygen pills. Was this altitude? When on a parched ten-hour walk one eliminated wine, beer, chilled martinis, and settled for a vision of cold water, there were no streams, or they ran lukewarm. When iced water cascaded about, as it does above 8000 feet, it was hot toddy and chocolate in tall steaming glasses that occupied our dreams.

There was plenty of drama in those first days: Sir Edmund bravely facing the rugged 120 miles with his size 12 feet crammed into size 11 tennis shoes. He had taken pains to see that everyone else was properly fitted and overlooked himself. (Tennis shoes are light, give good traction in normal conditions, and dry easily.) Do size 12 feet make brilliant mountaineers?

And infants brought to Dr. Tom, their bodies puffed up like water-filled balloons, their faces pinched and solemn. At one of our halts a father brought two such children. "Will one live?" he asked. "Let this one die, but save the other." Hard? Cruel? Inhuman? The father himself was wasted with malnutrition. All he could feed himself and his children on was the native beer—a potent brew made from rice. Tom Nevison learned to ask all cases of unnatural puffiness whether the cause was "chang." Inevitably it was. Children are fed chang to keep them quiet but as often because it is the only "food" available to a pathetically poor family.

There was the old Gurkha soldier cheerfully striding out on a particularly difficult stretch of track that crippled most of us— with a false leg. He had lost it in the last war, in Burma, fighting the Japanese. And there was the day when as we crossed it a stream flooded as a result of torrential rain in the mountains above us. To our heavily laden coolies this was a dangerous obstacle. The rushing water was waist deep and carried stones the size of tennis balls. Balance was easily upset, and to slip would mean certain loss of stores and equipment, possibly loss of life. So Hillary, Lowe, and I planted ourselves in the stream and, though not too stable ourselves, handed the porters across. Fortunately, as suddenly as it flooded, the stream subsided and we went on our way, delayed by a couple of hours.

Later the same morning we stopped for lunch in a village beneath tall trees. There was promise of tough climbing ahead; a forested spur leaped steeply from behind the house in which we rested, and zigzagging up it till lost in cloud was our track, a crazy thing designed by a mountain goat, nothing less. Watching us eat was the woman of the house and a child both strangely grave and withdrawn for the friendly local people. In the familiar way of the East I asked her if the child was hers. Yes, she said, the only one left after the calamity.

What calamity?

Only a few days previously her house had stood in terraced fields across the valley, high above the river, with a cattle shed and fruit trees and a family of eight in the earth-and-stone building. "There was my husband, my eldest son and his wife, their child, my daughter and another son. And this child, my youngest, and myself. It had rained for days and the cattle

hadn't been properly attended to. So I went out in the evening
to have a look at our cow—she was in calf—and this child ran
after me. Suddenly the earth shook, there was a great noise, and
I saw our house slide down the hillside. My husband ran out of
the house as it began to move and shouted to me. Then the
house fell about him and the whole mountain seemed to pour
down on top of it. Only my youngest child and I remain. This
is my brother's house."

We collected together a few rupees and gave them to her
without words.

There was the drama of great Himalayan peaks, shrouded
during our approach by late monsoon clouds, suddenly towering
above us on a morning of brilliant sunshine, unbelievably close,
unimaginably beautiful. And forests of writhing rhododendron,
their distorted carmine branches like a pink-stockinged, undis-
ciplined *corps de ballet* viewed at leg level. And the mysterious
scurrying of a lesser red panda, speckled blue lizards sunning
themselves on speckled blue rock, and a colorful burst of ceremony when we camped one evening in the grounds of a Buddhist monastery.

Our Sherpas prostrated themselves before an altar in the main
chapel, a room full of warm shadows and jeweled detail: serene
gods in gilded meditation, fierce gods in violently colored dis-
tortions, flickering butter lamps and peacock feathers, painted
scrolls, brocade, and lamas so deep in devotion they might have
been carved by the same hand that shaped the ornate pillars
and the shelves on which the sacred books were stacked in
silken shrouds.

When on behalf of the expedition Sir Edmund Hillary made
an offering, a boy reincarnate was brought out in all his brocaded finery, rather like a family heirloom, and posed for our
cameras in a gesture of appreciation. Six-foot horns of brass
and silver honked and blared for our benefit. Bells tinkled. It
seemed we had hardly fallen asleep when a pre-dawn service
woke us with the low chanting of prayers and the rattle of hand
drums. "*Om Mane Padme Hum* [Hail to the jewel in the lotus]."
When the sun came it was like Norbu, the flaming jewels seen in
Tibetan paintings. The sky was green. A stream ran gold.

But mostly we walked in mist and rain. The monsoon was
not yet done.

A Tomb for Massive Burial

Two days before Beding the landscape changed abruptly. The mountains closed on us; we were in rather than on them, and there was a strange feel of confinement, a powerful smell of rock and earth and rotting vegetation, the vibration of torrents and waterfalls, a sense of vulnerability as if Nature suddenly was preparing to be cruel and had forced us into a tomb for massive burial. Cliffs reared above us, their rock churned in some forgotten age, gray and steel-blue, violet and terra cotta. They were veined by milk-white waterfalls, thousands of them, as if the mountains bled their substance. So high were several of these falls that their water was dissipated in mid-air and we could pass directly beneath them and feel only a vapor on our faces and hands.

There was a bridge where the gorge was narrowest, a few tree trunks propped up on an enormous rock in midstream to form a double arch. The whole thing shook with the rush of water below it and was enveloped in a perpetual mist. We crossed and scrambled for hours up cliffs the other side on which a family of Himalayan langurs appeared to be at home. This was our first look at a possible contender for the Yeti title and the setting was perfect: perpendicular cliffs, the dense silent forests immediately below the tree line, snow peaks beyond, and a few isolated villages like humanity's outposts to record the secrets of the unknown.

A couple of weeks later, when we were established in Beding, Sherpa trappers brought us a young langur caught near these same cliffs. Its black face and jet eyes were like those of old women waiting death by the cremation ghats in holy Benares and the temple of Pashupati Nath in Kathmandu. The monkey was all sadness and chattering appeal, wrapped in a fawn coat the texture of nylon. The long tail, black hands, and feet were perpetually frozen in the cold of Beding, which made us doubt that langurs would of choice stray beyond 12,000 feet.

When one day our young langur temporarily escaped it loped away with its tail held high in the air. One of the arguments against langurs leaving "Yeti" footprints in the snow is that they would leave signs of their long tails as well. More than one person claiming to have seen a Yeti has mentioned a long, sometimes bushy tail, a detail that has dismayed ardent followers of the Snowman legend.

Our pathetic langur eventually died of a stomach complaint. The Sherpas looking after it were moved to feed the creature every time it whispered and looked more than usually sad.

WE DREAM OF MONSTERS

We were happy to reach Simigaon, a mean village of some two hundred people above the langur cliffs. It had been a difficult climb, often in chilling rain, so that when my Sherpa, Pasang Tenzing, told me that he had secured the best place in the village for my bed, I was overjoyed. While others wrestled in rain-soaked fields to pitch their tents, I lay relaxed in my sleeping bag on the veranda of the bed-sized monastery.

John Dienhart shared the monastery with me and was well pleased. "God dammit, Aila, old boy, you've done it again," he kept telling his toothy Sherpa between sips of tea, and who was more proud of the other was anyone's guess—the Sherpa of his sahib for wallowing in comparative luxury (a reflection on his own genius), or the sahib of his Sherpa for providing it.

Ed had just grunted as he passed by that we boys believed in doing ourselves well when John screamed like a peacock and flapped into the evening outdoors. I thought I heard "monsters," and there, true enough, were blue-green monsters crawling all over the monastery walls. They oozed out of great cracks and clucked in anger at our intrusion. Not a lover of giant lizards myself, I fled after John in the time it took to unzip my sleeping bag. Long after the others were abed, Pasang Tenzing and Aila were plopping about in a quagmire—the only level space available—in an effort to raise our tent. Both John and I dreamed of dragons.

From Simigaon the track climbed relentlessly. It grew more and more cold; the brief morning sun had been devoured by cloud, and mist packed the forest. It rained. And the rain was a torment, freezing and penetrating. I had long ago torn my plastic raincoat and my umbrella had snapped when I used it to brake a fall. But I was in warm clothes and the remnants of my raincoat did keep me fairly dry. The Nepali porters in contrast had the most ragged of cotton clothes. Most of them were barefooted; a few possessed threadbare blankets which they now used as waterproofs. This was one of those days when I felt acutely embarrassed to be dressed so adequately and to have a dry tent and bedding and a change of warm clothing awaiting me in camp.

Camp that evening was made immediately below a 14,000-foot pass, and though we could not see them in the forested depression we occupied, the great snow ridges of the Mahalangur Himal* were just beyond the pass. We could feel their closeness. As the evening deepened from ice-blue to sapphire the cold advanced and flung itself through the pass. We were camped in a forested depression and the cold poured into it, filled it, and froze it solid, so that the trees were of glass and the earth lead under a sugar coating of ice. The stars were wondrously bright and close that night, and Pasang said they caused the frost. Star dust on our tents at 14,000 feet, with the mountains across the valley like luminous whales in a sea of low cloud and the moon a copper disc with a silver edge.

Our unhappy porters sang and clapped their hands around a dozen fires to keep themselves warm. Tomorrow their job would be done and they could return to warmer altitudes with money in their waistbands. Tonight they could afford to sit up singing.

> Oh my brothers,
> I can see the reflection
> Of the white Himalayas,
> On the night of the full moon
> As we sit on this mountain pass.
> How can we ever forget
> The song we sing tonight?
> How to forget, my brothers,
> How to forget?

Rarely before had a Himalayan expedition employed so many porters. There were two hundred with us, over three hundred with Hardie. Old men, young men, boys, and men who would have looked happier in hospital—they were so obviously anemic or tubercular or undernourished. We knew a few of the porters

* Interestingly *langur* means ape. *Maha* means great. So Mahalangur Himal means "mountains of the great apes"—Snowmen?

by their names. Ghale, a strapping fellow like a Mongolian
David; Harkabahadur, a youth with pale looks and a keen intelligence who begged to be taken to the plains, India, anywhere, to get work where he could attend school; and Naike,
the shrew overseer who looked a crook and turned out to be
one. He drew advances on behalf of the porters, and days later
I was told he had kept the lot himself. Only a vicious form of
blackmail dissuaded the men from revolt. Naike represented
the Nepal Himalayan Society and, more, was in with it. All
porters and Sherpas must be recruited through the society in
Kathmandu. Anyone giving any trouble would never find employment again, Naike threatened. But Harkabahadur had the
angry quality of the intelligent young everywhere. He it was
who told me, and he didn't care a damn about the consequences.

Next morning we toiled to the pass, feeling for the first time
the breathlessness of high altitude. At the top was stunning reward: Gauri Shankar, the great goddess among mountains, only
a narrow valley away, so close we could hear the uneasy rat-
tling of its moraines and watch the coursing of its minor avalanches. What a magnificent pile it was, all rock and ice cliff
and brooding overhang. Its ridges were bayonet sharp, its summit like an oyster shell stood on end, pearly and fluted, and
mysteriously beautiful.

All day, as we walked up the valley of the Rolwaling, the
mountain was above us. But with every mile its character
changed, from humpbacked giant to towering sliver of ice. In
the village of Beding only one of Gauri Shankar's many ridges
is visible, and that in itself is a magnificent mountain, as thrusting and sharply pointed as a lance. We decided that there was
no way unto it.

SAVAGE YETIS AND A FRIENDLY HERMIT

Twelve years ago a great snow avalanche swept through the
village of Beding. A mother and child cowering in their small
rock-and-shingle hut were buried alive. And that, the villagers
of Beding remember, was the year Yetis were most frequently
heard, calling in their strange whistling way, quarreling through

the cold nights, and leaving their footprints in the fresh snow
every morning.

"I think they were after the corpses of the avalanche victims,"
the head lama of Beding's small but beautiful monastery told
me.

On another occasion, only two winters ago, a couple of Snowmen descended on the monastery at the time of evening prayer.
It was already dark and snowing lightly. The creatures snuff-
snuffled about the building, at one point threatening to enter
through a window. The terrified lamas clashed their ceremonial
cymbals with more than devotional fervor and the Yetis went
howling away into the night, "sounding like humans in great
pain."

Yet again some years ago a Nepali official visited Beding with
a retinue of servants and trappers. Between them they had a
vintage gun, and woe to the plentiful musk deer and pheasant
in the area. The time was winter and a light snow fell every
evening. As the head lama of Beding tells it, "The party was
settling to sleep one night when they were startled awake by
the sound of a heavy animal padding around the hut they occupied. Unmistakably it was a Yeti, and suddenly there was its
head, large as a bush, with two flaming eyes, at the window.
Not one of the party dared move, not even reach for the gun.
We lamas, hearing the din from our monastery—the Yeti was
screaming with frustrated rage—began to blow the big copper
horns, and eventually the creature took off in noisy alarm."

So the insignificant village of Beding, locked deep in a lovely
and seldom visited gorge, was an appropriate base from which
to hunt Yetis. It is small, even as Sherpa villages go, some
twenty stone houses, crudely built and strung together by a
complex of stone walls that delineate, rather than protect, the
village potato fields. The entire village, but for a finely proportioned Buddhist stupa (a dome-shaped mound, a shrine, usually built over sacred relics) of carved stone that testifies to some
local skill, might be a fall of rubble from the heights above. And
what heights! Cliffs leap dramatically upward for a thousand
feet or more and are concave so that clouds are sucked into
them to boil and be shredded and stream like ghostly waterfalls in reverse, up, up to the thrusting peaks where they are
worn like pennants. Tibet is just two miles away, over a high
pass.

There were so few people in the Rolwaling that even the villages seem deserted. And the people were quiet and unhurrying as if they had just woken from hibernation. We occupied the village green, a stretch of level weed-blown ground near the river, with the unexpected suddenness of an invasion from space. Our multicolored tents and our exotic activities were of endless interest to the villagers. They stayed with us so persistently that we suspected every family took it in turn to watch our goings on, so that not one delicious detail of our alien ways was lost to the evening gossip. In fact, the center of the village activity was now our camp.

The monastery, carved and painted and flying tall prayer flags, had emptied itself of its lamas and nuns. The local hermit descended from his hermitage, an impossible eyrie clinging to a precipice five hundred feet above the monastery. Apparently the great mystic and Tantric saint, Guru Padma Sambhava, meditated there nearly two thousand years ago, and the spot has been hallowed ever since.

It was the jovial hermit who first welcomed us to Beding. For fourteen years he had lived alone in the hermitage, giving lie to the belief that every recluse is necessarily an introvert by his friendliness and lively interest in all we did. Within minutes of our meeting he drew me aside and with an impish wink and dig in my ribs with his elbow suggested we take a drink together. We did, too, but later, when our camp was well established and day drained from the valley and the smoke from our fires formed a canopy above our tents. There were others drinking. Women from the village came and went with large pots of chang, at first surreptitiously, then openly, and the singing and laughter in our Sherpa tents got louder.

The next morning they were drunk, despite the sobering rain that fell that night.

THE QUARRY

Already established and accepted is the fact that there is not one breed of Snowmen. There are three: one very large, one medium in size, one small.

To Sherpas, and our search was made in the Sherpa highlands

of Nepal, all three breeds of Snowmen are generally known as
Yeh-teh (Yeti).

The Sherpas of Solu Khumbu, and again it was in Solu
Khumbu that we largely conducted our search, know the three
varieties of Snowman as:

DZU-TEH (pronounced chu-tay): A large (6-foot to 8-foot)
blond, red, black, or gray shaggy bearlike creature, that appears as
happy on all fours as it does on its hind legs, is vegetarian but preys
on cattle, has long claws, and is found at altitudes above 13,000 feet.

In Sherpa *Dzu* means cattle, *teh* is an ape: the inference of the
name Dzu-teh is an ape that preys on cattle.

MIH-TEH (mee-tay): A biped, the size of a small powerfully
built man, black or red in color, shaggy, with a sharply pointed head,
carnivorous and a man-eater. The male has a long mane that hangs
over its eyes. The female has noticeably pendulous bosoms. Both
have a high-pitched wailing call and often make a strange whistling
noise or chatter.

This is the true Snowman, the savage, extremely intelligent anthropoid of the high Himalayas. From all account Mih-tehs are not seen
much below 15,000 feet, are more at home above 18,000 feet. Legend
rather ruins things by having the Mih-teh's feet turned back-to-front.
Mih in Sherpa means man. *Teh* is ape. Mih-teh is "apelike man" or,
more sinister, the ape that preys on man.

THELMA (tuh-helma): A sad-faced, dwarf-sized beast, red, gray,
or black in color, found in dense forests below 10,000 feet. A tree-
climbing biped that looks like a monkey and probably is. It hoots
and often moves in large colonies. To see a Thelma is very bad luck.

The Sherpas of Langtang in north-central Nepal know their
Yeti as:

NYALMO: Giant sized (up to twenty feet tall), manlike, hairy,
and given to shaking giant pine trees in trials of strength while other
Nyalmos sit around and clap their hands. Otherwise like the Dzu-teh
and probably the same creature.

RIMI: Similar to the Mih-teh, but much larger; has yard-long
teeth and flaming eyes.

RAGSHI BONPO: A wizened, manlike creature, the size of an
average fifteen-year-old boy, found in dense forests.

Interesting here is the word Bonpo. Bonpo are priests of the
ancient Bon religion: the original cult of witchcraft and sorcery
that prevailed in Nepal and Tibet before the advent of Bud-

dhism. Ragshi derives from *rakshas*, the Indian and Nepali word for demon. So Ragshi Bonpo could be demon-wizard.

WARNING: These three improbable creatures of Langtang may be the figment of a certain powerful lama's imagination. It is from him, in Kathmandu, that visiting anthropologists, writers, and tourists have learned of Langtang's outsize Snowmen.

THE HUNT BEGINS

Over dinner—boiled Sherpa potatoes, lightly curried stew, chapatties (flat, unleavened bread, tortilla-like), tinned fruit, and Ovaltine—Ed disclosed his plans for the Yeti hunt. His idea was to set up two observation camps on each side of the valley, two sahibs, four Sherpas, and two tents to constitute a camp. The camps would be self-contained for a week so that, once established, there would be no movement around them. Each was to be equipped with powerful viewing glasses, capchur guns, rifles, and Yeti whistles. Marlin Perkins and Larry Swan, our zoologist, gave the scheme their blessing, and after three days of reconnaissance the camps were sited high up on the valley walls, just below the snow line.

In the meantime stories of Yetis and Yeti sightings poured in. A lama in the Beding monastery had seen one, black haired and powerfully built, about five feet high, "like an-idiot-man." Sadly, Beding is full of cretins. Sleeping one night near the window of his house, the lama was awakened by the sound of heavy breathing, and scratching, and a powerful stench. It could have been one thing only.

The lama began searching his mind for a protective prayer, and as his chanting grew in volume the Yeti retreated into the night. Next morning there were the familiar footprints, like a man's, only larger.

The story sounded convincing until the lama invited me into the monastery to view paintings of the Yeti. The whole building was vividly muraled: gods and goddesses in endless manifestation, Buddhist heavens and hell, the Wheel of Life, and horrifying friezes of severed human limbs. In a dark corner were a couple of strange creatures the lama said were Snowmen. They bore little relation to the popular conception of Yetis and plunged one bodily into the realm of fantasy and myth. Even an animal-headed manifestation of the god Dorji Tsempa was described by the lama as a Yetini, the female of the Snowman species.

Blood on the Gompa Steps

John Dienhart was in charge of our tape recorders. He knew their ins when they were out and their outs when they were in. He also knew the requirements of some distant complex of which most of us had never heard—"Monitor." By agreement, Monitor's countless listeners were given a blow-by-blow account of the expedition's progress on tape. John's voice intoning, "This is John Dienhart with the World Book Encyclopedia's expedition to the Himalayas led by Sir Edmund Hillary . . ." became the expedition's reveille and retreat. Everyone and everything was committed to tape. Ed Hillary was catch number one. "Sir Edmund, what comments have you to make on today's march?" "Sir Edmund, do you believe in Yetis?" "Sir Edmund, what's that you're eating?" "Sir Edmund, how do you plan to climb Makalu?" "Sir Edmund . . ." But the tapes and Ed Hillary were not fated to fuse together. Time and again a brilliant take was reduced to a series of hiccups or a length of silence when played back via the earphones. John despaired. When the recordings of a ceremony in the gompa (monastery) suffered similar treatment, John decided the recorders were faulty and new ones must be acquired posthaste. He would return to India with his faithful Aila, to make the purchase.

Ed agreed, and suddenly there was John in his red Bermuda shorts and under an umbrella, striding out for Kathmandu and looking terribly alone and vulnerable in the rain.

Two porters were to accompany him. And of course Aila.

But our Sherpas and Beding's inhabitants to a man were still drunk after the celebration in the monastery—the very celebration that defied the genius of John and our recording machines.

So when John walked bravely from the camp with only his umbrella, no one followed him. This we were to learn hours afterward, in the late afternoon, when I saw Aila still with us. But worse. Out in the middle of the rain-soaked village green were John's three loads, one containing his bedding and clothes, the other his tent and rations, and the third his private pharmacy. Even now, miles down the valley, he must be sitting under some coldly dripping tree, awaiting their arrival.

Ed was informed and he sent for Urkien, our head Sherpa. Urkien was clearly drunk but was allowed the courtesy of being considered sober, was ordered to do something, hiccuped, and withdrew. Nothing happened.

An hour later John's loads were still there, looking forlorn and more wet. There was much noise from the direction of the gompa but no sign of life. So Ed and I decided to investigate. Halfway to the monastery we met Urkien, smiling happily and in a state close to levitation. It's all, all right, he told us, shoving me playfully in the chest; the porters would be leaving immediately. But Ed and I decided to walk on, and we were immediately below the monastery when there was an explosion of people: lamas, nuns, and drunken villagers. Out of their midst staggered a man. He was frightful to look at.

Blood streamed down his face and over his clothes. A white messy substance, obviously his brains, slopped all over with the blood. The apparition moaned and came straight at us.

"I'm dead," it said. "He killed me."

The crowd built a solid wall about the drama. We were closed in tightly with something frightful, something sinister. I asked what had happened. No one spoke. Then Urkien lurched into the arena and, giggling stupidly, said the man was mad, we should take no notice of him.

The crowd found its voice and said one of our Sherpas had hit the man with a log. "He's dying," they chanted.

Who, we asked, was responsible? All our Sherpas were there now, but none of them answered. They shuffled, looked vacant; Urkien giggled. The crowd demanded justice. It pressed on us; it threatened; it began chanting, "Blood for blood." Then suddenly a child materialized beside the bleeding man and, pointing dramatically at Urkien, screamed, "This is the man who killed my father." As if some animal judgment had been pronounced, the crowd fell silent. It waited, a wall of bodies, limp arms, and expressionless eyes. The boy was very small, Urkien as large and strong as a bear. The wall of people sucked breath through its teeth. And waited. For a moment I thought Urkien was going to hit the boy. But he only giggled.

We got the man and his son and Urkien and our Sherpas
back to our camp, fighting a verbal rear-guard action all the
way. We even got Aila and two porters, all very drunk, to
stagger away under John's loads. But the villagers were far from
appeased. They had produced an eloquent spokesman, a lama,
and he kept demanding justice, mob justice, since not only had
Urkien killed a man but apparently had caused blood to flow
in a monastery. "There is blood on our gompa steps and Urkien
must cleanse it, with his blood."

Happily we were able to correct the boy's and the lama's and
the villagers' inaccuracy. The man had not been killed. Dr. Tom
Nevison had made a good job of a five-inch head wound—the
"brains" had turned out to be ash, a lama remedy for bleeding.
To prove our point we produced the assault victim, looking
groggy but cheerful. The man, who we nicknamed Splitso, was
our guest for two days and nights. "He might be done in by
bad characters in the village to get you into trouble," my friend,
the hermit, advised. So he and his wife and children occupied a
tent near mine, and I hardly slept because of the limitless attempts at assassination I imagined at night.

At the end of two days Splitso was fit enough to carry expedition stores on his head. Urkien was sober and repentant. The
prosecution lama, who we dubbed "Blood on the Gompa Steps,"
came asking for work and got it, and all was well with the world.
But it had been a narrow shave. Trouble like this can have an
expedition's permit withdrawn. It also can leave behind animos-
ity that other expeditions will reap.

It was some time before we discovered what had caused the
trouble—our Sherpas were either too loyal to Urkien or too afraid
of him; I suspect the latter. The two porters who were to carry
John's loads had decided to celebrate whatever was being celebrated with everyone else. They soon were drunk—and that's
allowing them ever to have been sober. Until Urkien got a blast
from Ed (when I discovered John's abandoned loads), they all
had been pals in alcoholic togetherness. Then, in one of those
chain reactions so well known in the army where the colonel
strafes the major and the major the captain and captain the
lieutenant and the lieutenant the senior non-commissioned officer
—all the way down the well-defined ladder of rank until the
final rung is reached—the mess boy or the bugle boy, Urkien
conducted Ed's wrath, adding a great deal of his own. People

were pushed about; one yelled at another. One stupidly got in
the way of Urkien's direct venom. He was pushed over and
kicked. Then he received a *coup de grâce* with a large hunk of
firewood. Testimony to the toughness of Sherpa skulls is the fact
that Splitso kept his intact. Anyone else's would have split wide
open, like a walnut under a hammer.

Aila saw John through to the next village. By that time the
two porters arrived, sobered, and Aila returned to the expedition. John worked for two months, flying back and forth to
Calcutta, freeing our skis, scientific equipment, and radios from
customs, got the new recorders and sent them on to us. Then he
had to return to the States.

3

FURS AND FOOTPRINTS

From my reports and diaries.

Beding. October 1—We are wildly excited. And all because of
the friendly old hermit of Beding. This morning, in a sudden
impetuous show of affection, he slipped his hand into mine and,
drawing me aside from a group of locals with whom I was
discussing the Snowman, whispered, "There is a Yeti fur in the
village."

In a moment we were surrounded by people and our exciting, unexpected conspiracy had to end there—one of the most
tantalizing moments of my life.

Is there really a Yeti fur in the village? Was the lama drunk?
(Impious thought.) Did the whole strange affair happen at all?
Because even as he spoke the lama was aloof and walking away,
and my efforts to resume confidences met with an inscrutable
smile—and silence. I have told Ed and he is jubilant. Marlin
and Larry have been summoned from their observation camps.
Although it is supposed to be hush-hush—too much excitement

and interest may jeopardize our chances of buying the fur—
everyone seems to know. Ed tells me George will be back by
nightfall with his cameras to photograph the trophy. But we have
to acquire it first.

October 2—This morning, in another burst of sentimentality,
the head lama added a few more conspiratorial fragments to
yesterday's bombshell.

The Yeti fur is owned by a nun. She lives in a house close by
the monastery. Her husband is away, and in his absence she
might deny owning the pelt. On the other hand, she might let
us see it for a price.

Would she sell it?

The old man was immediately a sphinx in magenta robes,
aloof, smiling a Mona Lisa smile and apparently struck dumb
with shock. Another chapter in the strange affair was obviously
closed.

This afternoon I decided to visit the monastery accompanied
by Bhanu Bannerjee and one of our Sherpa runners, Ang Temba,
who in a week's association I have come to appreciate as a
Houdini-cum-Mandrake in Sherpa clothing. Temba is an engaging character, small even for a Sherpa, with cross-eyes, a nose
that sweats abundantly when he is excited, and a crackling
laugh. He is up to his uncombed hair in the Beding Yeti conspiracy. He has been promised a bonus if we get the fur.

Our invasion of the monastery was something of a holdup.
The old lama, for once alone, indicated the owner of the fur—a
gentle, middle-aged nun wearing turquoise and coral in her ears,
who had been attending Tom Nevison's impromptu dispensary
every morning because of sinus trouble.

Ang Temba went into the attack. The nun in almost pained
surprise first denied having the fur or knowing anything about
it. Bhanu and I closed in, making pleading noises; Ang Temba
more bluntly started naming prices.

At this delicate moment the inevitable inquisitive crowd
closed in, the nun began telling her rosary and walked distantly
away, and chapter three in our little drama came to an end.

October 3—Today a new bombshell. Some of the other lamas
of the monastery have obviously got wind of our interest in the
"Yeti" fur. With quick, unholy profit in view, and unknown to

the nun, they burst into our camp today and offered a look at the fur for Rs.1000* ($132).

Ang Temba was hurriedly dispatched to contact the nun, to persuade her to make an outright and quick sale before the lamas trespassed onto her preserve. We waited—and waited, and then Ang Temba returned to say the nun would see me, alone.

I went, covered by one of our viewing glasses, past the houses of the opposition lamas, past the monastery, surreptitiously, and into the nun's small house. As I entered the rock-walled courtyard, Ang Temba, who had preceded me, closed and bolted the wooden gate behind us by laying a heavy log against it. A holdup? I had a bag of expedition money with me and no hope of secreting it in my clothes.

I was invited into the house. It was pitch-black, full of unseen snares and whispers. Ang Temba and the nun were in urgent conversation; money was a frequently used word.

I could see the fur for Rs.1000 ($132), Ang Temba explained at last.

How was I to know it was a Yeti's?

It was a Yeti's, the nun insisted.

Could I buy it outright?

Haggle haggle. No, but I could see it for Rs.500 ($66).

Could I buy it outright?

No, but I could see it for Rs.200 ($27), and no further reduction.

Could I buy it outright for Rs.250 ($33)?

No.

Rs.300 ($40) then, and no further increase.

Haggle haggle, and then finally the fur was being pulled from a box made of semi-cured yak hide, a dark fur with a golden glint to it and an ivory band across the shoulders.

It was the fur of a rare Tibetan blue bear.

"Yeti, Yeti," the nun insisted, and already Ang Temba was stacking our rupees into painstaking piles of ten. The money paid, the fur was stuffed into an old potato sack. On top were arranged a few boiled potatoes. Our nun was obviously equal in primitive cunning to the opposition lamas.

As we left, passing the monastery, there was the old head lama, smiling his unfathomable smile. If he knew, our secret was in good hands.

* Nepali rupees, worth at that time, 7.6 to the dollar.

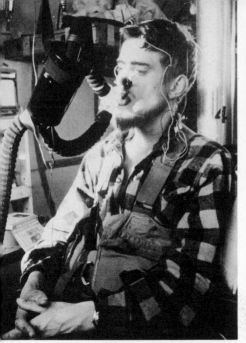

9-10. *Scientific tests: tubes and wires recording the effects of altitude.*

11. *Dr. Milledge checks the effects of vigorous bicycle pedaling on Bishop's heart and lungs.*

12.

15.

13.

16.

14.

17.

12. *Michael Gill on the left and Wally Romanes preparing dinner in the Silver Hut.* 13. *Christmas in the Silver Hut—back from left: Milledge, Romanes, Gill. Front: Nevison, Bishop.* 14. *George Lowe cutting Hillary's hair in Rolwaling.* 15. *Hillary holding hand of child who is a reincarnate lama. Outside Risingo Monastery.*

21.

22.

0.

23.

16. *Cooling off during march-in; Hillary in middle and Nevison on right.* 17. *Mulgrew.* 18. *Hillary and Ortenburger operating small radio.* 19. *Glacialogical work.* 20. *Special jacket equipment.* 21. *Wind speed indicators at Silver Hut.* 22-23. *Setting up the tent, starting preliminary tests.*

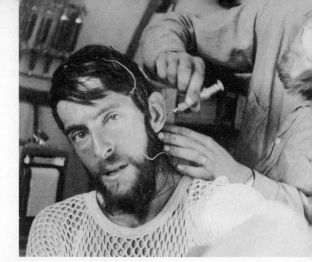

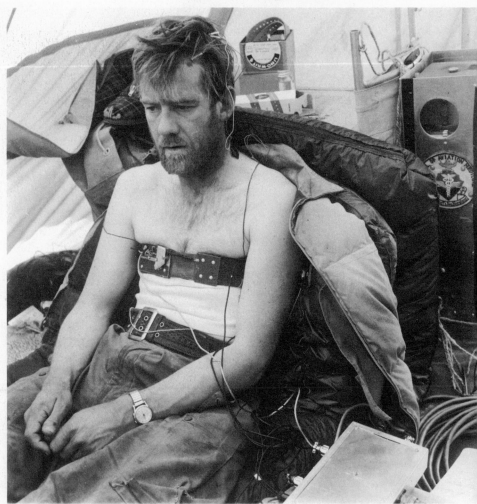

24-25. *Wires taped onto the scalp of Dr. Milledge and the chest of Michael Gill record effects of lack of oxygen.*

October 10—A week after the transaction lamas and laymen of Beding come asking confidentially if we would like to purchase a Yeti skin, owned by a certain nun in the village of Beding.

BLUE BEAR OR YETI

The fur is a dark smoky black in color with distinct reddish tints. Across the shoulders is an ivory band, interrupted by a hump of black hair at its center; that would be between the animal's shoulder blades. Unfortunately the skin is incomplete, having neither hind nor fore legs, but the upper part of its face is intact: a golden, slightly sinister mask, and distinctly a bear's, though without the prominent ears of a bear. From just below the eyes to the base of its tail (there is no tail) it measures exactly sixty inches. Its width is just short of three feet.

It is unquestionably a blue bear. But is it a Yeti?

Our fur has been labeled Mighyu, Dzuteh, and Yeti by the local people and our Sherpas alike. We are still uncertain where it originated, though the nun who owned it insists that it came from the vicinity of Chor monastery in Tibet, just four miles directly north of Beding. There is an 18,000-foot pass between Beding in Nepal and Chor monastery in Tibet. The people of Beding point it out as the direction from which Yetis come in the depth of winter to prowl through their village.

A Sherpa I have just met, and I have no reason to doubt his sincerity, described how a Yeti carcass was brought into his village, near Namche Bazar, the Sherpa capital in Solu Khumbu, some years ago. The people who skinned it could not rid their hands of its foul stench for days. "I felt sick at the smell," he said. In time the owner of the skin began selling it by the small piece, it being considered powerful medicine, a panacea for all ills. My informant bought a square and still has it. We will examine it when we reach his village next month.

Asked to describe the fur, he said it was bluish-black with red tints, about five inches deep. The animal he remembered had a white collar.

Interesting is this Sherpa's allusion to the foul stench of the animal, which in all probability was a blue bear. Most descriptions of Yeti sightings and visitations include the detail of an overpoweringly strong and unbearable odor. And the man remembered the creature's feet—"like a bear's but much longer."

Sir Edmund Hillary tells how in 1952, while climbing in the
Cho Oyu region of the Himalayas, his Sherpas found a snatch
of skin on which were coarse long black hairs. "Yeti, Sahib,
Yeti," his Sherpas said excitedly. Then one of them, snatching
the piece of fur from his hand, tossed it over a bluff, explaining
as he did so that it was "Bad luck, Sahib, very bad luck."
Examining the fur we now possess, Sir Edmund feels strongly
that the few hairs he saw in 1952 might well belong to the same
animal.

Blue bear or Yeti? Or the one and the same creature?

"So Sorry, Good Morning"

Before we left Beding for the higher, colder reaches of the
Rolwaling Valley, the lamas invited us to a small ceremony in
the monastery—we liked to think it was our farewell and hatchet-
burying party combined. We were welcomed by an exceedingly
expansive, fur-hatted gentleman who shook us warmly by the
hands and bade each of us, "So sorry, good morning." It was past
seven of a cold evening and quite dark.

There was nothing very special about the ceremony itself, but
what made the occasion memorable was the head lama's decision
to expose, for our benefit, the monastery's relics. Now Buddhist
relics, which usually comprise the remains of some extremely
venerated lama or saint, are very rarely exposed. That we were
to be shown the relics of this little monastery was a signal honor
and we were as touched as our Sherpas were delighted. The
relics, we were told, belonged to Chor Gompa, a monastery just
across the frontier in Tibet, which had been sacked by the
Communist Chinese. The eight lamas of Chor had fled to Nepal
by way of the 18,000-foot pass between Chor and Beding on
an improbably moonless night. They were at that time the temporary guests of the Beding monastery but hoped, in some
miraculous manner, to find the means to build a new gompa of
their own.

The relics they showed us were of the Tibetan saint who
founded their monastery, the most sacred among them an ex-
quisitely carved piece of "stone" compounded of the hearts of
successive reincarnations of the founder lama. There also was

the tooth of a sacred yak that gave milk from which the butter
for the monastery's butter lamps had been made and a bone
shaped like a deity that was found in the animal's brain when it
died. And a miraculous image of the Buddha that could turn
the tide of floods and prevent earthquakes and other calamities
but somehow had failed to halt the Communist forces of anti-
religion.

All these were looked upon with great awe by our expedition
Sherpas who, in a show of deep devotion, touched their foreheads to each relic in turn.

When eventually we left, to the sound of the sonorous five-
foot monastery horns blasting irreverently through the continuous murmur of prayer, there was the cheerful, expansive gentleman under his fur hat to bid us good-by.

"So sorry," he said, shaking us all warmly by the hands, "good
morning."

Up Valley to Na

On October 3 a French expedition to Chobutse moved into
Beding as we prepared to leave the village. Ed had been understandably upset about the French being given permission by the
Nepalese authorities to stomp about our field of operations. Five
men, one woman, and seventy-six Sherpas and porters was a
large number of intruders into an area one hoped was a Yeti
sanctuary. If Yetis are the intelligent anthropoids some suspect
them to be, the more activity there was among the mountains
and valleys of the Rolwaling, the less likelihood there was going
to be of seeing even a Yeti track.

Already the head lama of Beding had declared that we
smelled wrong and looked wrong and behaved wrong for the
Yeti. We readily agreed with him, but apart from our smell,
which improved every day, there was little we could do about
our shortcomings—our un-Sherpa size, our un-Sherpa beards,
our un-Sherpa equipment. Mountaineering clothes have undergone revolutionary changes since General Bruce assaulted Everest in tweed jacket and plus fours. We were decked out in
flame-orange down jackets, vividly checked woolen shirts, scarlet
Balaclava caps, turquoise, emerald, and gray pullovers. No Yeti

would be fooled into thinking we were locals. The French were, if anything, more colorful.

We moved up valley to Na village on the fourth of October. It was a magnificent six-mile toil, up the river dwindling to a stream, through forests bright with autumn tints being reduced by altitude to scrub. The gorge narrowed until it contained only the stream and the puny trail we followed. Gradually, so that we did not notice it at the time, the shrubs disappeared and we were in a world of tumbled rock and coarse frost-burned grass. Some of the rocks were a city block in size. Many were beautifully carved with Tibetan characters, *Om Mane Padme Hum,* or crowned with cairns of stones and shredded prayer flags. One of these was pointed out as being a table of the gods. It was vast and flat-topped and in so lovely a bend of the valley that I could well imagine it being singled out by the gods for divine picnics. Not far beyond was another rock like an inverted ice-cream cone. This, Pasang told me, was the fossilized hat of the Guru Rimpoche and had been hollowed out to make a shrine. "But lamas no longer live there. Two who did died of some terrible complaint. It is now full of demons."

Na is a Sherpa summer settlement, Beding's satellite village, abandoned when the first snow flurries convey the threat of winter. This can happen early or late, and when we were there the snow was late so that there was a great deal of activity about Na. Herds of yak and sheep still roamed the slopes above our camp, slopes that lead directly to a ring of spectacular peaks, unclimbed, some unclimbable, many unnamed. Most dazzling among them was Chobutse, 21,870 feet of fluted, precipitous snow which the French hoped somehow to climb (but which still stands inviolate). Nor were the yaks and sheep alone on the mountains. The villagers clambered after them, to harvest wild hay that grew on the very snow line.

George Lowe, Pat Barcham, Mike Gill, and Tom Nevison, who were on reconnaissance above the snow line, kept sending back reports of numerous tracks seen at heights close to 19,000 feet. In most cases yaks were responsible, sometimes wolves and wild dogs, occasionally snow leopard. But Yetis, no, which was disappointing.

According to the villagers of Na and Beding who breed them in quantity, yaks often stray so high and far that they either perish in the intense winter cold or return after months, all skin and bone and a bovine determination to reach shelter. Stray yaks have been known to cross the high passes into Tibet and vice versa, leaving their ungainly footprints behind them— to be called Snowman's?

"It is likely that the best our automatic tripwire cameras may record," I wrote at the time, "will be photographs of surprised domestic animals and the busy villagers of Na. Nevertheless observation camps have been set up at altitudes of 16,000 feet on the Ripimu glacier, where fresh-water shrimp have been found in quantity, and at 17,400 feet, where Larry Swan has noted an abundance of jumping spiders. To Larry this is almost as exciting as finding Yetis. If he could discover a lizard above the snow line his joy would be complete. Lizards are Larry's first love, frogs a close second.

"Bird life abounds in the valley: enormous enameled ravens, sad-sounding choughs, black and white snow pigeons, jaunty hoopoes, wagtails, pheasants, and a surprising variety of smaller breeds, often brightly colored and innocently tame. In the three weeks spent at Beding and Na we have seen few animals, but there is evidence of musk deer and wild dogs, wolves, blue sheep, and occasional bears in and above the valley. We now own four lesser red pandas, two of them tame, brought in by trappers.

"They are the most delightful of creatures and would be everyone's choice of a pet if they could be house trained. Bhanu let one share his sleeping bag with disastrous results. The bag may dry, but the smell will last forever."

DOCTORS AND WITCH DOCTORS

Ed decided with characteristic suddenness to move us again, onto the Ripimu glacier where even yaks are afraid to tread. The Ripimu adjoins the Menlung glacier, and it was there in 1951 that Mr. Eric Shipton saw and photographed the most widely talked-about set of Yeti footprints. As we were preparing to leave we heard that the French were forcing the Ripimu ahead of us. We were immediately suspicious and irritated. What were they up to? Watching us? Or after Yetis themselves? Irritation comes easy at high altitude and is the first recognizable sign in the mysterious process of deterioration that occurs somewhere above 16,000 feet.

The French, as it turned out, were inoffensively trying to find a route onto Chobutse, and when they entered the Ripimu Valley they could not resist going on to the high watershed at its northern end. Over the top was Tibet. Will Tibet, even the modernized Communist Tibet of patriotic songs, blue-uniformed comrades, and propaganda progress, ever fail to attract the romantic in man?

An intriguing incident removed the tension. The French did not have a doctor with them, and one of their Sherpas, Ang Namgyal, was suffering an acutely painful heel which might need surgery. Ed Hillary persuaded them to leave the man with us for observation and treatment. The pain had soon spread from Ang Namgyal's left heel to his wrists, his back, and then to his left knee. There it stayed, manifest in a vast swelling that threatened to burst through his pale skin. Tom Nevison diagnosed rheumatic fever.

As his agony increased and sleep became impossible, Ang Namgyal was more and more certain that he would die. Our Sherpas, suspecting the same thing, consulted the lamas of the local monastery and had a horoscope cast. It was very bad. The man was doomed, and stupidly they told him so. Poor Ang Namgyal's reaction was immediate. He wept; he moaned, and his temperature soared. Even we began to have doubts about his recovery.

So witch doctors and lamas were called in. A crumpled hag purified our camp with staccato chants and scattered milk. She washed Ang Namgyal's clothes in the stream below Beding monastery to alleviate his pain. Nothing happened. She was followed by a lama dragging a sheep behind him. With great ceremony the evil spirit in Ang Namgyal was persuaded to enter the animal via an incision made in its neck with a sacred knife. Apart from the excitement this provided for us, our Sherpas, and the unfortunate sheep, nothing happened. Ang Namgyal lay writhing in a fog of pain and fear.

There followed a visitation from an ancient lama reputed to possess great powers of healing. He perched by Ang Namgyal's tent just as our doctor clambered out of it, pills, stethoscope, and syringe in hand. After spending a long while in prayer the old lama reached into the tent, took Ang Namgyal's bloated knee in his gnarled hands, and began spitting on it. The sheep was still bleating out in the field and the old witch sat brooding apart, rocking gently on her thighs and never taking her eyes off the sick Sherpa's tent.

Ang Namgyal recovered soon after this combined display of skills. But whose victory was it—doctor's, witch doctor's, or lama's?

Among Unchartered Mountains

On October 11 Base Camp was shifted from Na at just over 14,000 feet to the Dudh Pokhri, or Lake of Milk, at 15,700 feet on the Ripimu glacier. Our route lay across a gigantic tumble of moraine that would make a combined pile of the Egyptian pyramids look puny in comparison. It was pleasant going. The monsoon was dramatically done, its last few clouds held captive in the valley or skewered on toothy rock pinnacles far below. We climbed into the sun, and there before us was a whole new complex of great mountain peaks, many in Tibet. George Lowe pointed to a group of them and then to his map. Representing those glittering summits on the map was a blank space. "Unchartered," he said. "God, how I'd like to have a crack at them."

It is an act of worship to just sit and look at high mountains, to feel lost in smallness. We relaxed on boulders warmed by the sun and munched chocolate and swilled lemon juice spiky with ice crystals from our water bottles.

Immediately about us was a nightmarescape in which it would seem all the world's bulldozers had gone berserk, piling rubble with monstrous abandon and tearing at the granite foundations of surrounding peaks with blasé disrespect.

Every here and there the gray rubble yawned open to reveal polished gums of ice, saber-toothed with icicles. Pools were cradled in the ancient ice, some so frozen they were emeralds among the tumbled rocks, others dark and evil, their water dripping audibly into some bottomless chasm. And as exhilarating as it was intimidating was the feel that everything moved, writhed, gigantically shoved, as if the primordial forces that flung these mountains to the sky were still active, as if even we were being propelled by other than the power of our limbs.

The Dudh Pokhri is considered sacred by Buddhists and Hindus alike. Tradition has it that the god Vishnu bathes in the lake of milk and sometimes lazes where our tents were pitched.

On the day we arrived a group of Nepalis from a village five
days' march away circled the lake three times, made offerings of
rice, flowers, and incense at a flag-festooned cairn of stones by
the water's edge, and immediately began their tedious journey
home. We were not left long in wonder at their speedy retreat.
The lake is closely surrounded by three precipitous peaks:
Chobutse, 21,870 feet, Landartsubugu, 21,970 feet, and Takargo,
22,250 feet. As soon as the sun dips behind Chobutse, which it
does in midafternoon, temperatures tumble and the cold is intense. It is almost visible, a writhing phosphorescent blueness
like mist with the sun behind it. Anyone caught in the open and
not adequately clothed would be in danger of freezing to
death. Yet while the sun shone we enjoyed almost tropical heat
and used to roam about stripped to the waist.

Our Sherpas even took to the freezing lake on their air mattresses when the sun was out, in imitation of the maker's label, a
swim-suited lovely sailing a swimming pool on her Lilo. We
stuck to a sauna steam bath built by Tom Nevison of stone and
clear plastic sheeting. While we sweated away a month's ac-
cumulation of dirt in this revealing contraption the Sherpas
came to watch—the closest I've been to sympathizing with gold-
fish in bowls.

But neither sauna baths nor the comparative comfort of a
fire-warmed mess tent were calculated to divert the enthusiasm
of Ed Hillary, who saw elusive Yetis and unscaled snow peaks
as challenges to be met—constantly and forcefully. Even before
our base was fully established he, George Lowe, Peter Mulgrew,
and Pat Barcham were manning higher observation camps at
16,200 and 17,400 feet.

Marlin Perkins set up his automatic tripwire cameras and
photographed a scold of surprised ravens. Larry Swan built a
laboratory, Dr. Tom Nevison his solarium-cum-dispensary, and
Bhanu Bannerjee and myself an office, all in an abortive show of
permanency. To no avail. Ed had our Sherpas carrying loads far
up the Ripimu glacier to establish yet another camp, at 18,000
feet, before we could take root. We made off like a tribe of
refugees on Sunday, October 16.

At 17,000 feet I had my first depressing brush with the forces
of high altitude. After walking well all morning I felt suddenly
dizzy and was forced to sit down. I saw double, even treble,
and everything I looked at exploded and vaporized except my

own hands and feet. These extremities, when I looked at them, were a mile away, no longer a part of me, certainly not on my brain circuit. They obeyed no commands so that when I tried to walk half of me went ambling away and the other, with my brain attached to it, remained behind. There was only one thing to do—retreat, and that I did. When I forced the 17,000-foot barrier again, I fared better but arrived at our new 18,000-foot camp feeling as limp as a chewed string. The sickly smile I tried to effect deceived no one. Only Bhanu fared worse. He, poor fellow, blacked out and temporarily lost his sight. I was with him, and his terror was easily transferred to me. For what seemed an eternity we sat together in the snow, feeling deserted. Then Ed came looking for us, and his rough assurance that every-, thing would be all right seemed to restore the sight to Bhanu's eyes. But I can still remember him suddenly floundering in the snow and wailing, "God, Des, I'm blind."

WITH TOES ON THEIR HEELS

Ed was still restless, and so it was that, while half our number was gratefully prepared to settle into the snow of our glacier camp at 18,000 feet with some of the most spectacular scenery the Himalayas had to offer piled about us, he was planning a higher camp, on the Ripimu Pass, at over 19,000 feet. Off he went on the seventeenth, with George Lowe, Peter Mulgrew, and Tom Nevison, to establish the camp, leaving Mike Gill and Pat Barcham to pioneer a route up the glacier to a col overlooking the Menlung glacier and Tibet. Larry Swan, Marlin Perkins, Bhanu Bannerjee, and myself remained to scout around for Yeti footprints.

On October 15, with the snow perspiring under a brilliantly hot sun, we discovered our first tracks, an unmistakable, undisturbed file of footprints. At first glance they were made by naked human feet—size elevens or even fifteens, broad across the instep, fallen arches, and a big toe that protruded inward. They were twenty to thirty inches apart. We were at 18,000 feet at the head of the Ripimu glacier, in an amphitheater of unscalable peaks, awesome tumbles of ice, and banks of deep brittle snow. A lethargic half-frozen stream wound its way through this new-found Yetiland, and it was on the stream that the tracks converged, growing shapeless and confused on the downhill slope, then disappearing completely in a precipitous rockfall over which the stream trickled in a tinkle of icicles and spray.

"The nearest description I would venture would be bare human feet," Ed Hillary said after he examined the tracks, "but that's not saying they're Yeti. I would like a lot more convincing proof."

Sir Edmund considered the tracks to be several days old and was certain he had noticed them before, when establishing a high-altitude observation camp in the area. At the time he had dismissed them as the tracks of a quadruped such as snow leopard, wolf, or wild dog.

Other opinion was undecided. Peter Mulgrew was distinctly skeptical. The tracks, he thought, were his own, made four days before when he had accompanied Ed. But a comparison of his booted footprints and those of the naked "Yeti" shook his arguments. By no stretch of imagination could our heavy rubber-soled climbing boots sprout toes, balled insteps, and smooth, elongated heels.

To me a number of the footprints appeared human with one glaring dissimilarity: they had toes on their heels. At the same time this peculiar phenomenon made the footprints more authentically Yeti, as a wealth of local legend has the feet of the Snowman facing back to front, a detail that has implicated the ape more than the bear in Yeti lore.

It is well known that the great apes rest their forelegs on the folded knuckles of their hands so that the digits face backward. When they walk the impressions of their feet and knuckles often coincide, giving the confusing impression, to the uninitiated, of their feet being turned the wrong way round.

To our Sherpas the footprints were without doubt a Snowman's. It was they who discovered the tracks while moving between the Lake Camp and an observation camp at 18,000 feet. Leaving their loads behind them, they descended the three difficult miles to Base Camp in an avalanche of excitement. It took only minutes to ignite equal enthusiasm in camp.

If Ed Hillary had blossomed into a many-headed, many-armed manifestation of himself he could not have reacted more quickly. All at once, it seemed, he had me questioning the authenticity of the tracks; George Lowe armed to the teeth with cameras; Tom Nevison and Peter Mulgrew equipped for a couple of days' tracking if necessary; Mike Gill, Pat Barcham, himself, and most of the Sherpas halfway up the nearest mountainside. Larry Swan, Bhanu Bannerjee, a very excited Marlin Perkins, and myself brought up the rear with things like plaster of Paris, sketch books, measuring tapes, and more cameras. There was also a gun, just in case.

I had always believed that excitement is a force knowing neither boundaries nor obstacles. How wrong I was. Possessed with sufficient quantity of the stuff to set me off like a rocket, I almost killed myself in the effort of scaling the three miles of moraine and rockfalls to where the tracks had been seen, at speed. My immediate companions were equally undone; even Marlin began cursing Yetis in general and the one responsible for our agony in particular before we were gone three hundred yards. Many of the tracks had been obliterated by the stampeding of our Sherpas, but a few good individual footprints remained. I even managed to make a plaster of Paris cast of one of the prints (eleven inches in length by five inches across), no easy feat in porous snow. Unfortunately, in the process of drying it out on our crude mess fireplace, it became irretrievably fused to a slab of local stone.

Three days later, at 18,400 feet on the Ripimu glacier, Larry Swan happened upon another track of Yeti footprints. In his own words, "I had just climbed a peak, dunghill as mountains around here go, but a virgin peak all the same, and was enjoying myself in the sun, when for heaven's sake, there right below me was a trail of footprints, and a biped's at that. Gee, I couldn't have been more excited. There must have been thirty of them, and a good many apparently made by a naked human foot."

As always happens in circumstances so extraordinary, Larry was almost out of film, daylight, and breath. So it was left to Marlin, Bhanu, and myself to explore the tracks next day, amply provided with photographic equipment, tape measures, and other implements of Yeti tracking. Some Sherpas who preceded us ran into tracks below those discovered by Larry and a great bellowing, chattering, stampeding excitement exploded above our heads.

Annullu, a personality-plus Sherpa who knows almost as much about Yetis as he does about women—he is now married to his third wife and has seven children—declared the tracks to be those of a Snowman, "and no better could we hope to find any-where," he said. The other Sherpas agreed, pointing out where the creature had walked on its hind legs, then on all four, then sideways because of the brittle depth of snow.

To us, alas, they were plainly and obviously the tracks of a small quadruped, the pug marks placed close enough together to form one large imprint. Conniving with the Yeti legend was the remarkably fierce sun, fusing the small pug marks together and enlarging them out of all proportion to their original size. As we followed the track we were confronted with "footprints" that on the shady side of a snow ridge were unmistakably a rosette of small pug marks but on the top of the same ridge were expanded by the sun into vast fifteen-inch "feet," the slightly misplaced pugs forming toes and heel. On the downhill slope the "footprints" either reverted to bouquets of pug marks or took on the appearance of small elephantlike tracks mentioned by Shipton.

When the tracks were on a single plane of snow, and where their angle of exposure to the sun was the same, they kept their huge Snowman shape with convincing regularity. Anyone hap-pening upon such a stretch of track would be justified in claim-ing they had happened upon the footprints of a giant biped: sub-human, mountain gorilla, or the abominably elusive Snow-man. Such ideal conditions are to be found on gradual slopes and at the top of passes, where most "Yeti" footprints have been seen.

The very next day (Tuesday, the eighteenth) George, Bhanu, and I came upon a half mile or more of perfect footprints trailing over great swells of hard snow. They appeared comparatively fresh, not more than a day old. We all were of the opinion that they belonged to the animal that had prowled our camp the night before, sniffing and snuffling outside our tents and nosing about some discarded sardine tins.

We were on the deep of the Ripimu glacier, the ice grooved and folded and so fantastically formed that it was a frozen ballet sequence many years bewitched, a ruined city turned to glass. We walked through lanes and streets of sequined alabaster, and there were public squares and heroic monuments, pillared ar-cades and cathedrals of jade run through with icy fire, all deserted but haunted with the running screams and groans and that tinkling laughter of ice. It was enthralling, a world of pure fantasy, but where in this impossible landscape did the Yeti live? Even the Sherpas didn't know, though they invest this frozen wilderness with snow dragons and mountain lions and accuse the ice spirits of soughing like the wind.

As we followed the tracks the same extraordinary artifice of a high-altitude sun, melting snow, and an innocent small animal's footprints combined to baffle us. In the course of several hundred switchback yards the selfsame tracks contained "foot" impressions two inches and fourteen inches in length and from two to seven inches in width. Fascinated, we watched small paws become giant feet, claw marks turn to toes, enormous "Yeti" feet become the pug marks of an animal no bigger than a fox. In all probability it was a fox!

Was this then the explanation of a legend and the demolition of a colorful myth? We hoped not, even as we were forced to accept that it most probably was.

If a fox or wild dog can make Yeti tracks acceptable to Sherpas, most avid supporters of the Snowman legend, then so can enormous high-altitude ravens, snow leopards, bears, and wolves.

Wherever we found them, and they had by now became commonplace, it was the same story—tracks the Sherpas swore to be authentic Snowman were quite obviously those of some small unsuspecting quadrupeds promoted by sun and local imagination into the realm of Himalayan fantasy. But this still did not preclude Yetis, too, from making Yeti tracks.

4

ONTO THE TOLAM BAU

Winter now was more than a threat. It grew chokingly cold on the Ripimu glacier and our far-ranging reconnaissance parties kept running into difficult, often dangerous, conditions. The trouble generally was on the northern slopes where deep accumulations of snow were soft and ever ready to avalanche, and the cold was intense.

Ed and George spent a morning floundering in waist-deep snow and returned complaining of headaches. It could have been worse. After struggling to the top of a high snow col that commanded superb views of Menlungtse, a mountain of sheer white granite and ice, the northeast slopes of Gauri Shankar, the Menlung glacier and Menlung lakes, all in Tibet, George dropped his snow glasses. A Sherpa proverb has things lost on mountains traveling far: George's glasses slid over an ice cliff. There was only one thing to do in that vast wilderness of dazzlingly sunlit snow, retrieve the glasses or risk snow blindness. In Ed Hillary's words, "We roped up and went to look for them but found the snow very loose on the steep slopes. Then we decided to try a different route, but as we were crossing a comparatively flat area there was a whoomp and all the snow around us subsided in a rather alarming fashion. We decided to call it a day."

George somehow protected his eyes from the glare, and an abstract fancy allows me to believe he used his ample beard. Sherpas who find themselves on blinding snow without glare glasses cover their eyes with a plait of their hair, leaving windows in it to peep through.

Here is an interesting example of tradition becoming innocently extinct. Sherpa men are rapidly forsaking their long hair and plaits in preference for "the Western cut." But the "Western cut," or its umpteen variations, can no longer be called upon to protect the eyes from snow blindness. Snow glasses have become a necessity. It could be argued that the advent of snow glasses has ousted long hair; certainly with the buttered plaits have gone the beautiful variety of male earrings—from four-inch-long turquoise pendants to large rings of gold set with coral, or turquoise, or both.

I once asked a Sherpa why he was trying to sell me his earrings. Didn't he realize they were an important part of his character, that this was Sherpa tradition going by the board? Very simply he replied that earrings looked and felt silly without long hair. Or didn't I think so?

So once had a student in Kathmandu dealt with my exaggerated Western approach to native culture. I had deplored the tearing down of several traditional Kathmandu houses with their carved windows and balconies and their pagoda roofs. And I grew patronizingly heated over the haphazard electrification of the city, the neon signs near temples, the unsympathetic bulbs that burned nakedly where votive oil lamps had once glowed, the building of jazz-moderne monstrosities beside ancient palaces.

"You should try living in our artistic old houses," the student said. "After bumping your head on the low ceilings and slipping down dark stairways you would think again about the evils of modernization. And if I remember rightly, you British are particular about your lavatories. Most of our houses have none."

HIGH-ALTITUDE SALMON

October seventeenth was memorable as the day Peter Mulgrew cooked fish cakes at 19,000 feet. The fish were Canadian salmon, out of a tin, and Peter had no pretentions about being a cook. But they were good and, though eaten with a great deal of rude banter, were a welcome change in the diet of boiled potatoes, stew sometimes called curry, chapatties, honey and jam. Besides, the fish cakes have a sort of mystic bearing on the expedition timetable. It was never ascertained whether they or the altitude, or both, were responsible for Ed, George, Tom Nevison, and Peter himself having a miserable night following the feast. Whatever it was, Ed was prompted by his immediate misery to pull out of the Ripimu. To search for tracks on the Menlung glacier, he argued, would be futile. The snow conditions were plainly bad: the wind howling up from over the Tibetan plateau was razor sharp with cold, and there had been another of those unnerving subsidences of surface snow, while even the most unambitious walk would deteriorate into a wallowing scramble by those who made it. Besides, sitting around at 19,000 feet might tempt Peter to cook again.

We withdrew to the Lake Camp, discovering "Yeti" tracks as we went. At one point our own track lay across a disintegrating slope down which rocks rolled continuously. Ed advised us to run across, using our ice axes as balancing sticks. True, it was not too far to go, perhaps thirty yards, but just walking at 17,000 feet is agony; running is to cut out one's lungs with a blunt instrument, a hara-kiri without honor. And the earth crumbles under one—imagine running on a three-foot depth of assorted cricket balls, footballs, golf balls, marbles, and sand. There's no standing still. When you started there was a brief lull in the downpour of rock and earth and you hoped with a prayer that it would hold. There was no looking up, no stopping; to do either was to slip, unbalance, fall headlong in a rock avalanche of your own making. Our Sherpas, heavily laden, hesitated, then went over at a gallop. Nima Dorji, our cook, was halfway across when the hillside over him moved, rocks separated themselves from it and whirled toward him, pursued by cartwheels of dust. It looked for a moment as if Nima's good luck on Dhaulagiri had deserted him; he was carrying an ungainly load of cooking utensils and tinned food in a basket and didn't seem to be aware of the threat. But even as the rocks thudded about him he flung his basket to the ground and lay behind it. Miraculously he was unhurt.

As the rest of us paused to go over I began cursing the frivolous fate that had brought us so far and so painfully only to hit us over the head with an avalanching stone. Why the hell today, when everything was so beautiful and we were returning to safer heights and safer temperatures? What silly impulse ever got me tied up with this crazy adventure? I suddenly hated the mountains, the whole blasted lot of them—silly, white, detached —and did Hillary or our distant sponsors or the whole herd of armchair adventurers who read about us with a small stab of excitement in their guts care a damn about us right now? Why the hell should I risk my neck on a ridiculous rockfall? Marlin was going across now, and even from behind he looked terrified. Was he thinking of his neck, of his wife, of his fickle television audience, of anything? The poor bloody idiot. How did he at his age get mixed up in this circus? What would I do if anything happened to Bhanu for whom I felt personally responsible? What could I ever say that would reconcile his parents to the unnecessary tragedy?

There was a shove in my back and, turning, I found Mingma, one of my runners, standing close behind me. He smiled broadly. "Don't worry," he said. "Today is a good day. Nothing will happen." Beauty flooded back into the valley. The sun reached quickly through my fear and warmed my forgotten sense of humor. Marlin finished his scramble like a circus chimpanzee and was gayly joking with Nima Dorji on the other side. "Come on, Mingma," I said. "I'll race you across." Not even a pebble threatened our crossing. For us it was a good day.

Not quite so for Larry Swan. He had been experiencing some difficulty with his breathing and Ed advised him to cross the slope further down, below the reach of most rock avalanches, where he could amble across in his own time and not strain his lungs by running. Alas, as he crossed the lower rockfall a tremendous avalanche swept down toward him. It gathered strength and more rocks as it went and for a horrifying few seconds buried Larry in clouds of dust. Fortunately for him, he was near a large boulder and sat out the avalanche behind it. He was understandably shaken.

Sahib Ghosts in Puttees and Felt Hats

The close brush with disaster prompted us to talk of mountaineering accidents. Mingma told of a party of Sherpas that had been swept away by an avalanche while on pilgrimage to Tibet. "Woosh and they disappeared just like that, leaving no sign. We believe that when avalanches bury large numbers of people it is the vengeance of some god. It is the same when people are swept off mountains by high winds and vanish forever."

I asked him if the disappearance of people was generally associated with divine wrath. What, for instance, if Sherpas or sahibs were killed on a mountain but their bodies were found?

That would be mere *leh* or *karma*—a fate that was as likely to catch up with one in bed as in a potato field, Mingma said.

"When people disappear completely they are apt to leave their spirits behind them. The party of Sherpas I told you about has often been seen like a flock of shadows on the moonlit snow above Rongbuk. And there are the ghosts of two sahibs on Everest seen quite often by the lamas of Rongbuk monastery. They wear puttees and cloth hats."

I was reminded immediately of a photograph of Mallory and Irvine taken shortly before they vanished on the great pyramid of Everest. In it they wore felt hats, tweed coats, plus fours, and puttees, as if out partridge shooting.

"How long have these two sahib ghosts been seen?" I asked.

"For many years," Mingma replied. "Long before the expedi-

tions began coming to our villages from Nepal." Nepal is the
Sherpas' name for Kathmandu. Like most Nepali tribes living
outside the valley of Kathmandu, the Sherpas do not have any
conception of a united Nepal. To them each Nepali race inhabits
a separate country; theirs is Solu Khumbu.

"There was the sahib who went to Everest alone," one of the
Sherpas said. "He went with only two porters and everyone
considered him mad. At first it was thought that he was on a
pilgrimage and would not go much further than Rongbuk monastery. But when it was certain that he meant to climb the
mountain without proper equipment and companions, he was
killed."

This sounded a strange way of relating Wilson's solo attempt
and death on Everest, but our Sherpas had a simple explanation.
Apparently Wilson's porters were Tibetans and unknown ones
at that. Certainly they were not Sherpas, and they were required
to expose themselves to inordinate risks. "It is quite impossible to
climb a great mountain alone—everyone knows this. Besides it
was Lonak, a black year, when nothing important should be
undertaken; it always ends in disaster. Either the two porters
were afraid of their lives or they were bandits. It is a common
rumor that they killed the sahib. They were selling his things
long after he died, in Tingri bazaar." This still sounded cruelly
unreal to me, unless of course Wilson had unfortunately signed
up two professional Tibetan bandits. "How would the men have
killed the sahib?" I asked. "Perhaps by pushing him over a
precipice, but most likely by simply deserting him on the mountain," was the reply.

Not all were in agreement with this story. Some hadn't heard
it. Others thought Wilson did have Sherpas with him. What did
lend credulity to the story for Sherpas was the occasional sight-
ing of a lonely "sahib spirit." Murdered people, like those whom
the gods destroy, leave ghosts behind them.

Back at the Lake Camp, we prepared to leave the Rolwaling
Valley and push on into Solu Khumbu. Short of actually seeing
or capturing a Yeti, our hunt so far had gone well. We had
reaped a rich harvest of local legend; we had the fur of a creature
that was partly, if not wholly, responsible for the Yeti myth, and
we had come upon a satisfyingly large number of "Snowman"
tracks.

In Solu Khumbu was important Yeti evidence; two ancient scalps that had mystified all who had seen them or the hairs plucked from them, a mummified Snowman hand, and a great deal of apparently authentic detail of Yeti sightings.

Our Sherpas, almost all of whom came from Solu Khumbu, insisted that their high mountains and forested valleys would be much more profitable than the Rolwaling Valley for Yeti hunting.

"We know all the spots where Yetis have been seen," Urkien argued. "We will introduce you to the people who have seen them." Had Urkien seen a Yeti? No, but he had heard one. Many people in Khumjung, his village, had heard Yetis, a long shrill whistling that certainly belonged to no known creature. What did he think were our chances of seeing a Yeti? If we used our present, to him clumsy, methods, our chances were bad. Observation camps were all very well, but they had to be more isolated. A minimum of people should occupy them, at the most one sahib and two Sherpas, and once they had set up their post they should cut movement to the barest necessity. He was against the use of tents unless they were cleverly camouflaged. A much better idea would be to occupy a Sherpa house or sangar, the high-altitude summer hut that has fairly permanent stone walls but a temporary roof of felt or shingles, as these would be familiar to Yetis. Tents would make any intelligent animal suspicious and send it on a circuitous detour or hastily back the way it had come. If we moved outside at all we should wear *bakhus* over our expedition clothes—*bakhus* being the voluminous yak-hair robes worn by Sherpa men—and fur caps.

I passed Urkien's advice on to Ed and Marlin. Both agreed it made good sense and that we ought to give it a try once we got to Solu Khumbu.

Once we got to Solu Khumbu! There was a 19,100-foot pass, the Tashi Lapcha, between us in the Lake Camp and Solu Khumbu, and we had been going in some dread of it. On our maps the Tashi Lapcha was shown as open only during the months of July and August—high summer. We would cross over in late October, and God help us. The Sherpas were not in agreement about weather conditions at this time of the year; some spoke of snow "this high," indicating a point below their armpits; others predicted an inch or two at the most. Annullu, a soothsayer among his other accomplishments, played eloquently safe. "If it rains now it will snow. If it snows on the

58 IN SEARCH OF SNOWMEN

pass the crossing will be very difficult. If it doesn't snow we will
be lucky. This is a time of snow."

Ed tried to comfort the fainthearted among us by saying that
yaks often crossed over the pass; so did sheep. Frankly I have
never disputed the superiority of yaks, as far as I'm concerned,
on a mountain or of sheep on precipitous rocks.

RUNNERS

It was decided to send out mail runners the day before we
left the Lake Camp. An old milk tin was labeled "Mail" and
stuck in the entrance of the tent I shared with Bhanu. Everyone
started writing with the desperation of people who are doing it
for the last time or people in love.

We began the expedition with four runners, signed on in
Kathmandu: Ang Temba of the cross-eyes and sweaty nose from
Namche Bazar, now promoted to Yeti sleuth extraordinary;
Mingma, a pale tubercular youth married to Ang Temba's sister;
and Pasang Que and Dhanaru from the Rolwaling. Dhanaru
was huge, pimply, and simple in the head. Pasang Que was an
elderly faun sporting a felt cloche, and there was something of
the Gay Twenties in the way he wore his shapeless clothes. His
trousers were split at the sides from knee to hip and had a let-
down flap at the rear, of the kind children have—an object of
much coarse humor among our Sherpas. I have never seen Pasang
Que look even remotely upset. Vacant perhaps, but more usually
wistful, as if he was on the verge of tumbling to some half-
understood joke. By his own confession he was a "spoiled
lama"—a monk who had broken the vows of celibacy and
abstinence. He was happily married and had three children.

When Ang Temba was considered too valuable a Yeti hunter
to send on long runs to Kathmandu, he was replaced by Nima
Tshering, another spoiled lama of Na village. Nima was all hair,
yak felt, and cherubic smiles. He had the good old Tibetan
habit of sticking out his tongue in greeting, a habit not immediately appreciated by some of us who dismissed him as mad
or at the best rather soft.

It takes good Sherpa runners six to seven days to cover the
120 miles between the Rolwaling and Kathmandu and eight to
nine days to do the 170 miles between Thyangboche monastery

and the Nepali capital. The record is five days for the Kathmandu–Thyangboche run. This in terms of distance is impressive
enough, but it's the sharp variation in altitude and the difficult
nature of the terrain encountered that made these runs extraordinary and of deep interest to our physiologists. Kathmandu is
4000 feet above sea level, our Rolwaling and Thyangboche
camps anywhere between 13,000 and 17,000 feet. Between our
remote camps and the city were high freezing passes and valleys low enough to be tropical, so that our runners were subjected to severe changes of altitude twice or even three times
in a day.

They ran light, in pairs for company and protection, without
the comfort of a tent or bedding. They carried meager rations
to see them over the uninhabited reaches of the track and otherwise ate in the villages in which they rested. Often their sole
sustenance was chang. When their runs piled up—340 miles, 680
miles, 1360 miles, 3000 miles—the strain clearly showed. All of
them grew blotchy with pimples; they lost weight, and after one
particularly strenuous run two runners developed noticeably dis-
tended stomachs. This run set a record in both high achievement
and foolhardiness.

In cloth boots and without special high-altitude clothing two
newly employed runners, Rin Norbu and Lakhpa Tshering,
made a crossing of the formidable Tashi Lapcha, in mid-Jan-
uary, when temperatures drop below zero and freezing gales
can lift a man bodily off the exposed knife edge of the pass.

No one dares the Tashi Lapcha in midwinter, and it is only
since foreign expeditions blazed the way that the pass has been
used at all by locals other than during the two "open" months.
It has a reputation for treacherous snow conditions, avalanches,
high winds, and lethal cold.

"We were almost carried away by the wind," Lakhpa told
me when they arrived, rather dazed, after the ordeal. "It
screamed at us all the while; our faces froze, and we thought
we would die. Fortunately Rin Norbu remembered the right
prayers."

Ed declared the adventure a record and himself deeply impressed. "But what they obviously didn't realize was that they
might have left their bones up there."

Rin Norbu, twenty-two, came to us as a trapper, selling two
lesser red pandas and begging medicine for his painfully

cracked feet, at a time when we were desperately in need of more runners. He is large and good-looking but not particularly tough—that's what we thought. In fact Ed, taking one quick look at his sideburns and carefully trimmed mustache, considered him a gigolo and despaired when I signed him up as a runner. I considered his obvious intelligence and desire to buy a pair of shoes and see Kathmandu ample qualification; besides, there was not much choice in the village of Na, where the only others in the running for our job were a one-eyed lama who was perpetually drunk and a dwarf with a goiter so large and misshapen that it looked as if he had gourds hanging about his neck.

Lakhpa we took on in Khumjung. He looked like a Siamese boxer who had been kicked repeatedly and hard in the nose. He walked up to me one day and, after exchanging greetings, asked for a job. He could cook, read a little Tibetan and Nepali, and knew that London was the capital of England and New Zealand was on the other side of the world. Did he know that the world was round? He wasn't sure, but round or flat, New Zealand and England weren't the same place, even though all sahibs looked the same. He said he was twenty-one, and was I sixty? This unflattering assessment of my age was enough to ruin Lakhpa's chances of employment for all time. But then all Sherpas think bearded foreigners to be antique. Ed had a mat of white hairs on his chest so he was sixty too, "or a little more, certainly an old man." Mike Gill, our youngest member at twenty-three, was thought to be the oldest among us because of his very blond hair. To the Sherpas he was gray and excessively ancient, which somehow made us all feel a little better.

The compelling motive behind Rin Norbu's and Lakhpa Tshering's epic run was mental anguish. Just before they left for Kathmandu, Rin Norbu got the news that his house in an adjoining valley had been burned down. His family may have perished in the blaze. So without second thoughts, and persuading the reluctant Lakhpa with wild promises of compensation, Rin Norbu decided to visit his home on the way to Kathmandu. To do this meant crossing the Tashi Lapcha.

Fortunately the cold that might have killed them worked to their advantage. It froze solid the loose rock and bulging ice overhangs that cause avalanches and provided bridges of hard snow between rock ledges and over crevasses. They carried only a fistful of millet flour each and chewed snow to quench their thirst. An unclouded sun warmed them over the pass. Had the weather changed, as it can within minutes in the high Himalayas, Rin Norbu and Lakhpa Tshering would never have survived. The incredible thing is that even after laboring across the pass, to spend a day poking around in the ashes of Rin Norbu's home, they still did the journey in nine days. Rin Norbu's family had happily escaped the blaze that consumed their house but lost everything.

After only three days' rest these two runners were back on the trail again, unsuspecting that they had found a niche in the history of Himalayan mountaineering and quite unaware that they had done anything more extraordinary than feel "very cold and a little frightened."

We sent runners to Kathmandu every week with mail and news bulletins. They returned with our eagerly awaited letters, newspapers, and "goodies" (request parcels of sweets, pickles, nuts, Chap-sticks, and nose drops). For each run made on time our runners were given a bonus of Rs.40 ($6). For an exceptionally fast run they received an extra of Rs.20 ($3). Their monthly salary was Rs.192, not quite $28, and that, by some, was considered to be a lordly wage. "You're spoiling them," I was told again and again. Such is the price of innocence and the degree of advantage we take of it. At the end of the expedition we had two of our runners suffering tuberculosis, and although there was no proof whatsoever that the strain of running had caused the disease, it certainly had aggravated it. Happily both men have recovered after treatment provided for them by the expedition in conjunction with the Kathmandu Mission Hospital. Modern drugs can work miracles among people who never have known Western medicine.

CHINESE PYROTECHNICS

Contact between our two main parties and between base and observation camps was kept by radio. The small orange sets that often had to be warmed by the fire (one was inadvertently roasted by an eager Sherpa) to get going had been carefully selected by Hillary. Peter Mulgrew, a naval radio officer, kept the sets chattering under all conditions except one—jamming by the Chinese in Tibet.

The Chinese first began searching out our frequency on October 20, but we got through to Thyangboche where Norman Hardie was pushing ahead with the construction of the Silver Hut. On October 21 we were completely scuttled. As soon as our call signal went out, down came a deluge of Chinese sound. It best can be described as a singing duel between a gong-accompanied Chinese female crooner and an Oriental tenor, fortissimo. By bearing with the sound and then hastily getting a few words through in the intervals when someone somewhere changed a record, we managed some sort of contact on our morning schedule. The afternoon attempt was hopeless. We were drenched with interfering sound.

But why bother to jam a radio contact as innocent as ours? There surely was nothing in our "Tell Ed that fourteen Sherpas are on their way down" or "Marlin wants his number two sleeping bag" or "Hello, old cock, how's the dysentery?" to either alarm or upset the Chinese. Or did they honestly believe that we were an expedition of imperialist spies, as Peking had more than once suggested, and that our morning and evening contacts were vital exchanges of border information in code?

We were discussing just this on the twenty-first evening by the fire in our mess hut, when Ed in obvious excitement called us out to see an aurora. The prospect of seeing anything so unexpected as an aurora was secondary to our snug comfort and warmth, and it took us some time to get out of the hut. Certainly when I stumbled into the freezing night there was nothing to be seen. According to Ed, he first saw "sweeping lights in the sky to the north. It was a bit like an aurora or the reflection from a very bright light over the border in Tibet." Tom Nevison, the first to emerge in answer to Ed's call, thought he saw a bright ball like a satellite disappear behind a peak to the west of us. He expected it to reappear within a few minutes, but nothing happened. The cold destroyed further interest, and for once Ed could have been imagining things.

Next morning we left the Lake Camp to begin toiling up the Tolam Bau glacier toward the Tashi Lapcha Pass. It was hard going, over Gargantuan tumbles of rock and below moraine walls like ruined battlements that spewed rubble continuously. There was dust everywhere, rising like sulphurous smoke from

26. *The village of Pangboche.*

27. *Our way into a Nepalese village.*

28. *Lama dancing in courtyard of Thyangboche Monastery.*

29. (ABOVE) *At Thami, a shelter belonging to Tibetan refugee. Clearly a rich man's tent.* 30. (BELOW) *Two of our laden porters commencing march in village of Banepa. Red "chillies" drying in the sun.*

31. (ABOVE) *Mask used for lama dancing at Thyangboche.*

32. (ABOVE) *Hillary welcomed by headman when he returns Yeti scalp by helicopter to Khumjung.* 33. (RIGHT) *One of our porters passing through a Nepalese village.*

the valley walls, the rocks, the glacier itself. We might have stumbled into a volcano or landed suddenly on another planet, so remote was this clattering, dusty, hot, and tortured world from the serenity of the heights about it. There was a lake, deeply gouged from the glacier, with copper for water and mud castles for icebergs. It hissed and bubbled as the muck poured into it, and we added to the confusion by rolling the biggest boulders we could unseat into the freezing water. It was a mad impulse that psychiatrists would explain as letting off weeks of nervous steam, and it was spontaneous. All of a sudden everyone was rolling boulders or throwing stones, and I retain a vivid picture of Mike Gill kicking at an elephant-sized rock while Hillary held him by the scruff of his neck and Peter Mulgrew and Tom Nevison hung onto his arms. Here was a facet of the sahibs' personality that Sherpas hadn't seen before: perhaps this was how we amused ourselves at home, or was there deeper significance?

On the top of every pass in Sherpa Nepal is a cairn of stones, often a stupa or a prayer wall designed to propitiate the gods and spirits of the surrounding valleys and mountain peaks. We learned that these stupas or cairns of stones must be kept on our right when passing, a consideration that often sent us on tortuous detours. And we learned to sing out "So So" in the way the Sherpas do when making an offering of stones or wild flowers at the top of a pass. Sometimes the patron spirit to whom we made obeisance was a long-dead bandit or ruthless official who over the years had assumed the proportions of a deity.

By rolling boulders at the expense of great energy we may well have been making a votive offering to the lake. Almost certainly there were spirits in it: it looked sinister enough to house the legendary demons and monsters that share the eternal snows with Snowmen.

We camped that evening below the intimidating cliffs of Chobutse, with the glacier still a muck heap below us. It was not much of a place, but it had water and there was a sufficiency of stunted azalea bushes to burn. This was important because the sun would leave us to freeze at 4 P.M. We were huddled about our campfire at 7 P.M. when Pat Barcham, who was grubbing about for something to burn, called our attention to a blaze in the sky. There was no doubt about it this time. As we watched a bright round object swept up from behind the wall of mountains separating us from Tibet, went into a wild snaking wobble, and then seemed to explode and dissolve high above us. Behind it ribboned a luminous vapor trail that hung diminishing in the sky for almost half an hour.

In his diary Ed Hillary describes the phenomenon as "something whizzing like a pencil across the eastern sky. I looked up in time to see a broad wiggly trail flash again and then fade, leaving a dimmer but distinct smoke or vapor trail where it had been. This trail curved upward into the sky and then bent over backward toward Tibet again, making almost a complete circle. Then it faded. It was a most astonishing sight, and the only explanation seemed to be some form of rocket. We wondered what the Chinese were up to."

What had we seen? Had this and the aurora of the evening before any connection? Could it really have been a Chinese rocket or "Chinknik" launched successfully into the night sky? It so happened that we had with us two men with rocket experience, Tom Nevison of the United States Air Force, a space physiologist, and Peter Mulgrew of the Royal New Zealand Navy, fresh from a rocketry course. Tom was prepared to stake his reputation on it being a rocket and a powerful one at that. He put its launching site at about a hundred miles northeast of where we were—that would be in the region of Lhasa. Peter Mulgrew was as certain that we had witnessed a spectacular but nevertheless natural phenomenon, but he didn't know what. He doubted the rocket idea but admitted that he was not as familiar with rocket launchings as Tom, who had come almost directly on expedition from Cape Canaveral. To me the snaking wobble and then the explosion far out in space were significant, similar to a number of films I have seen of rocket launchings.

The "Chinese Rocket" was seen that night by Dr. Pugh, the leader of our physiological team, from a point at least forty miles south of our camp. He dismissed it as a meteorite. The people of Namche Bazar recorded it as a comet with an excessively long tail, and the lamas in the local monastery were moved to recite special prayers.

Perhaps it was coincidence, but a day later we were freed of the radio interference. The powerful Chinese songsters fell silent and were even missed by our Sherpas who had found endless amusement in the woozy voices.

5

KHUMJUNG

For three days we camped below the Tashi Lapcha, waiting for porters from Solu Khumbu to come and lift us across. Although every able-bodied man, woman, and child in the Rolwaling Valley had been coaxed into our service, they were far short of our needs, numerically and physically. We had seldom seen such a sadly deficient lot of people as those of the Rolwaling. The cause may be inbreeding, the lack of iodine in their water, a sad history of venereal disease, or merely the stultifying forces of undernourishment and isolation. At least 50 per cent of the population suffered from disfiguring goiter; many were stunted, the way plants are stunted for lack of nutriment, and a pathetically large number were genuine cretins.

Yet they all wanted work, and our expedition was a godsend since it brought with it the opportunity of ready cash (barter meets the Rolwaling's usual needs) and luxuries like tins and bottles, empty crates, discarded food, and sometimes discarded clothes.

To get as far as we had with only local help had not been easy. Urkien had cajoled and bullied his way through Na and Beding trying to raise a sufficiency of porters. What an extraordinary collection they were when they arrived! One old woman was clearly too feeble to walk, let alone carry loads. But she insisted that she be taken on, or were we going to deprive her of urgently needed assistance? Not only did she shoulder a normal sixty pounds but added a few abandoned crates and tins to it so that her load stood as high as herself. Another had brought her newborn infant along and cradled it in a cardboard box atop her load.

Three good-looking young nuns from Beding were conspicuously the center of our expedition Sherpas' attention. They were given less cumbersome if not lighter loads to carry, were loaned

Balaclava caps, snow goggles, and gloves, and given a share of
the much coveted chocolate and cigarette ration. One of the
nuns was genuinely sophisticated, and it was interesting to
watch her use sunburn cream—offered by one of our Sherpas,
of course—in the artfully studied way that fashionable women
apply make-up.

When one of the women Urkien had rounded up suddenly decided to return home to Na we stumbled upon one of those little
dramas that illustrate the ruggedness of Sherpa existence. She
had two young children, one little more than an infant; her husband was away somewhere, and there was no one else in the
house. So she had stuffed her children to capacity, given them a
good swig of chang to make them drowsy (even she resisted
the harsh word drunk), and locked them in a room of the house.
Now, after seven hours, she was in an understandable panic.
Her children must be awake and restless: they may have
burned themselves in the open fire, or fallen out of a window, or
cut themselves, or done any of the myriad things that anxiety
can visualize; certainly they would be hungry. Urkien had told
her she would be needed only for three or four hours, but with
our shortage of labor he was now wanting her to cross over the
Tashi Lapcha, an undertaking of several days.

On October 25 the Solu Khumbu porters began arriving. There
was a shout from the cliffs high above us, and Pasang Tenzing,
who has the most remarkable eyesight, began intoning, "Two
men, a woman, that looks like Phu Dorji from Khumjung; four
more men, yes, I'm sure that's Phu Dorji; three women—hey,
Aila, your sister-in-law is coming. . . ." To us when we spotted
them at last on the rock ledges two thousand feet above us, the
newcomers were an antlike swarm hardly recognizable as
humans. Yet Pasang was correct. When after an hour they
scrambled from a deep *couloir* (a steep gully) and were at
last close enough for us to recognize individuals, there was Phu
Dorji, a veteran of Everest, in the lead. And Aila began yelling
greetings—or good-natured abuse—to his sister-in-law. By late
afternoon all sixty of the imported Sherpas had settled themselves into our glacier camp, most of them in rock shelters
blackened by the smoke of countless campfires. Scoops under
large rocks, often fortified by rock walls, provide excellent shelter for the traveler in these uninhabited wilds. Often there is

space enough for thirty people or more around several fires. I
once spent the night in a similar shelter with tons of rock a few
inches above my face. It was wonderfully warm and comfortable, the rock retaining the heat of a fire that had burned in the
shelter several hours before. But quite suddenly I discovered the
horror of claustrophobia. What if there should be an earthquake?
What if out of a formula of age the rock that had given shelter
to Sherpas since they first began coming to Nepal from Tibet
several centuries ago should subside without warning? Sleep
went by the board, but the alternative to possible death by
burial was certain death by freezing. I chose warm burial.

WHERE RAVENS HONK LIKE VINTAGE CARS

Sixty porters had just crossed the Tashi Lapcha without incident. It helped allay our worst fears. Sixty pairs of Sherpa boots
must have trampled a well-defined track through the snow. We
had been warned that the rock ledges above us were in an unstable condition, but again, if they had withstood the trample
of 120 feet, they almost certainly would bear with us.

Personally I was somewhat relieved. I even managed to sit
down and compose a news dispatch while sunlight flooded the
glacier and two runners leaving for Kathmandu sat to a hearty
meal.

"Tolam Bau October 26, 1960. By Runner.

"Marlin Perkins and George Lowe with four Sherpas are halfway up a precipitous ridge leading to the pass. They have been
in their precarious camp for four days, on a shelf no bigger than
a carpet, a flying carpet, hoping to catch a glimpse of the elusive
Snowman without seeing anything that could even remotely be
mistaken for a Yeti. There is nothing alive up here but ourselves,
a couple of almost tame ravens that honk like vintage cars held
up at traffic lights, and a few sad choughs condemned, it would
seem, never to rest. The ravens adopted us in Beding and have
been with us ever since.

"None of us would blame Yetis for avoiding the area. Apart
from an icily reserved, formidable beauty, it has nothing to
offer, not even the hardy plump mouse hare considered to be

favorite Snowman food. Water coaxed from beneath thick ice in glacier pools is free of the fork-tailed scarlet midges we have discovered and swallowed in water at higher altitudes than this. But when the sun warms the great tumble of rocks on the glacial ice, whole colonies of unexpected insects begin to swarm; silver fish of a size that would alarm housewives anywhere, flies, black jumping spiders, and tortoise-shell butterflies.

"We are now at the foot of the formidable Tashi Lapcha Pass, like fleas below the pyramids—Ed Hillary, Peter Mulgrew, Bhanu Bannerjee, Mike Gill, myself, and half a dozen Sherpas. Tom Nevison and Pat Barcham have gone ahead over the pass on a Yeti-hunting diversion of their own and will join us at our final Base Camp, Thyangboche. We did not see them go. We could only believe they went up these disintegrating cliffs and gullies and across the beds of cracking, splintering ice and are now safely on the other side of the pass. An army could pass this way and leave no trace; an army could be deployed behind the rock piles and moraine towers and in the craters about us and give no sign. Nor would they be heard among the rattle and groan and crash of all this restless rock and ice.

"We envy Tom and Pat, looking up the cliffs and icefalls toward the pass: their ordeal is over; ours is yet to begin, and as if to rub in the inherent difficulties, rock avalanches sweep the cliff we must eventually assault with that type of lordly exhibitionism one cannot ignore; the icefall (only alternative route) explodes and subsides alarmingly. Ed and Pete have tried to force it, failed, and declared it too dangerous, though to me it looks kinder than the cliffs.

"We are fully aware that the route up the cliffs is hazardous, our first real obstacle to date, particularly where it enters a deep *couloir*. There, apparently, the only usable ledge narrows to the width of a human foot, no more.

"To make matters worse, snow and rock avalanches pour down the *couloir* with disheartening frequency, so that George Lowe has advised us from his eyrie to climb with our hands over our heads to protect ourselves from the falling muck.

"What worries people like myself is that we usually approach such situations, if we must approach them at all, on all fours. Sir Edmund has promised us a fixed rope across the bad patches, and Mike Gill, in Hillary's estimation "a brilliant rock climber," left early this morning with Sherpa Phu Dorji, leader of the Solu Khumbu porters, to fix a rope in the unnerving *couloir;* I wish I had his cheerful assurance. Peter Mulgrew and Bhanu Bannerjee followed soon after, ahead of thirty porters, one at least carrying a load bulkier than himself. George Lowe, courting disaster in the *couloir,* and Marlin Perkins, on the cliff above, are well toward having a field day photographing the drama of the difficult ascent. We may live to see the film.

"Tomorrow, with the remaining thirty Sherpas from Namche Bazar, and twenty-five from our old base, Beding, plus the few expedition Sherpas with us here (the biggest lift over the Tashi Lapcha, according to Hillary), we will face the precipices and the pass. The Rolwaling Valley will settle to its winter sleep.

"The ravens, I like to think, will miss us."

TASHI LAPCHA

According to Ed Hillary, who was the first European to cross over (in 1951), the Tashi Lapcha is probably one of the world's most spectacular, and difficult, passes. On one side are precipitous rock slopes swept by avalanches and the track is a series of crumbling ledges; on the other are sheer icefalls.

We got to the top of the pass on October 28 without incident and only a loss of breath and occasional nerve. And then, as if to deliberately steal our thunder, there at the very top of the impossible pass were a herd of goats and another of yak, making the crossing with dumb unconcern. Some paid the price of their slavish devotion to man: we found stragglers left in the deep snow to die, terrified and using their small remaining strength to bleat and bellow after us as we passed. I was told it was unprofitable to worry about the sickly few, and besides, what could be done about them? There were half a dozen men with the two herds, all of them well laden. Carrying their exhausted animals was out of the question, and besides, speed over the pass was essential. Should a storm suddenly blow up all could be lost. What amazed us was that yak and sheep could be taken across the pass at all. Yak apparently are coaxed over obstacles such as the crumbling rock ledges and the *couloir,* one at a time, held onto by horns and tail.

Behind us was the vast Tolam Bau glacier on which we had spent a fifteen-hour night, huddled in our double sleeping bags, eating little because of the altitude, doing little because of the cold. The Sherpa porters had slept on ice, a blanket of yak hair beneath them and a canvas awning above, without any sign of discomfort. Our own Sherpas enjoyed the protection of expedition equipment—tents, air mattresses, sleeping bags. So did a few favored women.

Ahead were the valleys and spectacular mountains of Solu Khumbu, the true land of Sherpas; immediately above us, a mountain all snow and ice like a well-whipped meringue. Ed Hillary sat at the top of the pass, his shaggy mane riding a near gale and icicles forming in his beard. For the rugged, unemotional character we considered him to be he was suddenly and unexpectedly nostalgic. He confessed to being moved, excited, experiencing a feeling of "coming home"; in fact, to all the things that are the powerful Himalayan bug and Sherpa Siren. The mood was infectious. We were all soon wallowing in the heady atmosphere of Solu Khumbu, romping like school children, forgetting the wear and fatigue of the weary haul to the pass.

We had hardly started down from the pass when we ran into trouble. To avoid an impossible icefall we had to crawl down a long treacherous gully onto a 1000-foot slope of unstable scree (loose, small rocks). We had just begun descending, the route pioneered by Hillary, when there was a crack and rumble high up above and within seconds a rock avalanche crashed about us. I had stopped in the middle of the gully to take a photograph. Ed Hillary and some Sherpas were below me, George Lowe above. There were shouts from below, a "Look out" from George Lowe. As I flattened myself into the gully wall, arms folded above head, a small stone thudded into my pack; others, some the size of suitcases, went hurtling by. The terrifying business might have lasted minutes or seconds, I don't remember; fear is measured in eternities.

More terrifying was the silence that followed with dust swirling about and the mind braced to bear the shock of calamitous news. Were Hillary and his Sherpas safe? No reassuring sound. What had happened to George? Where were Marlin Perkins and Mike Gill and their Sherpas? They had been behind me, but no sound. Suddenly, as if in answer to my fears, there was a shout from somewhere above, and out over the lip of the cliff towering behind us sailed a basket from which tumbled tins and blurred objects to explode on the rocks below. All of us who saw it expected a body to follow. None did. Rocks crashing about some of our porters who had remained above the *couloir* had swept down one of their loads, but the man came through unscathed. In the basket was one of our precious radios, looking like a broken crate full of scrap. We had to abandon it.

Down on the scree slope, congratulating ourselves on having escaped so lightly, we were electrified by another, more violent explosion, another shriek of "Look out," and another vast spiraling, whirling tumble of rocks. Somehow we survived, but not heroically. By now we all were distinctly unnerved, and the rest of the descent was made with our eyes constantly on the heights above and our hearts thumping with more than the strain of altitude. To aggravate our fears, there at the bottom of the scree slope was a rock cairn topped by a wooden cross. What previous calamity did it commemorate?

Marlin Perkins and Mike Gill had watched the drama from above. It is creditable that they ever made the descent through the *couloir*, having been so spectacularly warned of its dangers. All that seemed to worry Marlin was that he did not have his camera handy at the time to record the dangers of Himalayan travel for TV audiences back home in Chicago.

The rest was an easy, delightful descent through Sherpa villages and fallow potato fields, across streams of wondrous clarity, and through forests of stunted rhododendron, juniper, and pine. What a joy it is to see grass and flowers again after long weeks of snow and barren acres of moraine. I had a sudden wild impulse to roll in the grass like an animal, to tear at leaves and flowers and make the lot into some giant salad into which I could plunge headlong. I wanted to bathe in the first stream, but the impulse was cured by the shock of cold.

Always there were great peaks towering above us: Amadablam; Tamserku; Khangtega, the "Yak's saddle"; and Makalu, hugely formidable even in distance, its rock summit dark among the other glittering peaks, as somber and prophetic as a black veil at a white wedding.

CHARITY ANOTHER NAME FOR DOLLARS

Norman Hardie awaited us at Thami, the first village of importance on the Khumbu side of the pass. Celebrations were
being held in the monastery to welcome the arrival of an important reincarnate lama from Tibet, and we decided to join in
them briefly. Our Sherpas were most anxious to pay their re-
spects to the lama and offer prayers for their safe passage over
the Tashi Lapcha. To us the monastery with all its new flags,
rather like a ship dressed for ceremonial, was a distinct attraction after the lonely weeks in the Rolwaling.

The reincarnate known as the Thulshig Rimpoche sat in the
main shrine of the monastery, on an elevated throne by the
gilded altar. Before him in two rows sat lamas in order of
seniority, and every other inch of available space was occupied
by Sherpas and Tibetan refugees from all Solu Khumbu.

We were offered tea, most thoughtfully tea in the Western
style, as our Sherpas knew our aversion to the soupy Tibetan
variety.

It seemed at first that the reincarnate was observing a day of
silence because, despite the long and often excited explanations
of our presence being made by lamas and our Sherpas alike, he
remained unspeaking, smiling and folded carefully in the lotus
position of meditation.

All of a sudden he summoned an interpreter and asked if he
could go to America.

I said I thought he could.

How much would it cost?

I told him.

Would he have to pay in dollars?

I said I thought not. Indian rupees would do.

But dollars were essential to a trip abroad, or was this not
true?

Dollars, I admitted, were helpful.

How could he get some dollars? Did we have any?

Tom Nevison thought he might have a few cents and began
rummaging through a battered purse.

Were any of us Americans? the reincarnate wanted to know.

I pointed to Tom and Marlin, and immediately all attention was focused on them.

When was America going to liberate Tibet?

Neither Tom nor Marlin were quite sure.

But America would hurl the Chinese from Tibet, wouldn't they?

Silence, full of whispers and scarlet embarrassment.

It didn't matter. Dollars were the immediate problem. Could Tom and Marlin arrange to procure some?

Marlin at this point played the perfect diplomat. People back home would love to know what the Rimpoche looked like: familiarity breeds charitable interest; charity is another name for dollars. Could he take photographs of the Rimpoche?

So we all adjoined to a sunny courtyard where a throne was hastily erected and the reincarnate posed in great dignity for a dozen cameras. He insisted on wearing a pair of gold-rimmed spectacles that had originated in Calcutta, but whether they were his or a prop considered necessary to his important position, we never discovered. He also insisted on posing with one of our movie cameras, and did.

In the courtyard in which the Rimpoche posed a large bee-hive-shaped furnace was being constructed of stone and earth. In it, I was told, the remains of another important lama would be cremated within days, and would we like to attend the ceremony?

According to our Sherpas, the reincarnate of Rongbuk mon-astery in Tibet had died seventeen years previously, and in keep-ing with tradition his body had been embalmed and encased in a stupa of copper decorated with gold and precious stones. When the Chinese invaded Tibet a miraculous safeguard against bul-lets, sword thrusts, indeed death in any violent form, was in-creasingly talked about. It was nothing less than eating the re-mains of renowned lama saints, such as the embalmed body of Lama Nawang Tenzing Norbu, piece by little piece, like swal-lowing pills. And so the lama's stupa in Rongbuk was broken into and his corpse removed. Somehow the need to devour it was never necessary; the Tibetans who bore it to Nepal escaped without opposition from the Chinese—a miracle in itself. Now it was being given decent retirement; after cremation the ashes would be kept against the day that a new stupa could be built about them. Cremation had been ordained by an oracle.

THE SCALPS

Two days later we were in Khumjung, the Sherpa village that is home to most of our expedition Sherpas. We were given a great reception; everyone turned out to welcome us; every household insisted on entertaining us to bouts of drinking, feasting, and dancing. We accepted the lot and did the equivalent of a pub crawl, growing weaker as we progressed. At every party where the abandoned, stamping dances of Tibet and Sherpaland were performed a fur-hatted, blue-eyed, and delightfully animated village elder was the undisputed champion. He claimed to be the dance champion of Lhasa, a distinction won by performing nonstop for twelve hours. His name was Khunjo Chumbi.

Khumjung is outrageously lovely, particularly in the tangerine and lavender hour when we approached it through a miniature landscape of carved rocks and stunted pine trees festooned with trailing lichen. Above the village is the stark rock and ice pyramid of Khumbila, god to the Solu Khumbu Sherpas, a peak which because of its religious significance must forever remain unscaled. Beyond is Everest and the Lhotse-Nuptse wall piled enormously together, and Amadablam, magnificent in isolation.

Agitated prayer flags ride the roof of every house so that the massively proportioned buildings appear unsubstantial, to shiver in the cold; and to heighten the feel of movement huge shaggy yaks stride ponderously between the houses, and black mastiffs with marble-blue eyes strain at heavy chains, and goats swarm in and out of front doors, and children, like an invasion of grubby cherubs, frolic everywhere.

Above the village and directly below the highest pinnacle of Khumbila is a small stone monastery where for seven days in the year is enacted the legend of a great Snowman slaying and the miraculous acquisition of the monastery's most cherished relic—a Yeti scalp.

We arrived in Khumjung on October 30 and, impatient to examine the Yeti scalp, went in a body to the monastery on the following day. The place was deserted, and when eventually we gained entrance there was no sign of the scalp. We were to learn that afternoon that the people of Khumjung guard their extraordinary treasure with more than ordinary zeal.

Three village elders have to be present when the scalp is exposed. Each must affix his personal seal to the box in which the relic is kept when it is closed after exhibition. The box is kept in the house of a nun, an ancient crone believed to possess mystic powers. Since the three elders can be doing things as diverse as grazing yaks, visiting a neighboring village, or drinking deeply in any one of 150 houses, getting them together is no easy matter. The antique dame is almost always at home, but should she be out the whole thing becomes impossible.

It took us a good three hours to get the elders assembled in the monastery. When we did, the scalp was brought from the nun's house, worn in turn by the village elders, thrust onto the head of Hillary (looking like a self-conscious Robinson Crusoe), and then for good measure given to Marlin Perkins and myself to wear.

For all of us, long unkempt hair and all, the scalp was a size or more too big. It was a mystifying object, dome-shaped and sparsely covered with black and henna bristles, obviously of some age, and to all appearances the scalp of a powerful anthropoid—most likely contender the mountain gorilla. From sawn-off base to pointed crown it was eight inches deep, seven inches in width, and ten inches long at its oval base. The thickness of the tough, blackened hide was from 3/16 to 1/8 of an inch, the circumference of the base twenty-eight inches. Once the entire scalp must have been covered with coarse bristles, but now the mange of considerable age had reduced them to shaggy patches above what would have been the eyes and the ears and along the distinct, slightly raised median crest, like a stubby mane. The scalp was pierced with holes around its base to allow a brocaded frill and a chinband to be attached when it was worn during the ceremony commemorating its acquisition. Usage, the touch of the devout, and age had caused it to split and crack. But, since tradition invested it with a life of two hundred years or more, it was remarkably well preserved.

Was it genuine? Most of us thought not, though there was no sign of it being joined or sewed or otherwise contrived.

According to the three guardian village elders, the valleys about Khumjung were once overpopulated by Yetis, a considera-

tion that did not worry the Sherpas until the creatures took to
man-eating. So one day, two hundred and more years ago, when
a man, his son, and daughter had been slain and eaten by a
Snowman, the people of the Sherpa valleys decided the Yetis
must be liquidated. But how? Yetis were powerful creatures;
they were in a distinct majority and had acquired a taste for
human blood. A certain learned lama, Rolwa Dorji by name,
formulated a somewhat irreligious plan, considering lamas must
never take life. Large vats of chang were brought out in full
view of the watching Yetis; the villagers pretended to drink
their fill and then to fight to the death among themselves. The
swords the villagers used for their mock battle were made of
wood; at dusk when they stole from the battleground where
they had been simulating death all day they took the precaution of leaving genuine, well-sharpened swords behind them
and, of course, the chang.

Alas for Yetis, they were splendid mimics. At nightfall they
descended from their rocky fastness where they had occupied
a grandstand view of the Sherpa battle, drank the potent chang,
and, getting drunk, fought to the death. In the morning only one
rather dazed Yeti remained. This Lama Rolwa Dorji personally
slew and carried its carcass back to his monastery in triumph.

The monastery in this case was the one at Thami. Some fifty
years later the people of the Sherpa valleys rose in dispute one
against the other and those of Khumjung won the battle, ran-
sacked the Thami monastery, and carried away the scalp. The
rest of the creature had apparently been given to other monasteries and purloined piece by piece by visitors.

Thus the famous relic came to Khumjung where it has remained ever since. The only improbable part of this story, which
is current in several widely separated areas of the Himalayas, is
that the Sherpas pretended to drink the chang and feign drunk-
enness. From my knowledge of Sherpas they would have been
beyond caring when evening came and, had the spirit of peaceful coexistence been as rife then as it is today, Yetis and humans
would have had a good old binge together and lived happily
ever after.

There is a similar scalp in the monastery in Pangboche, a
village eight miles from Khumjung in the direction of Everest,
but whereas the Khumjung scalp is held in superstitious regard,

the Pangboche scalp is considered sacred and, as such, quite impossible to buy or borrow. If we wanted one of the scalps, and we did, it would have to be Khumjung's.

The story of Pangboche's acquisition of a Yeti scalp is less convincing than the one associated with Khumjung's. It seems the founder of the monastery, a certain Lama Saywa Dorji, was given to meditation on a mountain high above Pangboche village where he was kept alive by the generous administrations of a Yeti. The creature used to bring the lama food and drink, and this arrangement lasted for years. Then one day the lama felt pangs of hunger reach through the insulation of his devotions and realized the Yeti had not fed him for days. He at once went out in search of his benefactor, only to discover the Yeti dead in a cave.

The Lama Saywa Dorji brought the Snowman's scalp to his monastery, and there it has remained, a relic eventually sharing the same chapel with the lama's own sacred remains, eyes, tongue, and intestines, enshrined in a jewel-studded, gilt casket.

The Pangboche monastery also boasts a "Yeti" hand, which more than one expert (examining photographs and a flake of skin) has declared to be human or part human. The hand is skeletal; the heavy, markedly squared phalanges are wired together and the palm partly covered with brown, leathery skin. It is possible that some of the bones are not human, but almost certainly the best part of the hand is. It is a large but slender human hand, a woman's perhaps, but more possibly a young lama's. More than one of our expedition members had been moved to remark on the delicate, sensitive fingers of important lamas we met.

It is not unusual for the hand or heart or skull of a dead lama to be preserved as a relic in his monastery. Skulls are made into ceremonial cups; trumpets are made from thigh bones. What should have turned suspicion on the Khumjung and Pangboche scalps from the very outset is the fact that they are without supporting skulls. Much more significance would have attached to the skulls of Snowmen, which undoubtedly would have become articles of genuine religious import, whereas the scalps are merely good-luck charms.

The Pangboche hand might well have begun its mysterious existence as a relic, a displaced companion of the Lama Saywa Dorji's other morbid remains.

6

ARTICLES OF
AGREEMENT

On looking back, our arrival in Khumjung was the point at which we abandoned our open-minded attitude toward the Snowman legend and frankly disbelieved.

There was cause.

On the way down from the Tashi Lapcha I met two women in a small village who told me that the remains of a Yeti had been found on a nearby hillside only a month previously. When news of the find reached the Nepalese check post at Namche Bazar, two miles below Khumjung, the captain in charge promptly ordered that the remains be taken to him and, quoting a government order which made all Yetis and Yeti relics the property of the King, promptly seized them. I for one was wildly excited. Here was fate playing right into our hands, giving us, short of a living Yeti, the most convincing proof of the Snowman existence we could hope to find—a skeleton. We lost no time in visiting the captain at Namche Bazar. It was on our way, and in any case we had to report our arrival in Solu Khumbu to the captain.

Yes, he said, he had the complete skeleton of a Yeti, also some hair from the carcass. He had preserved the lot most carefully for us since he was certain we would wish to buy it.

We assured him we would if it looked promising, but we must see it first. With great ceremony an old sack was brought into the captain's sitting room and its contents carefully emptied onto the floor. There was no doubt about it whatsoever. The skeleton belonged to a dog, a large dog, probably a Tibetan mastiff.

Anyway, here were bones and fur belonging to something that the locals were ready to declare was a Yeti. As such, we wanted to photograph the phony remains and asked the captain if we might do so.

No, he said. If we neither thought the remains to be a Yeti's nor did we want to buy them, then why should we bother to photograph them. If they were important enough to photograph, on the other hand, they were worth buying.

We declined, and the bones were returned to their sack with exaggerated care. We were ready to stake anything on the "Yeti remains" being free on any of the numerous village refuse dumps next morning.

An easy day's walk from Khumjung is Thyangboche, a monastery village built on a spur in full view of Everest and devoted to contemplation of the world's greatest peak. I risk a cliché to declare it one of the most enchanting places on earth, exquisite in any mood, at any time of day. In cloud its tiered pagoda roofs and stout walls are a fabled castle, shrouded in mystery; on a day of sparkling clarity, as only days at high altitude are clear, it is the mystic jewel in the lotus, the great peaks arranged all about it like petals, as delicately shaded, as pure. Nowhere have I felt such exhilaration, such wondrously primitive joy, as at Thyangboche. Man here has enhanced, not desecrated, his surroundings.

The monastery is built over a stone on which a long-departed lama saint slipped and fell, and visitors are shown the imprints of his heels in the rock. *Tingba* in the Sherpa language is heels; *jay* is imprint. *Tingba-jay* is literally "the imprint of heels."

So the beautiful monastery village is understandably sympathetic to legend and local tales. These myths have been given credence, certainly prominence, by visiting foreign journalists who have invested Thyangboche monastery with a particular Yeti mystique. Apparently Snowmen have descended winter after severe winter to play in a forest clearing near the monastery and in full view of the resident lamas.

There are the classic details: Yetis being frightened away from monastery precincts by trumpet- and cymbal-playing lamas; Yetis carrying away village belles, mating with them, producing children. Invariably these children have been destroyed by the villagers in unholy wrath or they have conveniently died of natural causes "just a few years ago; so unfortunate."

There is even the story put out by a recent journalist visitor to Thyangboche that a Yeti killed a man within full sight of the monastery and its lamas two days before he and some companions arrived. The story was complete with details of Sherpa timidity, the Snowman's savage unconcern, and a sorrowful if colorful cremation recorded on film.

Naturally we were most eager to investigate. After all, the report had the validity of Western observation and it bolstered local legend.

It was something more than an anticlimax, therefore, to discover from the reincarnated head lama of Thyangboche monastery the day we arrived that the alleged Yeti killing was a drama staged by certain interested locals, mostly porters, for the benefit of their sahibs. The young lama was positively embarrassed when we pressed for details.

"We had nothing to do with it," he said. "It so happened a man had died and was being cremated. That is not unusual; all people who die in the area are cremated here. But I am positive the dead man was not killed by a Yeti, or bear, or any other animal. I know some such thing was said at the time and a lot of pictures were taken of the cremation."

Had the head lama or any of his lamas seen a Yeti, perhaps in winter when the creatures were said to play about near the monastery?

He could not speak for the others, but he personally had seen nothing. Two old lamas who helped build the monastery fifty years ago and had been there ever since were equally certain that they had never seen the Yetis that visited Thyangboche, but it was said that many years ago . . .

So it went. Every person who was rumored to have seen Snowmen in the vicinity of Thyangboche extricated themselves under close questioning by explaining that Yetis *used* to be seen, by their forefathers. Nowadays they are only heard, an unfamiliar high and sorrowing cry not unlike a chough's. Marlin Perkins felt certain that snow leopards were responsible for the mysterious sound, and we hoped that when the first winter snowfalls brought the high-ranging animals of the area down to observable altitudes (Thyangboche is 13,000 feet above sea level) we might record and classify the "Yeti" sound. Of course, we didn't. Not once during the many months we were in and about Thyangboche did we hear anything even approximating the call of a Yeti.

Introduction to the Serow

Our full concentration was now turned on the Khumjung and Pangboche scalps, though after repeated and detailed examinations of both we were more and more of the opinion that they were artifacts ingeniously molded from the hide of some animal possessed of a mane. What animal was anyone's guess, but we were fairly certain that the scalps had originated as ceremonial hats and somewhere in their long history had merged with the powerful local Snowman legend.

Working on data supplied by previous expeditions, hairs from Khumjung and Pangboche scalps had been checked in America and the United Kingdom against the sera of rodent, cow, giant sloth, Asian blue bear, gorilla, ape, horse, goat, pig, panda, and the human animal without proving anything. This wide area of prior research left us precious little to conjure with, and we would have gone on being mystified about the origin of the scalps but for an unexpected and happy coincidence.

The day after we examined the Khumjung scalp our special fur-and-oddments sleuth, Sherpa Ang Temba, shook Marlin Perkins, Bhanu Bannerjee, and myself (sharing a tent) into a freezing, anemic dawn to inform us that he had discovered another Yeti fur and a few "other things." True enough, there was a splendid blue-bear fur, complete with all four feet and musk, spread out before our bleary eyes. It was the lightest-colored fur we had yet seen, so blond that it was platinum in places. Yetis, by people who claim to have seen them, have been described as white, gray, rust, red, and black.

We were just getting over the excitement of this important acquisition when Ang Temba asked if we wanted another, quite ordinary hide. Even as he unrolled it we felt certain it was the raw material for the Yeti scalp in the local monastery: a dark mane reaching the entire length of the large body, coarse red and black bristles, a firm thick hide. Under a magnifying glass bristles from the hide compared exactly with the hair we had begged from the Khumjung scalp. The hide, we discovered later, belonged to the serow, a wild goat-antelope (*Naemorhedus*).

Among the "other things" that Ang Temba brought for our inspection that morning were some highly "mystical" objects described by him as the horn of a horse, "lightning's excreta" (literal translation meaning a thunderbolt), a petrified lama's penis, and a human tail: the lot were pebbles. Ang Temba looked most disappointed when I pronounced them phonies and worthless. The human tail was expected to raise at least Rs.1000 ($143) by the lamas who owned it.

That night I wrote in my diary, "Almost certainly the Khumjung and Pangboche scalps are twins, made on the same mold of serow's hide. The shape, color, and essential dimensions are identical; two conical, balding caps of black-and-henna-colored bristles with distinct median crests and punctured with holes about their bases which look suspiciously like those made by nails used to hold the scalps onto their mold."

In an endeavor to prove that the scalps would be molded artifacts, even if our guess at the fur was incorrect, we set about making two of our own, sacrificing one of three serow hides we had acquired, and employing an unsuspecting lama to carve the molds from a freshly felled pine log. So expertly and immediately did the old man fashion the conical molds, using a crude local tool, that it almost looked as though he might have manufactured the originals. The results were excellent. After four days of experiment we possessed two distinctly anthropoid "scalps," unlike those in the Khumjung and Pangboche monasteries only in their newness and wealth of hair.

On Ang Temba's advice we conditioned our rather old hides by soaking them in a mixture of hot water and mud and beating them pliable with hammers. A fresh hide would have been the answer, but all our efforts to obtain one failed.

We sent bristles from our fakes and the original Yeti scalps to Dr. Osman Hill of the Zoological Society of London for investigation, without giving him any clue to their origin, and we did so with certain excitement. If the two samples were declared identical, the scalps would be fakes and an important argument in favor of Yetis would have been defeated. Until proved otherwise the Khumjung and Pangboche scalps were impressive proof that Snowmen existed. We might think them to be fakes, but we could not be certain until a thorough examination by experts could be made. One of the scalps must be taken abroad, but how? Even if we could coax or bribe our way past the elders of Khumjung there was the old unbending witch to contend with.

And what if some calamity did befall Khumjung or Sherpas anywhere while the scalp was being exhibited abroad? We would be blamed, and the whole happy relationship of Sherpas and sahibs might be in jeopardy.

"THE BOY MUST DIE"

One of the very first persons I met in Khumjung was Khunjo Chumbi, the dancing champion of our welcome parties. He told me that he owned a Yeti relic and thought I might be interested in it. From a chest in his house he took a basket, from which he took a tin, from which he extracted a copiously bandaged object. It was a single claw which on examination turned out to be from the left rear foot of a Tibetan blue bear.

While we bargained, because naturally the relic had a price, Chumbi told me that two of his children had actually seen a Yeti only a few months before our arrival while they had been grazing the family yaks.

"Over there," he said, indicating the slopes of Tamserku, a 21,000-foot mountain of fluted snow rearing above Khumjung.

"The children were playing together when suddenly the creature walked out of some rhododendron bushes and stood watching them. They thought it was a nun at first. It was so human in appearance and its rust-red color was so exactly that of a nun's robe that they thought it was a nun collecting firewood. They even called out 'Ani' (Sherpa for nun), whereupon the Yeti—what else could it be—turned slowly and walked back into the bushes. The children grew frightened and ran for home. We are very worried, because people who see Yetis usually die shortly after the encounter."

I questioned the children, a grave-eyed boy of fourteen and a girl of eight. Yes, they had seen a Yeti; their descriptions were very exact and I believe authentic. I have no doubt that they saw a bear, probably the elusive blue bear of Tibet, or something unfamiliar.

When I visited Khumjung months later, Khunjo Chumbi's son

lay seriously ill, dying of pneumonia. His labored breathing filled the smoky gloom of Chumbi's house so that the building seemed to breathe. He lay by a window, wrapped in blankets, his eyes glazed and deep in their sockets, his cheekbones almost bursting through his sallow skin.

Why, I asked Chumbi, did he not send to us for help? We had doctors with us, as he knew; they would have come immediately.

"It's no use," he said. "The boy must die."

I could have struck him in sudden anger. Why the hell should the boy die?

"Because he saw a Yeti."

Chumbi told me that he had consulted lamas about his child's condition since the malady was in their spiritual province, but they had offered no hope.

All this was said in front of the boy, probably for the umpteenth time. He whimpered but otherwise received his father's and the lama's prediction with stoical calm.

I did all I could to assure the boy he could recover and then, using all the abuse I could remember, lashed Chumbi and his wife into making a broth of yak's meat, vegetables, and eggs. Fortunately I had a bottle of assorted pills with me, and from among the vitamin, water-purifying, sleeping, and dysentery tablets I fished four lozenges of chloromycetin. For a moment I felt real panic. What if the pills killed the child in his exhausted state? It was a risk that had to be taken. Besides, his parents fully expected him to die, no matter what was done for the boy. I prescribed one pill every two hours, with soup or milk, and administered the first dose myself, praying hard.

By evening the boy was much better; his pulse was steadier and his breathing closer to normal. I retired, deeply relieved, but was wakened before dawn to be told that something had gone wrong; could I come at once?

Chumbi's son was bleeding profusely from his nose. "An hour already," his mother said, holding a copper drinking pot under his chin. It was alarming to see how quickly the vessel filled; there was no doubt about it, the child was bleeding to death.

"It's no good," Chumbi kept telling me. "He saw a Yeti and now he must die."

In desperation I sent a runner to our camp six miles away to ask assistance from our doctors, fully aware that it might never arrive in time. Chumbi sent for the lamas. Suddenly Mrs. Chumbi had a primitive inspiration. Fetching a hunk of yak dung from outside, she burned it over the fire and rammed it, hot, into the boy's nose. The bleeding stopped. Two days later the child was out of bed and Chumbi was having second thoughts about the infallibility of the Yetis' curse.

An Angry God

It was to Khunjo Chumbi that I first broached the subject of borrowing the Khumjung scalp. If he was shocked at the idea he showed no sign. On the contrary, he appeared quite intrigued and promised his co-operation. At the same time he warned that it would be a long-drawn-out and difficult transaction, if not altogether impossible. At least one bid for the scalp had been made previously and almost ended in riot. The gods that protected the scalp (human or otherwise, I wasn't sure) could get very angry.

At this point I sent a message to Ed who had pushed on to supervise the building of our Silver Hut.

"Would you be interested in obtaining Pat's red hat? Could be expensive business."

Pat Barcham was our code for Yeti; Pat's red hat was the scalp.

Back came the reply, "Go ahead, most interested," and negotiations began.

One by one the village elders of Khumjung and Khunde, a village immediately adjoining Khumjung and sharing the one monastery, were isolated and wooed. Each one feared the others' reaction but was willing to temporarily part with the relic at a price. The toughest opposition came from the Khunde "major," the headman of both villages who was rich, superstitious, and very conscious of his position, in this case custodian of the public good fortune. He told me that to remove the scalp from Khumjung, for however short a while, might cause a visitation of the plague, earthquake, failure of crops, a crippling disease among yaks, or disastrous avalanches from the heights of Khumbila.

But I persisted, bargaining now with the promise of considerable funds for renovation of the monastery. And didn't the village elders know of our desire to build a school in Khumjung? This was a gesture of friendship for the Khunde-

Khumjung Sherpas, and in the name of this very friendship we were asking the favor of being loaned the Yeti scalp. Just for three months; well, two then; all right, six weeks, but no less. Yes, we would take great care with it; Hillary and Doig would personally accompany it. It was difficult to make the elders understand the enormous distances involved in getting the scalp to America, France, and Britain, and at this point they were not exactly keen to know. Six weeks or not at all. We had to agree, fully conscious that the whole project would be possible only if we could get a helicopter to lift us in and out of Khumjung. The normal one-way walking distance between Khumjung and Kathmandu is measured in fourteen to seventeen days. Allowing even the minimum number of days in Chicago, Paris, and London for actual examination of the scalp, we calculated four weeks outside Nepal essential. We might even make it walking one way, but going and coming on foot was out of the question. We still said yes.

Just when it seemed we had won our prize, along came Khunjo Chumbi to say that one of the gods was giving trouble.

Which god?

Oh, one of the mortal ones—this said with a two-eyed wink.

Could the god's anger be appeased?

Yes, of course, but it would cost Rs.500 ($66).

Would the god consider a reduction?

Absolutely none. His anger was great.

Five hundred rupees were handed over with the earnest hope that no more gods would suffer fits of bad temper.

At this point we began having nightmares, horrifying nightmares in which we had procured the scalp but were without the funds to transport it anywhere, and appeals sent to our sponsors and friends drew a blank, and then when eventually we got away we could not return to Khumjung. The dream ended with Khumbila, the powerful Sherpa god, destroying Khumjung and Khunde in one colossal exhibition of divine wrath and our Sherpas hurling us down precipices.

Ed took warning. He sent cables to our sponsors advising them of our good luck and explaining that luck of this kind might cost them four air tickets around the world plus other Himalayan expenses. Between the lot of us and the expedition treasure box we did not have enough cash to pay the sum agreed for renova-

34. *Sherpa men and women working to build an airstrip. In the background, Mount Taweche.*

35. (LEFT) *A very old nun from the nunnery near Thyangboche.*

36. (RIGHT) *A Sherpa villager.*

37. (LEFT) *Sherpa girl dressed in her traditional finery.*

38. (TOP LEFT) *The head lama of Thyangboche (left) and one of his senior advisers.* 39.
(BOTTOM LEFT) *A boy of sixteen—the youngest of the 500 men to carry a sixty-pound load
eight days through a hundred miles of rain and leeches. The Sherpa is Gumi Dorji, who
later broke his leg on Amadablam.* 40. (TOP RIGHT) *An Indian fakir who visited the Silver
Hut and had an astonishing ability to sleep out in the open with bare feet and no bedding.*
41. (BOTTOM RIGHT) *Sherpa women overcome the baby-sitting problem by adding a child
to their sixty-pound load.*

42. (ABOVE) *Khunjo Chumbi and his family before his departure for Chicago with the Yeti scalp.*

43. (RIGHT) *Natives with their crafts.*

tions to the Khumjung monastery. Pause. Another desperate cable was sent to World Book Encyclopedia headquarters. But what if the money did not come on time or not at all? "Face" is of paramount importance in Sherpaland. If we could not rise to our agreement after all the fuss we had been making over the past several days, we would be eternally damned. We even began hoping that the transaction might be held up by more divine anger, but it was not to be. We were summoned to a handing-over ceremony in the monastery on November 18.

Poor old Ed became obsessed with the non-arrival of the runners and news from America. Our funds in the Nepal Bank, Kathmandu, were dangerously low. Besides, could we afford to risk everything on the success of the Yeti hunt just when a critical stage in the preparations for our physiological program had been reached? Opinions were sharply divided. For a while our physiologists and Yeti enthusiasts glared at each other.

OUR SHERPAS AS HOSTAGE

Postponed for twenty-four hours in acknowledgment of our bankruptcy, the handing-over ceremony was held on the nineteenth, when to our enormous relief our runners arrived with the necessary money. It was a rumbustious affair often menaced by superstition and the anger of the local "gods." But eventually Sherpa friendliness outbalanced Sherpa mistrust and the scalp was handed over to Sir Edmund by the village elders via the old nun, now a grimacing gargoyle.

Articles of agreement were drawn up in Sherpa, Nepali, and English. We had gone fortified with an agreement of our own, typed on the best paper we could raise and liberally decorated with sealing wax. It read:

ARTICLE OF AGREEMENT BETWEEN THE HILLARY-LED HIMALAYAN SCIENTIFIC AND MOUNTAINEERING EXPEDITION 1960–61 AND THE VILLAGE ELDERS OF KHUNDE AND KHUMJUNG.

His Majesty the King of Nepal and his Government have granted permission to the Himalayan Scientific and Mountaineering Expedition 1960–61, led by Sir Edmund Hillary, to temporarily remove to

America and Europe the Yeti scalp belonging to the villages of Khunde and Khumjung.

As is now known by the people of these villages, discussions have been held during the past weeks between ourselves, represented by Sir Edmund Hillary, Desmond Doig, and Marlin Perkins on the one hand, and Gnana Chumbi, the village elder of Khunde, and Khunjo Chumbi, Dorje Mundo, and Nima Tashi, the village elders of Khumjung on the other.

These discussions have concerned the following points and conditions, to which all parties have agreed.

1. That the Yeti scalp belonging to the villages of Khunde and Khumjung be loaned to the Scientific and Mountaineering Expedition led by Sir Edmund Hillary, for the purpose of examination by experts in America and Europe.

2. That the duration of the loan be six weeks, two weeks for transportation to and from Kathmandu, and one month for examination abroad.

3. That the above-named members of the expedition be responsible for the safe return of the scalp within the stipulated time.

4. That as a gesture of our good faith we are prepared to meet the following conditions and requirements of the above-mentioned village elders of Khunde and Khumjung:

    a. That one village elder accompany the Yeti scalp wherever it may be taken in America and Europe, and that his entire expenses be paid by the expedition.

    b. That a gift of Rs.8,ooo/oo (Rupees eight thousand only in Nepali currency) be made to the Gompa at Khumjung for the purpose of urgent renovations.

    c. That Sir Edmund Hillary and the members of the expedition put into effect an appeal to the sponsors of the expedition, mountaineering societies, and the general public to establish and support a school for the benefit of the people of Khunde and Khumjung villages.

As part of this agreement we the undersigned wish it to be understood by all in the two villages that Sir Edmund Hillary and all members of his expedition consider the generosity of the people of Khunde and Khumjung in lending their cherished relic a gesture of genuine friendship between the Sherpa people and the people of the West. In the spirit of this friendship we ask the elders of Khunde and Khumjung to affix their seals beside our own.

Signed on this the nineteenth day of November in the Year Nineteen Hundred and Sixty, in the village of Khumjung, Nepal.

The document was signed by Hillary, Perkins, and myself; Sirdar Dawa Tenzing, Urkien, and Annullu affixed their seals as witnesses.

Never had Khumjung's old and crumbling monastery, in the courtyard of which the ceremony was held, seen anything like it. It was mad, happy, emotional, slightly drunk chaos. Yet while persuasive argument and inculcative wrangling zoomed afresh, the lamas of the monastery sat unmoved in prayer, their chanting insinuating itself into the few near-silences the day enjoyed, like a swarming of bees.

We had asked for an extension of the loan period. Why? Where was our magic helicopter? Were we already going back on our given word? Why could not the scalp be transported to and from Kathmandu and be examined abroad in the space of a month? Were not Western scientists clever enough? Was there any reason for the privilege of being loaned the scalp? After all, other expeditions had made considerable offers and had been refused, even when they were prepared to accept the scalp for only a month.

We avoided a walkout by two stubborn village elders and— triumph for our methods of acclimatization—we outtalked the most garrulous in the rarefied atmosphere of Khumjung.

But the real heroes of the day were our three head expedition Sherpas, Sirdar Dawa Tenzing, Urkien, and Annullu. Whereas we had included them in our written agreement as mere witnesses, the village elders of Khumjung had decided to hold them and their estates as hostage. If we did not return the Yeti scalp in the time stipulated, a grudgingly won six weeks, the entire properties and effects of these three Sherpas would be forfeit to the village and monastery.

To their considerable credit, and as testimony to their faith and friendship, the three Sherpas, who had no reason to do more than their paid jobs demanded, did not hesitate to put their signatures to the agreements. They were openly embarrassed when we expressed our gratitude.

Celebrations took over where the ceremony left off. Old Sherpa custom demanded a party and got it. We slept where we drank our last drinks that night, and I'm damned if I can remember where that was.

STRANGE GIFTS FOR A QUEEN

In conformity with our agreement Ed decided that four of us
need accompany the scalp on its world travels: Marlin Perkins
as our zoologist, Khunjo Chumbi as the relic's guardian, myself
as interpreter and wet nurse to Chumbi, and of course Ed himself.

The choice of Khunjo Chumbi as the Sherpas' representative
could not have been a happier one. Forty-eight years old, Khunjo
Chumbi is as typical a Sherpa as one could hope for: strong
Mongolian features, plaited hair, turquoise earrings, embroidered felt boots, and a swagger that agitates his magenta robes.
He is the keeper of the village documents, deeds, and ancient
firmans (issued by the once all-powerful prime minister of
Nepal) demanding the allegiance of Khumjung's Sherpas who,
until then, had looked to Tibet and the Dalai Lama in matters of
law and order.

When Khunjo Chumbi learned that he had been selected to
accompany the Yeti scalp to America and Europe, he prepared
for travel—preparations identical to those he had made to visit
Lhasa, in Tibet. He sent for four bricks of Tibetan tea and he
ordered a new pair of high felt boots. What worried him was
food. Should he take the usual Sherpa traveling rations with
him: a full sun-dried carcass of sheep, a bag of wheat flour, at
least one wooden bottle of chang? We persuaded him to leave
rations behind, but he insisted on taking along his silver Tibetan
teacup and a Tibetan rug, plus a selection of fur caps and
turquoise and coral necklaces, some, we suspected, borrowed
from his wife.

And of course he had to take presents for Queen Elizabeth,
President Eisenhower, and the King of Nepal; strange gifts by
Western standards that included bags of finely ground *tsampa*
(wheat flour), sacred scroll paintings depicting the Buddhist
saint and mystic Guru Padma Sambhava, bricks of Tibetan tea,
and dried yak's tails. These, Khunjo Chumbi explained, were the
traditional gifts for important chiefs, and he would rather go
shamefully naked than without them. When informed that
Queen Elizabeth had a husband and three children, Khunjo

Chumbi was immediately worried about the quantity of tea and *tsampa* he had to offer. "But then they probably have a lot given to them every day by the people," he said.

Khunjo Chumbi showed me these gifts shortly after we left Khumjung on the trek to Kathmandu: the scrolls, the Tibetan tea, and yak's tails all wrapped in fine Nepali paper; the *tsampa* in a homespun bag typical of Sherpaland. I wondered about these gifts being introduced into the splendors of royal palaces and presidential homes; the raised eyebrows, the questioning glances, and then perhaps delight at presents so unexpected and unusual.

Chumbi had no doubt that he would be received by the Queen and President. He was a village elder, wasn't he? He was traveling far and risking the dangers of crossing the sacred seas beyond the earth, wasn't he? Besides, great chiefs were kind, weren't they?

I found myself being tortured with doubts and praying that our world of protocol barriers and well-defined social boundaries would be kind to this innocently naïve villager from Khumjung. Tibetan tea, it should be explained, is drunk with yak butter and salt. *Tsampa* is the "Sherpa's staple diet"; an offering of *tsampa* is an offer of hospitality and friendship. Yak's tails, adorned or embellished with silver handles, are used as fly whisks, and to Khunjo Chumbi there is no inhabited place in the world without flies.

Auspicious Day

Sir Edmund, Khunjo Chumbi, George Lowe, Pat Barcham, the Yeti scalp, and I left Khumjung on November 25, a day proclaimed auspicious by the old witch. The village elders gathered in the monastery; pledges were exchanged; seals were affixed to the scalp itself by almost anyone of importance who had a seal handy; vast quantities of chang were consumed, and suddenly this most enigmatic of strange relics was in one of our traveling boxes and we were on the switchback trail to Kathmandu. Our Sherpa porters matched the rather abstract history they were making: among them, quite unintentionally, was Sen Tenzing, the Sherpa who had been with Eric Shipton when he discovered the now famous Menlung Yeti tracks, two practicing witch doctors, two lamas, an artist, a bootmaker, and a tailor. On the hurried 170-mile dash from Khumjung the artist found time to fill a sketch book with drawings of mythical animals and Yetis. One of the witch doctors told how a powerful predecessor had reached up and pulled the moon into a valley we passed through in order to brighten it. His fingerprints can be seen on the moon to this day.

More practical was the bootmaker. He decided Ed Hillary's walking shoes needed urgent repair and had to be convinced that Sir Edmund's feet could only be contained in the undersized tennis shoes he was forced to wear with the judicious use of slits and windows cut into the cloth. I had ample opportunity to talk to Sen Tenzing, a jovial old-school Sherpa with the look of a pirate. When I questioned him about the Yeti incidents he had recounted to Shipton and again to a gathering at the British Embassy in Kathmandu in 1951, the old man looked apologetic. I could get him neither to confirm nor deny his stories, but I got the impression that he either had grown guilty of exaggeration or blasé about peddling his tales any more. But like all old Sherpas, he firmly believed in Snowmen.

7

KHUNJO CHUMBI, WORLD TRAVELER

The helicopter we had been relying on had not arrived in Nepal. As there was no knowing whether it ever would, we decided to walk out to Kathmandu and hope that the plane would be available when we returned, to lift us back to Khumjung. By double marching and traveling fast we did the fifteen-day journey from Khumjung to Kathmandu in nine days. On one particularly soul-destroying climb Khunjo Chumbi regaled us with a story of a Tibetan king who had twenty-seven wives. How each one was met, wooed, and married was a story in itself, and for some reason, in proving himself to each good woman, the king was required to carve pieces from his body, gouge out his eyes, and do other ghoulish things. He was saved from cutting off his head, and presumably from dying, by the twenty-seventh wife, who was really a goddess in disguise. She restored the king's decimated body to its original state, recharged him with youthful vigor, and king and wives all lived happily ever after. This happy conclusion was reached as we got to the top of the ridge up which we had toiled for hours.

Khunjo Chumbi told us that the story was a traveler's tale designed to take one's mind off the road and the Tibetan king might have anything from six to sixty wives, according to the length of the trail. We measured our climbs in wives ever after.

In Kathmandu, where happily funds, air tickets, and a warm invitation to America awaited us, we had an audience with the King, Mahendra Bikram Shah. In a small royal reception room, where two stuffed tigers mounted on opposing walls were prevented from crashing their heads together by a huge chandelier, we showed the Yeti scalp to the King, who took it into an inner chamber to show the Queen, suffering from a cold.

Khunjo Chumbi, who accompanied Hillary, Perkins, and myself to the palace, had been suitably prepared for the occasion with a lecture on kingship and protocol. I was mortified, therefore, when Chumbi, in a massive whisper, asked me who the person in dark glasses might be. It was the King.

He created a similar *faux pas* when we called on the then Nepalese Prime Minister, Mr. B. P. Koirala.

"Who is that thin man?"

Hush, the Prime Minister.

"What is that?"

The head of the government.

"Then he's the King?"

Fortunately Mr. Koirala has a fine sense of humor. We enjoyed his company and his tea. We found him most sympathetic toward the Sherpas and concerned about the growing communist influence in Sherpaland.

A few days later, in Chicago, we learned that the Koirala

government had been dismissed by the King and that Mr. Koirala himself was under arrest. Khunjo Chumbi understood immediately when I gave him the news.

"There cannot be two kings in a country," he said.

"MY, ISN'T HE SOMETHING?"

Chumbi had been in a plane before—in a Dakota—for the fifty minutes it takes to fly between Patna in India and Kathmandu.

But he had never flown over the sea, and this was to be a mystifying experience. To Sherpas the universe is flat, a great sea bounded first by a circle of flames and then by a girdle of air. Their known world, Lho, is an island to the south, with the happy reputation of being inhabited by the devout and God-fearing. Other islands of existence share the universe with Lho. In the center is an eight-tiered pyramidlike world, U-ri-gya-lhymbu, crowned with a heavenly chapel. Four floors of this world are above water, four beneath, and there live the Nye-Gin, people in a state between mortals and gods. The heavenly chapel is the abode of the Gyaltzen Rishi, the powerful lords of the north, south, east, and west. Immediately above this world are thirty-three heavens, in ascending order of importance, and in them dwell the vast concourse of Mahayana Buddhist gods.

In the north is the square world of Chang-da-mi-nyan, peopled by the godless and gossips; in the east Shar-li-pa-pho, lozenge-shaped and inhabited by people who once lived in great wealth and luxury on our earth, but days before their death were allowed to see their place in the hereafter. The vision upset them so much that they now live in perpetual misery in their new home.

To the west is Nub-Palang-Chhe, a world of unbelievers and misers who for their sins live in eternal distress.

The sea between these worlds is so vast that no one can effect a crossing except in the liberating moment of death. Yet here we were flying across the sea and apparently touching down in another world. Chumbi recorded the magical adventure on a Pan Am post card and, from the shape of the land he drew when we began settling on Bangkok, he thought we had fetched up in Shar-li-pa-pho, the eastern world of the universe. Watching the old man intently drawing away as Thailand filled our port windows, I wondered if he had any qualms about ever getting away from the dreaded island where people are damned to horrible visions. He gave no sign.

He could of course be praying that we land up in U-ri-gya-lhymbu, the enchanted island of semi-immortals, or even fly into one of the thirty-three heavens of eternal bliss. After all, he knew we were flying at a height greater than Mount Everest, and that, to Sherpas who live among divine mountains, is the ultimate abode of gods.

By the time we reached Honolulu, Chumbi was a seasoned world traveler, accepting seas and continents and a spherical world. His next trial was hysteria, the kind that swoons over crooners and tears the clothes off popular film stars.

We had hardly entered the Honolulu airport lounge for refreshments and the inevitable press and TV interview when a blond matron squealed delightedly and flung herself at Chumbi. He was beautiful, thrilling, exciting, so absolutely cute, marvelous—she must kiss him, could she? Yes, she would, there, and just once again—oh my, he was a honey, just once again, and Daddy, do take a photograph of us together, there now, isn't he something?

Chumbi's blue eyes popped, slid down his magenta robe onto the floor, were retrieved, then blazed. He got the idea. This was one of the thirty-three heavens.

The matron was seized by another series of generous impulses. Off came her earrings, then her necklace. They were given to Chumbi who quickly scratched them with his thumbnail to see if they were genuine or paste, smiled, and dropped them into the cavernous depths of his robe.

Come on, Daddy, haven't you got anything to give him? Oh my, he's so cute—is he married? What does he think of America? Does he like Americans?

Quite obviously Chumbi did. Daddy had fished a cigarette lighter from his pocket and handed it over. He also parted with a dollar bill and some silver for which Chumbi exchanged two Tibetan coins.

"Oh my, isn't that something?" said the happy matron. Our

departure prevented her from giving away anything more, but
she and Daddy followed us to the departure gate where Chumbi,
having learned the strange ways of the West with commend-
able speed, gave her a hug worthy of a Yeti. She squealed.

No Fleas on Chumbi

Chumbi's popularity gave Ed and me cause to worry about
the old man's new boots. They were beautiful boots, scarlet and
emerald embroidered felt, knee-length, and tied with gay rib-
bons. Unfortunately their soles were made of uncured Sherpa
leather that ripened like a good cheese as Chumbi sweated into
them.

At a distance they conveyed the correct concentration of Eau
de Sherpa: a combination of sweaty wool, yak's butter, smoke,
and scorched grass. We were spared garlic, because Chumbi believed garlic to be unclean; no one who ate the stuff could hope
to see Yetis, for instance. But at close quarters, hugging and
kissing and togetherness close, the smell of Chumbi's boots was
overpowering. On no account could we have our new idol lose
his attraction because of uncured leather.

A strongly perfumed atomizer came to the rescue. Chumbi
awoke one night to find me spraying his feet under the blankets
and to see deodorizing mist pouring from the top of his boots.
His expression accused me of witchcraft.

We learned in matters of similar delicacy to take Chumbi
directly by the horns and not practice an unfamiliar finesse.
There was the affair of delousing before we set out on our tour.
All of us at some time during the expedition contracted lice, or
fleas, or ticks, or the lot together. It was one of the things we
came to accept along with beards, dirt, discomfort, and cold.
But generally we managed to keep less verminous than the
Sherpas by using a variety of insecticides thoughtfully included
among the expedition's medical supplies.

Wanting to take no chances with Chumbi and yet not wound
his pride, Ed and I arranged to bring up the subject of vermin
very casually over dinner one night, at which stage I produced
a carton full of insecticide, praised its lethal properties, and suggested we all use it. Ed reached over and, taking a generous

fistful, began rubbing it into his hair and dusting it into his clothes. I did likewise. Chumbi looked deeply shocked. What? he exclaimed. Did we mean to say we were lousy? He, in grand manner, refused to emulate our example.

But if overheated American interiors and taxicabs did cause us moments of anxiety, Chumbi's growing popularity was never in jeopardy. From the moment we arrived in Chicago on December 11 till the time we left New York for Paris on December 18 the old village elder from faraway Khumjung enjoyed a triumphant progress.

In one of those vast caverns of the Merchandise Mart Building, Chicago, where our sponsors, the World Book Encyclopedia, seat a small army of women in front of identical typewriters, Chumbi received a nine-hundred-woman-power ovation. He walked through it with the stars bright in his blue sapphire eyes, receiving ear clips, necklaces, Christmas baubles off Christmas trees, ball-point pencils, and an ormolu flowerpot complete with a spiky plant.

He was particularly fascinated by one of John Dienhart's secretaries, a glamorous dark-haired individual who among other things was the keeper of our press cuttings. Accustomed by now to compulsive giving, old Chumbi was prepared to believe that the girl had been presented to him when I jokingly told him so. (He immediately lost interest in the cuttings that gave him more prominence than the scalp or even Hillary, headlines like WHO NEEDS SNOWMAN? CHUMBI'S IN TOWN, STRANGE HOWL OF THE YETI HEARD IN CHICAGO, MR. SHERPA GOES SHOPPING.) Welcome as the gift was, it was going to present problems: there was a buxom Mrs. Chumbi at home; the girl's high heels and slender stockinged feet would never carry her the 180 miles to Khumjung from Kathmandu; altogether the bird was too rare to keep in a grimy stone house in Sherpaland. Perhaps it was these considerations besides old Chumbi's generosity that prompted him to share the girl with me.

"I think she will do for both of us," he said in a whisper. Fortunately no one else understood Nepali in Merchandise Mart Plaza.

"PLEASE TELL THE QUEEN"

Living with Chumbi through those madly rushed days in
America, Paris, and London was a rare experience. There was
the morning we rang for breakfast and Chumbi, wearing only
a pair of briefs, answered the door when the waiter rang,
straight from his bath, long hair hanging about his shoulders,
mustache dripping. Did the waiter think he had disturbed a
bearded lady? Chumbi feeling the texture of a startled woman's
dress material where it stretched most broadly. Chumbi thinking God made skyscrapers. Chumbi watching himself on television at 7 A.M. one morning and wondering why he didn't
appear every following morning at the same time. Chumbi howling in imitation of a Yeti for reporters and television audiences.
Chumbi praying in every car, elevator, and airplane we boarded
to appease the local gods.

One morning in an elevator in the Executive House, Chicago,
a man wearing a rosette asked Chumbi what he was advertising,
what convention he was with.

In Paris Chumbi had something of his own bat. When Professor J. Millot of the Musée de l'Homme pronounced the scalp
a fake and cast doubt on the Yeti, old Khunjo delivered himself
of a delightful Chumbiism.

"In Nepal we have neither giraffes nor kangaroos so we know
nothing about them. In France there are no Yetis so I sympa-
thize with your ignorance." And why, Chumbi wanted to know,
were there so many naked stone people standing about in public? They were gods naturally, but why so poor that they were
without clothes? Over his remarks at a night club I draw a veil.

London had some of the best of Chumbi. He was invited to
Buckingham Palace on December 23 to present his gifts, unfortunately not to the Queen, who was in Sandringham, but to
a Royal Equerry deputizing for her. It was one of those dismal
London days when sky and street and buildings and trees and
people are all gray, all things of mist, so that one expects them
to dissolve in the sun. But the sun when it struggles through
the cloud is gray.

We passed a solemn plod of Household Cavalry on the Mall.

Chumbi was amazed by the size of the horses. They were the biggest he had seen.

At the palace we were received in a remote lounge that necessitated walking down miles of corridors piled with heavy furniture and hung with paintings. Chumbi was impressed. But the equerry was a disappointment. No representative of the Queen should wear anything so ordinary as a lounge suit. Even a snatch of ermine and the odd jewel were necessary to convey Her Majesty's commands.

"Her Majesty has commanded me to receive you and thank you and your people for their most generous gift and good wishes. Her Majesty is most touched."

"What about the children?" Chumbi wanted to know.

"The royal children are very well, Mr. Chumbi, thank you."

"Please tell the Queen that I am not too disappointed not meeting her," said Chumbi. The Royal Equerry was understandably surprised.

"Because," explained Chumbi, "the Queen and I have many thousands of lives yet to live. In one of them we will certainly meet.

"And tell the Queen that I think she must be a very great Queen because she has made me very happy today. It is the job of a Queen to make poor people happy."

I hope the Queen received these gems, along with the bags of barley flour, yak's tails, painted scrolls, and bricks of tea he brought for her from Khumjung.

On the twenty-fifth I had the pleasure of taking Chumbi to my home in Kent and introducing him to his first Christmas: to Santa Claus and Christmas trees and all the glitter and gormandizing that he at once associated with the Tibetan New Year. Father Christmas was Mei Tshering, the old man of good fortune. The Christmas tree was *torma*, a votive offering. Suddenly embarrassed that he had no gift to offer, he emptied his purse of all its remaining Tibetan coins and to my mother he gave one of his most treasured possessions, a small photograph of the Dalai Lama, worn as a brooch.

We were just about to begin Christmas lunch when Chumbi launched himself into a marathon prayer, every now and again throwing offerings of nuts, sweets, bread, and wine about the room. My nephews and nieces could hardly contain their impatience after suffering initial shock, but the rest of us were deeply impressed.

The Scalp Is Examined

Not all our time in the West was spent romping with Chumbi. The Yeti scalp had to be proved genuine or otherwise, and in Chicago, Paris, and London were inquisitions of scientists who would pass judgment on our collected relics and theories.

We took with us on our world dash three blue-bear furs, one complete with all four feet and mask, one Himalayan black-bear fur, Himalayan fox and wolf pelts, two serow hides, our fake Snowman scalps, and, of course, the Khumjung Yeti scalp.

Unfortunately the press and scientists shared one conference in Chicago and the tone was set by Chumbi demonstrating Yeti noises and we being questioned into repeating Sherpa Snowman fables. I believe the scientists came to the conference convinced that the scalp was a fake and, as a result, were not terribly interested in tracing its origin. They accepted our belief that the hide used in the manufacture of the scalp was a serow's, although experts in America had previously been recorded as declaring hair from the same scalp to be either porcine or anthropoid or belonging to some unknown animal.

Our Yeti relics had the benefit of critical examination at the Chicago Natural History Museum by Dr. Austin L. Rand, Chief Curator, Department of Zoology, and Professor Philip Hershkovitz, Curator of Mammals. Not being in possession of any Tibetan blue-bear (*Ursus arctos pruinosus*) specimens, the museum was apt to declare our furs belonging to the Himalayan red bear (*Ursus arctos isabellinus*). We resisted this suggestion most strongly for a very good reason. The red bear is a Himalayan animal, common to Kashmir and Punjab and rarely found in Nepal. Sherpas generally know only the collared black bear (*Selenarctos thibetanus*) and the tree-climbing sloth bear (*Melursus ursinus*). I do not remember meeting a single Sherpa who had seen a red bear; many do not believe such a creature exists, a point in favor of the red bear being mistaken for the Yeti.

Significant is the fact that Sherpas have no name for the red bear, but the large black bear is *Thom* and the small sloth bear is *Sing Thom*. They know the Tibetan blue bear as *Dremo*, which is also the Tibetan name, and *Dzu-teh* (pronounced chu-teh), one of the names for the Snowman.

The Tibetan blue bear is known to inhabit the eastern provinces of Tibet; according to Tibetans it is most commonly found in the mountains of Amdo. Zoologists with whom I have discussed the blue bear are quite adamant about the creature *not* being found in the Himalayas. If it is, then this in itself is an important discovery, and Sherpas can be forgiven for mistaking a creature so far removed from their conception of a bear for the Yeti or, more correctly, building a Snowman legend around it.

Professor Hershkovitch, who now agreed with the blue-bear identification, told Ed and me that he was considering putting our blue-bear relics on special display and labeling them the Yeti or Snowman. He would not have been wrong since every Sherpa who saw the blue-bear furs we had collected instantly declared them to be *Dzu-teh's.*

. . . AND DECLARED A FAKE

On Monday, December 19, we flew into Paris, and the scalp was subjected to scientific inspection within hours of our arrival—at Le Musée de l'Homme. The experts had prepared by laying out samples of hair from gorilla, chimpanzee, orangutan, and Himalayan langur. Also a wide variety of human hair and a somewhat gory exhibit—a shrunken human head.

The ancient scalp from Khumjung did not approximate any of these preconceived ideas. Its stiff red bristles made silk of great ape and human hair by comparison; its tough hide was several times thicker than mummified human skin. I believe the scientists were as puzzled as they were interested, though they were not long in slicing through some of the mystery associated with the scalp.

Present to examine the relic were Professor Vallois, honorary director of Le Musée de l'Homme; the present director, Professor Millot; Dr. Olivier, Professor of Anthropology at the Sorbonne; Professor Lehmann, of the Museum of Natural History; Professor Ceccaldi, hair specialist in the criminal investigation department, Paris Police Headquarters; and Mr. Francis Petter, Assistant of Mammalogy at the Museum of Natural History.

Present among the experts was the Abbé P. Bordet of the Catholic Institute of Paris, who in 1954 saw and photographed Yeti tracks in the Makalu region and was considered something of an authority on Yetis.

Small samples of hair and tissue were taken for closer examination in Paris, though it was generally agreed that the scalp was a fake and probably molded from serow hide.

Among those who examined the scalp in Paris was Professor Bernard Heuvelmans, author of an entertaining book, *On the Track of Unknown Animals*. In a chapter devoted to the "Not So Abominable Snowman," Professor Heuvelmans had written:

"Thus the unusual shape of the alleged Yeti scalps agrees better than one could possibly have hoped with what I deduced the beast must be on the evidence of its footprints alone."

Even after viewing the scalp Professor Heuvelmans was reluctant to forego his carefully built-up picture of the Yeti.

Before our arrival in Paris with the scalp Professor J. Millot had expressed an opinion on the Yeti footprint and Yeti hand when photographs we had taken of these strange phenomena had been shown to him. In a letter to M. Charles Ronsac of Opera Mundi, the French news and publishing agency distributing our dispatches, he wrote:

"Without waiting for the conclusions reached by my colleagues, which I will transmit to you as soon as I have them, I can send you my own conclusions so that you may kindly forward them to Sir Edmund Hillary.

"(1) Nothing serious can be deduced from the footprints in the snow. The experience which I have acquired in the African and Madagascar jungles, where I have followed the tracks of many wild animals, has taught me that, on very soft grounds, very disconcerting deformations are possible and the dimensions of the tracks can be amplified in the most unbelievable manner. On snow this phenomenon is certainly even more accentuated.

"(2) The hand is without doubt a human hand. It would be necessary to examine it or at least to have an excellent photograph taken from every close quarter to determine, without risks of mistakes, if some bone from another hand may have been introduced into it, but the whole structure is typically human.

"The poor Yeti has no luck!"

Experts in London gave the Yeti scalp a generous look over. We had left arrangements to Dr. W. C. Osmon Hill, of the Royal Zoological Society, an eminent expert on primates, and he collected together an impressive number of scientists to examine our evidence. The Kensington Museum of Natural History, where we met, was until then the only museum outside Russia that had a collection of blue-bear furs. The furs we brought with us were immediately identified as blue bear, though one, the rich gold fading to platinum and complete with all four feet, was viewed with initial reservation. The museum had taken the trouble to mold a scalp of their own from fresh cowhide, to the exact dimensions of the Khumjung and Pangboche scalps. It would have made any fashionable woman a welcome hat.

The consensus of expert opinion in London was that:

(a) the Khumjung and Pangboche scalps were fakes,

(b) they probably were molded from serow hide,

(c) they were old—possibly as old as was claimed (200 to 300 years).

Dr. Osmon Hill showed us microscopic sectional photographs he had had taken of the bristles from the Khumjung and Pangboche scalps and from our own fakes, molded from serow. Until then he did not know which was which—we hadn't told him the origin of the bristles when we sent them from Khumjung. Dr. Hill was confident that all the specimens belonged to the same genus of animal.

Chumbi's reaction to all this expert demolition of the Yeti legend was typical of his generous concern.

"I promise you that when I return to Solu Khumbu I will find a Yeti for you. I must. When you and the Burra Sahib (Hillary) have gone to such trouble and expense to prove the existence of the Snowman, it is up to us Sherpas to help you. We cannot have you doubted by your own people."

RETURN TO KHUMJUNG

The six weeks allowed us by the village elders of Khumjung and Khunde were almost done. Even if we started walking the moment we reached Kathmandu, there was no hope of reaching Khumjung in time to prevent the property of our three senior Sherpas from being forfeited. Only a helicopter could help us now, and happily a letter from Kathmandu assured us that the long-expected plane was at last operative in Nepal and open to charter.

We chartered it, two days before our time limit expired, the weather not right for flying, the brilliant Swedish pilot uneasy about making the trip. Taking off in intermittent sunshine, we leapfrogged ridges to pick our way between threatening pillars of cloud. Within an hour we had put a normal twelve days' trek behind us and entered Sherpaland. But there the weather failed us completely; snowfalls veiled our destination and, as the clouds closed more thickly about us, the fragile craft began to shudder alarmingly. There was no alternative but to return to Kathmandu.

Next day we tried again. The weather was perfect and we flew boldly among the great peaks about Khumjung with the same feeling of insignificance a dragonfly must experience among the skyscrapers of Manhattan.

All the people of Khumjung turned out to welcome us, risking decapitation by the helicopter's rotors. Here was a miracle if ever there was one, a plane dropping right out of the sky onto Khumjung, and out of it coming the magic scalp. The 'copter was shown the reverence reserved for deities in the gloomy interiors of Sherpa monasteries. People approached it with their heads bent and tongues out, offering ceremonial scarves. Only the pilot's vigilance prevented the helicopter from disappearing under a cairn of stones, pebbles, and wood—votive offerings from the delighted.

There is a sequel to Khunjo Chumbi's world tour that must be told. In January 1961 Queen Elizabeth, together with the Duke of Edinburgh, made a state visit to Nepal. The Duke had been invited to visit our Scientific Base Camp at Mingbo, below Amadablam, by helicopter, but had "most reluctantly" declined because the royal schedule allowed him no opportunity.

The Queen expressed a desire to meet Khunjo Chumbi and thank him personally for the gifts he had left for her in London; Mrs. Chumbi was invited too. The old man was back in Khumjung when the summons reached him, and he had just sufficient time to make Kathmandu on foot before the Queen and Duke arrived. What none of us knew when we sent instructions to Khunjo and Mrs. Chumbi to hurry down to Kathmandu was that forty-five-year-old Mrs. Chumbi was nine months pregnant.

Without hesitation the couple set out on the 180-mile walk to Kathmandu, along with some of our expedition Sherpas. Four days out of Kathmandu, while the men stopped to eat their morning meal, Mrs. Chumbi sat calmly by the roadside and produced her fourth son.

"I did not want to miss you," Mrs. Chumbi told the Queen when they met in Kathmandu at a British Embassy reception. "So I wasted no time about having the child and decided to keep up with the men when they walked on after their food. That was only five days ago." The infant was named Philip Tobgay Chumbi in honor of the Duke.

In keeping with his promise to us in London, Chumbi had gone searching for more substantial evidence in support of Yetis, and he brought a "Snowman" arm to show the Queen.

The shaggy, henna-colored limb that the Queen and Duke examined was without doubt the hind leg of a blue bear.

8

THE SHERPAS

To appreciate the full implication of the Snowman legend, in so far as it exists in Nepal, it is necessary to know something of the Sherpas.

They are a Mongolian people, claiming to have come several centuries ago from Minyak in Kham, in eastern Tibet: *shar* in the Sherpa language means east; *pa* is people, so Sherpas are the people from the east.

There are eighteen distinct Sherpa tribes, each with its own traditions and taboos, many speaking dialects of their own. The Sherpa language is very similar to Tibetan and employs the Tibetan script so that Tibetans and Sherpas have no difficulty in understanding each other. Men and women dress in the Tibetan style.

A rigid tribal law once prevented marriage between certain of the tribes, but this custom is rapidly dying out. Marriage between members of the same tribe is still not permissible. This is a necessary restriction since Sherpas already show degenerate signs of inbreeding.

Without making Sherpas appear depraved, it is correct to say they are sexually uninhibited. No one is shocked by premarital intercourse (which is common) or premarital offspring, and conjugal infidelity is considered neither outrageous nor necessarily grounds for divorce. Polyandry is practiced since it protects against carving up of property and, in a community where men are away from their home for long periods of time, it assures a man in the house. One of our runners had a wife and family in both his home village and in Kathmandu and made no secret of it. His village wife even welcomed the Kathmandu rival, declaring that it kept her husband from visiting prostitutes.

Both marriage and divorce are easy. Parents have only to signify an acceptance of the wedding by exchanging bowls of chang for a couple to become engaged, and that's more important than the wedding itself, which is excuse for lavish ceremony and feasting. Divorce is settled by the guilty party paying a fine or by all concerned having a good old beano and parting amicably. Children are no problem. Daughters go with the mother, sons with the father, unless otherwise desired and arranged.

Early Sherpa history, unrecorded and as yet unsupported by extensive research, has a Tibetan chief of Kham being commanded by a combination of visions and oracles' pronouncements to lead his people south. This chief has left behind him no name, only a title, *Thakpa Tho* (*Thakpa* means "Great leader"; *Tho* is "that which is above all").

At first this huge migration of people paused tentatively about Tingri in southern Tibet, forty-five miles from the present Tibet-Nepal border, but later it moved again south, through the Nangpa Pass above Namche Bazar, and settled in the high fertile valleys of northeast Nepal. This happened about five hundred years ago, although many Sherpas insist on a somewhat mystical 1008 years ago.

It is more than likely that the nomadic Sherpa tribes were persecuted in Kham by the warlike people found there today, or they may well have been the original inhabitants of eastern

Tibet forced south by invading Mongol hordes. Their entry into
Nepal was peaceful and unopposed. The valleys they occupied
were for the most part uninhabited. But there is a tradition of
struggle between them and the people of southern Tibet when
they began settling in the region of Tingri. These clashes and
disputes, presumably over property, must have prompted the
Sherpas to move into Nepal.

There is a more likely theory. Allowing the Sherpas to have
migrated from Kham in the first place (and there are traces of
their tribes in present-day Kham), they began dividing their
time between southern Tibet and northern Nepal. To this day
the Sherpas of Khumbu and the Dudh Kosi (including the
Rolwaling Valley) are seminomadic, having temporary summer
settlements at altitudes about 15,000 and 16,000 feet and permanent villages below 14,000 feet. It would appear that the
Sherpas spent their summers in Tibet and their winters in Nepal,
trading, grazing cattle, and crudely farming in virgin-forest
clearings.

Then came the potato. As soon as the Sherpas discovered it,
they settled permanently. Potatoes are the high-altitude Sherpas'
main crop and, together with barley and wheat flour, their
staple diet.

Sherpas are found today in many regions other than those
they originally occupied: in Khumbu, the complex of valleys immediately south of the Everest-Massif; in Solu, the slightly
lower region below Khumbu; in the valley of the Dudh Kosi,
west of Solu Khumbu; in Kulung, below Mount Makalu, east of
Solu Khumbu; and in Langtang and Helmu, directly north of
Kathmandu. But Khumbu is the real heart of Sherpa country,
and the Nangpa Pass remains the main doorway into the old
homeland. It is from Khumbu that most expedition porters are
recruited. On our expedition I discovered a couple of Solu
Sherpas suffering the effects of high altitude as painfully as I
did. One of our Khumbu Sherpas, on the other hand, was found
by our scientists to be nearly as physically fit at 19,000 feet as
the average person at sea level.

Although Sherpas are essentially agriculturists and cattle
breeders, their comparatively high standard of living is a result
of trade that once flourished between Nepal and Tibet. They
themselves had little to trade with: grain, locally made paper,
cattle, and butter. But acting as middlemen, they imported

kerosene oil, cloth, dyestuffs, and manufactured goods from Kathmandu and bartered them for Tibetan salt and wool. As there is no indigenous salt in Nepal, the Tibetan salt trade was a most profitable business.

After the Lhasa uprising in 1958, when the Dalai Lama fled Tibet, the border between Nepal and Tibet was closed by the Chinese and the lucrative trade between the two countries, through Solu Khumbu, came to an abrupt end. It is still too early to predict how this will affect the Sherpa economy. The growing number of foreign expeditions to the Nepal Himalayas will compensate in part, but widespread social and political changes almost certainly will result—changes that may send the northernmost Sherpas finding new homes and employment farther south or turn their interests north again. Communization of the Sherpa areas is more than a fear. It is a growing reality.

Sherpa villages are seldom compact. Their houses stand in their own fields; there are no shops and no public buildings other than the monasteries or chapels that serve as community centers. The nearest a Sherpa village gets to being built up is Namche Bazar, often referred to as the Sherpa capital, where houses are built end to end in horseshoe-shaped tiers. Khumjung, the home of most of our Sherpas, is a bigger village but widely scattered; Khumjung and its twin village, Khunde, have two hundred houses between them.

The distinctive Sherpa house is a solid affair; two storied, white rough-cast walls, gabled roofs tiled with shingles or covered with logs, and floors of rammed earth and wood. More often than not they are semidetached, the two or three sections unconnected and occupied by related families.

On the cavernous, windowless ground floor are rooms for the cattle, farm implements, firewood, and fodder. Negotiating these, and one has to, as through them is access to the stairs and the upper floor, is something of a nightmare. Animals snuffle and move in the dark; one may stumble over a sleeping yak or onto the sharp horns of a Tibetan sheep. Underfoot the floor is soft and uncertain with leaves and fodder, and other things; the stairs are precipitous, unseen, polished with usage. One always prays that the guardian Tibetan mastiff is not loose in the dark of the ground floor, and it is wise to inquire and have someone make sure before risking your calves, seat, and throat to the cultivated fury of these dogs.

The upper floor of the house is devoted to living rooms, most usually just one, but sometimes two, or even three, excluding the cubbyhole that is the emergency lavatory. Calls of nature are answered outside, and village scavengers are relied upon to keep the surroundings reasonably clean. Because of the close proximity of Khumbila, the most important of the Solu Khumbu mountain gods, scavengers are not permitted in Khumbu villages. How it's managed I never found out, but the villages are tolerably clean. Pigs are never raised by Sherpas who consider them too unclean even to touch. But pork is eaten and relished "over the first mountain" (outside the home valley).

The center of Sherpa family life is the open hearth, *thap*, in a corner of the largest living room, by the stairs. Here is the master bed; here the women of the house cook or nurse their children; here the men gossip and drink, and here the family has its meals. There is a formal arrangement of low seats and tables below the main window (all windows are in the front of the house) where visitors are entertained.

Furnishing is simple but impressive; carved shelves along the three windowless walls are piled with copper and brass utensils. Huge wooden chests contain the family's clothes and household treasures; a corner of the room is set up as an altar on which images are displayed against painted scrolls and butter lamps burn perpetually. Among the house "furnishings" it is appropriate to mention the carcasses of yaks or sheep that hang from the roof, smoked to a fine charcoal gray. Religious convictions will not have Sherpas slaughter animals, so once a year Tibetan butchers are imported to kill off a few yaks and sheep. Sherpas claim that they prefer dried flesh, slightly high, to fresh meat. Many of our men would not eat the flesh of anything freshly killed. They always insisted on waiting a day to allow time for the animal's soul to find peace. As Buddhists, Sherpas subscribe to the theory of reincarnation, and to deprive an animal of its right to be reincarnated would be deplorable sin.

An interesting feature of the Sherpa house is the *Kar*, the great central beam hewn from a single forest giant. It is likened to the husband or breadwinner of the family, supporting the entire household, and it is venerated with offerings of food, ceremonial scarves, fertility symbols, and sacred texts block-printed on local paper. The long horizontal beam that rests on the *Kar* is *Karju*, and is considered female.

Sherpa houses have no doors other than the one at the entrance, and that is seldom closed. People walk in and out all day, every arrival a cause for minor celebration. Chang or tea is served, and no matter what is occupying the family interest at the time, it is dropped or momentarily suspended while the guest is welcomed and made comfortable. Then gossip zooms or tales and jokes are told to the accompaniment of much ribald laughter. Suffering no inhibitions, the women suckle their infants or feed them with food chewed first in their own mouths, regardless of the company. It is not uncommon for Sherpa women to suckle children of three and four years of age.

Because Sherpas have not yet discovered the chimney, their houses are almost perpetually fogged with smoke and everything but gleaming copper utensils is black. Sooty stalactites hang from the wooden roofs; shields over the hearth appear made of black fur. As a result Sherpas suffer commonly from a form of conjunctivitis and hacking coughs but believe, on the other hand, that the smoke is medicinal and keeps all ills away.

A Sherpa's prestige is measured in the number of houses and yaks he owns. Khunjo Chumbi, for instance, owned eighteen houses—many of them temporary high-altitude summer huts, but property nonetheless—and sixty-two yaks, *naks*, *dzhums*, *dzopkios*, and *kirkos*.

All these strange-sounding creatures are related to the yak, which always is male. I remember once being told, "Please don't talk about yak's-milk cheese. Yaks are male."

The *nak* is a female yak. *Dzhums* are the much-prized female products of crossbreeding yaks with mountain cows; *dzopkios* are the infertile male offspring of the same union and are useful as pack animals. *Kirkos* result from breeding between *naks* and *zolungs*, *zolungs* being a variety of lower-altitude bulls. These are by no means the lot. Every possible product of crossbreeding has a name so that there also are *dimzos* and *dimsi dzums*, shaggy *tulmos* and *pamus*.

A great deal of good Sherpa time is spent looking after yaks, *naks*, and the rest of them, as cattle command a good price and butter is in huge demand for burning in votive lamps both in the monasteries and in private homes. Butter, often rancid, is an essential ingredient of the popular Tibetan tea. Cheese making for export is a growing industry, begun by the Swiss Technical

44. *Site of the Green Hut.*

45. *The Green Hut's framework.*

46. *Completed hut with firewood stacked around outside.*

47. (ABOVE) *Framework of hut was first overlaid with wire netting, then covered with aluminum paper for insulation, and finally by an outside layer of canvas.* 48. (LEFT) *Milledge operating one of our small radios at the Green Hut.*

49. (TOP) *Interior of Mess Hut*. 50. (BOTTOM) *Dr. Lahiri in his Green Hut bunk.*

Assistance, with considerable funds provided by the New Zealand Government.

Apart from the art of image making, rock carving, and scroll and mural painting practiced by a few lamas and lay individuals, there is little real handicraft among the Sherpas. Their weaving does not compare with that of their neighbors in India, Tibet, and Bhutan; their architecture, solidly impressive, cannot be accused of any real art. The beautiful silver drinking cups, silver and stone jewelry, gay felts and brocades that are seen in Sherpaland are almost all imported, from Tibet, India, and even China.

In Khumjung is a single family of artists, painting in the traditional Tibetan style, and their fine house is testimony to the profitable demand there is for their services. I met a lame lama artist in Junbesi, a large monastery village in Solu, who was required to travel miles to paint murals in monasteries all over the Solu and Khumbu regions. One of my Sherpa runners was an artist and an excellent one at that. With little prompting he produced a Christmas card depicting the Birth of Christ painted in the Tibetan manner and filled every book I could provide with charming drawings of villages, legendary beasts, flowers, and people, all set pieces learned in a monastery.

Rock carving is still a flourishing business. Sherpas commission rocks to be carved *in situ* along tracks and in the vicinity of their villages or have small tablets carved with a religious text or figure to offer at roadside shrines. Much of the really fine carving has died out. Whenever I tried to commission some, I invariably was told that the "master" was dead and his art with him, but there were many who still can carve the Tibetan prayer, *Om Mane Padme Hum,* in numerous styles of great beauty.

There could not be more than a dozen policemen in all Solu Khumbu, and they are a very recent phenomenon. Law and order is kept by village elders elected by the people of each village. When occasion demands, the village meets in assembly as it did in Khumjung to decide whether we might borrow the Yeti scalp and later to voice an opinion on how best to spend the money we presented to the monastery. We were interested to discover that 50 per cent of the money had been given out in loans at high interest and that, within a month of distributing it, the monastery had realized over Rs. (Rupees) 200. This initial profit was spent on butter for the monastery lamps, apparently in our name, but we managed to impress upon the village elders that there were more useful things to do with similar returns in future.

Moneylending is big business among Sherpas as cash is not always readily available. Interest is excessively high, even 25 per cent not being considered too outrageous. This goes far in explaining the popularity of mountaineering expeditions that pay wages, in cash, far in excess of anything that Sherpas could hope to earn elsewhere. On our expedition, for instance, there were very few Sherpas who drew much of their salary during the months they were with us. They let it accumulate and eventually left the expedition with a sizable saving. This they almost certainly invested in loans, cattle, land, tradable articles, and jewelry, in that order of preference.

Without exception Sherpas are Buddhists of the Kar-Gyud-Pa sect, the oldest unreformed church of Tibet. Until as recently as eighty years ago they looked to Lhasa for spiritual and temporal leadership, and even today the Dalai Lama and certain important Tibetan reincarnate lamas enjoy more popularity and respect among the Sherpas than the King of Nepal and his ministers. This is not out of any political disrespect for the Nepalese monarch or his frequently changing cabinets. It merely emphasizes the Tibetan origin and cultural heritage of Sherpas and the fact that until a few years ago communication with Tibet was easier and more profitable than with distant Kathmandu.

Religious practice and ritual are as natural to Sherpas as growing potatoes and breeding yaks, and the centers of their culture and learning are the monasteries. The greatest of these is Thyangboche, the spiritual core of Sherpaland and the home of the first Sherpa reincarnate lama. Thyangboche Gompa, to give it its correct name, was built only forty years ago by an old hermit from Khumjung, Gulu Lama, with money and free labor donated by all the villages of Khumbu.

Dawa Tenzing, our head Sherpa, remembers carrying stones for the monastery and helping to build it.

"People came from all over: men and women, and some brought their children along. So eager were we to build the gompa that the work went on in all weather and often at night, and in six months it was done, even the painting."

This is all the more remarkable because Thyangboche monastery is built on an isolated spur miles from the nearest villages. The voluntary labor force that raised it had to travel far and be self-supporting. Ten years after it was so heroically built it was destroyed by earthquake. The old founder lama was killed as he prayed in the main chapel and his body was cremated on the ruins of the monastery by hundreds of sorrowing people. That very day work on rebuilding the monastery was begun, and the new, much larger building is a monument to the generosity and undying faith of the Solu Khumbu Sherpas.

The present young abbot of Thyangboche was discovered in Namche Bazar twenty-four years ago. While still a very young child, he talked of a former home and friends in Thyangboche Gompa. When taken to the monastery, he recognized places and things he obviously had not seen before. The resident lamas were deeply impressed by the child's behavior; he could be a reincarnation of the old abbot. With his parents' consent the boy was subjected to the tests of all important reincarnates; his body was examined for blemishes (there must be none), and he was required to select from among several identical odds and ends the belongings of his previous body. This he successfully did and was installed in the monastery with great ceremony. At the age of fifteen he was sent to Rongbuk, the Tibetan monastery on the north side of the Everest-Massif, to further his studies and in 1956 returned to resume his place as the head of the monastery.

The young abbot is held in high regard by all Solu Khumbu Sherpas. We found him to be a most intelligent and charming individual, deeply interested in world affairs and eager to know about other religions.

A much older, apparently, three-hundred-year-old monastery is at Pangboche, the last permanent Sherpa settlement before Everest. It was built by Sawa Dorji, the lama who procured the monastery's Yeti scalp fourteen generations ago. The lama's fourteenth reincarnation, a two-year-old boy, was brought to Thyangboche from Tibet in 1960. He was yet to be installed in the Pangboche monastery.

The Buddhism the Sherpas practice has deep roots in the original Bon, a form of animism that employed sorcery, witchcraft, and cruel sacrifice in its ritual and had every cave, forest, valley, and mountaintop inhabited by fearful demons and gods. When

Buddhism came to the Sherpa valleys—and I now forsake historical fact for local belief—it came with flying and tiger-riding saints and was manifest in many miraculous ways. The divine Buddha shared his heaven with a vast concourse of gods and goddesses, many borrowed from India, many promoted from the ranks of local Bon spirits and demons. Bon worship and Buddhism became almost indistinguishable; lamas adopted the tools of sorcerers, sorcerers borrowed the trappings of lamas. Myth and fable were given religious authority, encouraged, written into the sacred texts.

On the two miles of track between Thyangboche monastery and Pangboche village there are half a dozen spots invested with religious fantasy: a stone on which the great Tantric Saint Guru Rimpoche sat, leaving an impression; the rock on which his dog romped (one is shown its pug marks); a spot where he slept and, feeling cold, pulled a rock over him as he would a blanket—it's there today, curled and crumpled and blanket-thin; and a cave where the saint meditated so long his reflection is cast on the rock surface.

In the Rolwaling are the fossilized saint's cap and the table at which the gods sometimes sit to eat. On a pass where the track plunges between two huge boulders is the story of a saint who passed by wearing a miraculous hat. The hat was so big it got stuck between the rocks, and the saint became so enraged that he flew back the way he had come walking, and the valley on the other side of the pass is considered unblessed and godless to this day.

Monastery murals are splendidly illustrative of the highly colored world of make-believe into which a Sherpa is born. If he has a lamastic education he learns to relegate his demons and horrifying aspects of serene gods to their proper place in life. But usually he will accept them for what they are, a host of visions so powerfully familiar that they color everything he does and sees. There is the popular frieze of all Tibet's animals found in almost every monastery, animals easily recognizable as yaks, leopards, bears, wolves, and camels. And among them are flying creatures half-bird, half-human, dragons and winged lions, and Snowmen. To the Sherpa they all exist, and I have been told about Snowlions and dragons with the same sincerity used to describe Yetis.

One day some Sherpas with whom I was traveling pointed out an eagle's nest and they told me how occasionally, very occasionally, a small doglike creature is hatched from an eagle's egg. To possess one of these is to have control over one's own fortune. A similar story concerns the lesser red panda. Hatched in the nest of an eagle, it promptly devours its parents and, armed with the strength of eagles, it takes to the forest.

And I was told of ectoplasmic *things* that exude from women at night and go ahaunting, and of women who are witches, and of men suddenly possessed by spirits who speak with voices of people long dead or like gods. On a mountain near our winter Base Camp dwelt a god who kept herds of ghostly horses. Every now and again the clatter of their hoofs could be heard in Pangboche, and their hoofprints were plainly left in the hard rock, sometimes in the snow.

But, where all this is dismissable legend, there are strange Tantric and Lamaist practices familiar to the Sherpas that make even myth appear colorless. All Sherpas, like Tibetans, know of the powerful spirits that can be begged from a monastery in Tibet to protect households and individuals. These spirits are contained in grotesque masks that are so charged with supernatural energy, they must be chained to the house. On occasion the spirit grows stronger than the person it protects and becomes so menacing that it is dangerous to keep. Spirits like this cannot be destroyed; they must be returned to their parent monastery where they are kept chained and made impotent by powerful spells cast by the lamas. And there are the *Lung-pa,* lamas who reach such an extreme state of purity through meditation that they become weightless and can travel as fast as the wind. They are credited with being capable of circumventing the area of Tibet's great monasteries, a matter of four thousand miles, in eight days. Levitation is accepted. Reincarnation is the basis of Sherpa philosophy—not just a reincarnation of mortals, but of all things, animate and inanimate.

Look at the Snowman against this background of superstitious belief and it becomes immediately acceptable: the bogey to frighten children with, the half-beast, half-human monster of the monastery murals that is manifest wherever fear and some unfamiliar apparition are fused together. When pandas can be hatched in eagles' nests, why not Yetis from the dens of bears?

9

THE YETI STORIES

By virtue of the serious scientific attention that has been paid the Himalayan Snowman the creature has been plucked from the realms of pure fantasy and given the status of an exciting possibility—an unknown and infrequent anthropoid, *Giganto-pithecus* still at large, the Indian panda or orangutan, like a coelacanth of the eternal snows fighting extinction in the remote regions of the Himalayas.

Scientists have shown interest because of the evidence that has supported the Snowman legend: sightings of an apelike creature not only by Himalayan people but also by travelers from the West; the huge footprints in the snow; the strange whistling call of something unidentifiable. Whatever one may think of the legend, however one may explain it, there certainly is *something* in the high Himalayas to spark the descriptions of a shaggy red monster, domed or square headed, walking usually on two feet, ferocious or extremely shy, and leaving behind it the evidence of droppings, kills, half-consumed meals, and those baffling footprints.

Traveling extensively in the Himalayas, I have come upon firsthand accounts of Yeti sightings in more than one region and country: in Bhutan, Sikkim, Nepal, and Garhwal.

"You will not be able to see Mighyus," said His Highness Sir Tashi Namgyal, Maharajah of Sikkim, when once I discussed Yetis with him. "They are quite invisible." Yet the Maharajah, who is distinctly psychic and an artist, has apparently seen a Snowman since he has painted one, half-ape, half-human, striding above the Himalayan snow peaks, carrying off a woman.

According to tradition, Sikkim was once plagued by Yetis, and there are any number of tales telling how the creatures were duped by the local people into setting fire to themselves,

eating poisoned food, or fighting to the death among themselves.

In the palace one night when our conversation turned to
Snowmen the Crown Prince Palden Thondup Namgyal, an extremely intelligent and sophisticated person, startled me by saying, "Do you want to interview someone who has had actual
firsthand experience with the Yeti? Here you are, ask him."

A personal retainer of the Crown Prince was at that moment
serving us with drinks, a pale pomegranate-cheeked hillman
who did not look the type given to illusions. He and a companion had been attacked by a Yeti only a couple of years ago,
within twelve miles of the capital.

In the high wind-swept tumble of peaks and granite ridges
that is Sikkim's border with Tibet, above the forests of stunted
rhododendron, the two had killed a deer. By an ancient Sikkimese tradition they immediately should have offered the animal's hoofs and entrails to the patron spirit of the hunt—the
Mighyu or Yeti; but eager to hunt on in the fading light of
evening, they postponed the ritual until after nightfall.

Hardly had they begun "before stones clattered above us,
footfalls approached, and suddenly the unmistakable stench of
the Yetis polluted the air."

Then the attack began. Stones and bits of wood were thrown
with surprising accuracy while the unseen creatures set up such
a whistling and screaming that it seemed there were hundreds of
them. The men fled, leaving their deer behind them, and did
not stop running until they reached Gangtok.

There was no doubt in the mind of my informant that he had
had a brush with Yetis. "We must have angered them by not
making our offerings in time," he said as way of explanation.
This is what makes Yeti stories so completely convincing, the
casual, matter-of-fact way in which they are told.

At this point it is necessary to briefly recapitulate on our
knowledge of Snowmen. To the Sherpas there are the three
Yeh-tehs: the large, shaggy brown, cattle-eating creature known
as Dzu-teh and seen at altitudes about 15,000 feet; the savage,
apelike Mih-teh, man-eating, black or red, with a conical scalp
and reversed feet, found at altitudes above 16,000 feet; and the
Thelma, a small ginger-colored beast found in the dense forests
below the snow line.

The Thelma is almost certainly a monkey or a gibbon; if the latter, it's interesting because gibbons are not considered to be at large above the Brahmaputra River, though common below it in the jungles of Assam and northern Burma. I disregard the Himalayan langur completely. This creature is far too well known to Sherpas who have excellent eyesight and are not given to mistaking known objects even at great distances. The Thelma corresponds to the Pyar-them of Sikkim, Bhutan, and southeast Tibet, a "little man" that hoots through the jungles, piling twigs and leaves into neat bundles on the forest floor. *Pyar* means hanging; *them* could be a bastardization of *thom*, the name for bear. A hanging bear or tree-climbing bear would point to the small sloth bear (*Melursus ursinus*) which I personally have seen running along a horizontal branch much like an ape, on hind legs and arms held out to balance it. This little bear is fast vanishing from the Himalayan forests.

The Mih-teh is the true Snowman, the intelligent anthropoid of the Himalayas. But does it exist? Until we proved them to be fakes, the Khumjung and Pangboche scalps were mystifying proof of the Mih-tehs' existence. So were the footprints in the snow, now known to be made by animals as insignificant as foxes and wild dogs and also, we believe, by snow leopards, yaks, ravens, and bears. Ruling out the possibility that Yetis are also making Yeti tracks, what bear is prowling about at 18,000 and 20,000 feet in a region where Sherpas claim bears don't exist?

Our guess is the blue bear of Tibet, though it could be the more common Himalayan brown bear (*Ursus arctos isabellinus*). The legends in support of the Mih-teh can be declared pure myth; we found them to be invalid everywhere.

But why this preoccupation with an apelike monster among people who have no knowledge of the great apes? Why do Sherpas invariably point out photographs of the gorilla, chimp, or orangutan as Mih-tehs when shown photographs of animals approximating the Snowman's description?

The answer is partly in the Hindu influence of the Mahayana Buddhist religion, the instinctive recognition of the ape as being related to primitive man, and, more down-to-earth, the peculiarities of the most obvious contender for the Yeh-teh's title—the blue bear.

Hindus, however far removed from the Himalayas and the

Snowman legend, believe that the Himalayas are the abode
immortal beings, the most famous among them Beeveesone,
brother of Ravana (the celebrated demon of the Hindu epic,
Ramayana). Beeveesone had been granted immortality by
Brahma, Lord of Creation, and it is generally believed he retired
to the Himalayas to meditate with such other immortal heroes
of the *Ramayana* and *Mahabharata* epics as Aswathama and
Mahabir Hanuman, the monkey-faced god. With Hanuman, according to some, went the monkey hordes that had helped rescue Sita from Lanka, the island of Ceylon, where she had been
taken by Ravana.

According to the Hindu Puranas, Beeveesone was born in the
age of Treta, an age when humans were much larger in stature
than they are today (twenty-one hands tall is the description
given, and a hand is measured as eighteen inches). Feet were
correspondingly larger than those of present-day man. It is the
prints of these huge immortal feet that are seen in the highest
reaches of the Himalayas, devout Hindus believe. The immortals
themselves are invisible to all but the deeply religious and those
who attain to a high degree of perfection by meditation at high
altitude.

What is important is that the belief exists, a Hindu belief
absorbed into Mahayana Buddhism along with the vast concourse of Hindu gods and animist spirits, its origin long forgotten.

We are now left with the Dzu-teh, and all the evidence we
amassed points to the Dzu-teh being the Tibetan blue bear.

My report, published in the *Calcutta Statesman* in August
1958, when I returned from a visit to Bhutan (a country still
closed to all foreigners) with the fur of a blue bear, details the
peculiarities:

Enter the Dremo. In his fur, and standing on his hind legs, six to
seven feet high, possibly more. Golden brown with bluish under-
tints; hair the quality of nylon: across his shoulders an ivory-coloured
band. Fur five inches deep, a hide a quarter of an inch thick, and a
large hump of dark fur atop his shoulder blades.

To so much deduced from a single fur add other scientific data.
Name: *Ursus Arctos Pruinosus Blyth*. Habitat: the remote mountains of Kham, Amdo, northwest China, where the Giant Panda
comes from and, according to one, H. Elwes, who discovered a skin

(now in the British Museum), "far beyond any of the regions accessible to Europeans."

Ursus Arctos Pruinosus Blyth has not been seen alive by other than those Tibetans who have dared to hunt him with flintlock rifle and sword. Nothing firsthand is known about his living habits. To the Western world and to India he is known by five or six furs, skulls, and bones, found in Tibet and now in private collections in Britain or in the British Museum.

He was named by Edward Blyth, first Curator of the Asiatic Society, in 1853, because of the blue tints in his fur and to differentiate him from a close but common relative, the Himalayan brown bear (*Ursus arctos isabellinus*). But though Blyth discovered him, the Asiatic Society never came by a specimen. There are none in India so far as is known.

The few known furs in existence (six have been recorded) were picked up by Britons rummaging through Tibet for one reason or the other, in Lhasa, Amdo, Tsaidam, and West Kansu. The most recent find appears to be that by Charles Bell in 1928. Exit Blue Bear.

Re-enter the Dremo. In Tibet he belongs part to fact, part to fiction. Tibetans value his fur for its beauy and warmth, and I have met two Tibetan officials who remember, I stress remember, having one or two furs in their homes. From their accounts I gathered that the furs were not recent acquisitions; that they were considered extremely rare and growing more and more scarce, which could suggest that the species is becoming extinct.

The wife of a senior Tibetan official I spoke to recently said she had actually seen a living Dremo. It belonged to the Panchen Lama and was a great attraction at his private zoo in Shigatse. It walked on its hind legs, had a face akin to bear and ape, and was the height "of a tall man."

In 1954, the *Calcutta Statesman's* Kalimpong correspondent reported a living Yeti in the Panchen Lama's zoological garden at Shigatse. She tells how immediately after publication of the story she was inundated by inquiries and cash offers for exclusive photographs by foreign newspapers and scientific bodies. Letters addressed to the editor contained similar requests. While excitement was still bubbling, Shigatse was swept by a disastrous flood. The Panchen Lama's zoo was washed away. The alleged Yeti perished.

Said the Tibetan official's wife who knew nothing of the *Statesman's* 1954 report and the uproar it caused: "I believe the poor creature was drowned."

In Calcutta a few days ago Mr. Peter Byrne, of the Slick Johnson Yeti expeditions to Nepal, revealed that an extensive search had been conducted some time later to try and discover trace of the animal's carcass in the silt left by the flood. Nothing had been found.

Here fact begins to mingle with fiction. Dremo means anything from golden bear to strayed mystic.

Sarat Chandra Dass, an eminent Indian Tibetologist, in his Tibetan-English dictionary (1902) says of the Dremo, which he calls the Dredmo: "One who has gone astray from a religious life; a yellow bear; a species of bear peculiar to the mountainous plains of Amdo and the Koko Nor region. It preys upon lagomys and marmots."

He gives its zoological name as *Ursus Lagomyarius* of Trejevalski. In another entry under Dredmo he describes it as "though born a human being he has grown an impious savage; a wild man; a savage."

Tibetans say more. They invest the Dremo with human qualities and supernatural powers. According to several Tibetans and Bhutanese I have spoken to the Dremo feasts off bamboos and berries, young birds, baby animals, the tailless mountain rat, frogs, and sheep. It has been seen carrying off the latter under its arms, walking erect.

Like brother Yeti, the male Dremo has a distinct liking for human females, carrying them off to love and life in the raw despite the jealousies of lady Dremos. If folk songs are to be believed, these forlorn captives spend their days composing verses with which to beguile their masters.

> My lord Dremo,
> tonight the moon is full
> and I
> would beg your leave,
> that I
> may to my home return.
> To my father
> and my mother
> and the others by the fire.
> To stay until the moon
> is full again.
> And should you doubt
> that I
> will come again,
> see I
> will make this vow,
> by my father
> and my mother
> and the others by the fire.

When this fat moon is thin
and the thin moon is fat again,
resting like a jewel
on the shoulder of the hill again,
I will return to you
however sad the parting.

In another song the captive woman expresses her fear of the female Dremos. She knows them to be jealous. She beseeches her captor to protect her or to return her to her home until their wrath is spent and he has need of her.

Do women ever learn to love their unnatural consorts? There is the song of a girl who, finding her "lover" trapped by her searching relatives, begs as her brother bends his bow to shoot the Dremo:

"He loves me as tenderly as you.
He is as noble as you are.
If you must for your arrow
    seek a heart
Let mine be the target.
Or slay us both."

The Dremo apparently is so aggressive the legend has grown that to see it is to die. To some it is an animal body possessed by a human spirit. To others, and the Panchen Lama's claim to possess a Yeti is a notable illustration, it is a "wild man of the rocky places" (one of the interpretations of Yeh-teh), but mostly I have heard it referred to as a monkey bear, by some invested with human face, hands, and feet.

Very recently in Bhutan, in the far northern province of Bumthang ("the place of spirits"), I discovered a Dremo skin in a monastery. It was draped over a lama's chair, and though it rained outside and the painted chapel was misted with gloom, the fur shone like burnished copper. I asked my guide what it might be and with massive unconcern he said he thought it was a migyu (the Yeti or Snowman). I asked to photograph it, and did, my hands jelly with excitement. The exposure suffered. And then, because it must have been easy to guess that I was more than ordinarily interested in the fur, the lama asked my guide if I would like to purchase it. Apparently he himself had bought it only a few days before from a Tibetan refugee.

The name the lama gave the animal was Dremo (Sarat Chandra Dass's Dredmo?). According to him, it had a human face and human feet. Quite obviously he was not trying to sell me the Snowman. He was innocent of the outside world's interest in the Yeti and the price he asked was not inspired.

Shown to several Tibetans and Bhutanese, the fur invariably was

described as belonging to the Dremo (in Bhutan Tremo) though
few, if any, of them had ever seen one. His Highness the Maharajah
of Bhutan, who is a keen shikari and knows his country's fauna
intimately, had never seen the animal or a fur. But he thought a few
might be living in the unknown northeastern mountains of Bhutan.

The official's wife in Kalimpong who had seen the supposed Yeti
in the Panchen Lama's zoo immediately identified it with the fur I
had discovered. Mr. David Macdonald, of Kalimpong, for many years
British Trade Agent in Tibet and a great authority on the country,
pronounced the fur a Dremo's. He knew a great deal about the
creature but had never seen one.

But confusion arises. The Calcutta expert who examined the skin
(Dr. B. Biswas who accompanied the Daily Mail Yeti Expedition to
Nepal in 1953) had not the slightest doubt about it being a blue
bear's. But Sarat Chandra Dass described the Dremo as a golden
bear.

Look at the zoological names. The blue bear is Ursus Arcots
Pruinosus Blyth, the Dremo Lagomyarius of Trejevalski. The skin I
now possess is by all accounts a Dremo's. Could the blue bear and
the yellow bear be the one and the same animal, named differently
by Blyth and Trejevalski? Both descriptions are tenable. The fur I
brought from Bhutan has a golden sheen caused by the tip of every
individual hair being yellow, and there is the pale yellow bar across
the shoulders. But under the gold is a distinctly blue tint. In some
lights the fur is blonde, in others brown, in others again a greyish
brown. It could be described as any of these colours.

More important, could the Dremo be the Yeti? He is extremely
rare and rare animals generate folk tales. He is "the height of a tall
man," does often walk erect, is shaggy gold or shaggy grey brown,
has a face unlike the normal bear, apparently is dangerous, his eating habits match the Yeti's, he is a high-altitude animal, and there is
the mythical business of his carrying away women to live with.

So far the Dremo has never been seen in the Himalayas, but the
Maharajah of Bhutan thinks there are a few in his country's remote
forests and mountains. Remember there never has been a Dremo in
any zoo other than the Panchen Lama's. The creature has not been
studied. Little is known about it. And if it is a shy, close-to-extinct
animal hiding out in the least accessible tracts of the Himalayas, it
is possible that here is the origin of the Yeti stories.

I have come to realize after weeks in Bhutan, often as isolated as
the man in the moon, that imagination can invest even the most well-
known object with wildest fantasy. Once at 17,000 feet I saw the
back of a blonde yak loom out of the mist. Had I fled, I would have
carried with me the vision of a Yeti.

The furs we found in Nepal were declared by some of the world's greatest living authorities to be Tibetan blue bear. None of these furs belonged to animals killed in Nepal, though at least one was from southernmost Tibet, just across the Nepal border. But we do know of one blue bear actually trapped and killed in north Nepal—the "Yeti" of Mustang, crushed by a crude stone trap in 1957.

The certain characteristics of the blue bear I find common to the Snowman legend and descriptions of Yeti sightings are:

The blue bear has a white or ivory band around its chest; Sherpas often describe the Mih-teh as having a bald belt about its middle above which the fur grows upward and below which it grows downward.

The blue bear has light-colored, extremely short hair on its face, and its belly is comparatively free of fur; the Mih-teh is described as having a pale human face and naked human stomach.

The blue bear has a conical hump of fur on the apex of its shoulders. Seen in profile or head on at a distance, this hump could be regarded as part of the head, the conical scalp of the Mih-teh.

Tibetans insist that the blue bear walks a great deal on its hind legs. Certainly when surprised or merely curious the creature could be expected to rear up on its hind legs.

A Tibetan who saw the live blue bear in the Panchen Lama's zoo described its "very big chest, straight back, square head, and swinging arms . . . it seemed to be singing a sentimental song."

I hope we are wrong about the Yeti. During our ten months in Nepal we never saw a bear of any kind. We saw surprisingly little animal life, nothing bigger than a wolf. If bears and snow leopards kept out of our way, an intelligent anthropoid certainly could. As I have said before, even our most convincing arguments are negative. Someone has yet to explain the commonly heard cry of a "Yeti" and keep looking for footprints in the snow that could have been made by an anthropoid or large bear and not a combination of brittle snow, a hot sun, and a small animal's tracks. And someone has to discover conclusively what it is the Sherpas and Bhutanese and Sikkimese and North Indians are seeing when they claim to see the Yeti.

But the hard fact is that one by one the supports to the Yeti theory have faded before our investigation:

Yeti tracks are readily molded by the sun from the footprints of other animals;

The Khumjung Yeti scalp is an interesting relic—but a fake for all of this;

The Pangboche Yeti hand is largely human in origin;

The Yeti skins, so positively identified as such by any Sherpa, are in truth the Tibetan blue bear;

And the myths and legends about the Yeti quickly move into the sphere of fantasy when carefully investigated.

What then remains?

When we were taking leave of the Abbot of Thyangboche, the same abbot who discredited so many stories of Yetis associated with his monastery, he said, "If you left a camera with me I might get you a photograph of a Yeti. While you sahibs are about they never come near us, but as soon as you have gone they will surely appear."

PART II

OUR LIFE IN THE CLOUDS

10

INTO THE

MINGBO VALLEY

THE SNOWMAN PROGRAM

Desmond Doig has related how we carried out our search for
the Yeti and how interesting and entertaining we found the
whole affair. To supplement his conclusions, here is a summary
of the evidence.

Our investigations were carried out almost exclusively among
the Sherpa people living within thirty miles of Mount Everest.
Tracks and sightings of the Yeti have been reported over a much
wider area than this, but a large proportion of the more tangible
evidence used in support of the Yeti theory comes from the
region we examined.

Tracks: The single piece of evidence which has been more
widely used than any other to justify the Yeti is the photograph
of a footprint found on the Menlung glacier in 1951 by Mr.
Eric Shipton and Dr. Michael Ward. (I was a member of this
expedition but was operating in another valley at the time.)
This print, a remarkably clear one among a lengthy line of less
distinct tracks, has been the source of much conjecture. From its
shape and dimensions some anthropologists have reconstructed
the form and characteristics of the Yeti in considerable detail.
We did not find any single footprint as remarkable as the Shipton one but did discover many that approximated it. It was
quite clear that our Yeti tracks had been produced in rather
mundane fashion—by the sun melting out the pug marks of
small animals. As our tracks were discovered at the same altitude, at the same time of the year, and within three miles of

Shipton's tracks on the Menlung Glacier, it is fair to assume that a similar effect could occur there. It is of interest to note a comment of Dr. Ward—that in following along the Menlung tracks they noticed animal tracks mixed up with them but didn't regard this as being particularly significant at the time.

Mr. Ralph Izzard, author of the book *In Search of the Abominable Snowman,* describes the many Yeti tracks seen by his expedition in the Khumbu area. His opinion has the weight of considerable personal experience (unlike the many Yeti "experts" who argue enthusiastically from armchairs), and he told me in London that he is now coming to the view that his tracks were made by the great Tibetan wolf. The Slick-Johnson expedition completed several journeys into the isolated Iswa Valley and reported tracks, noises, and animal droppings. Despite the use of a pack of trained dogs they were unable to capture a Yeti. The first exploration of this valley was carried out by two members of my NZAC expedition in 1954, Dr. Charles Evans and Mr. Geoffrey Harrow. On the snow fields at the head of the valley they photographed tracks—two sets side by side, one large and one small. Although his Sherpas accepted the tracks as having been made by Yetis, Dr. Evans reported that he could clearly see signs of claw marks in these very fresh tracks and suspected that a mother bear and her baby had crossed the area.

It is perhaps not generally realized that the regions up to 19,000 feet are by no means always devoid of life and food. Foxes, wolves, snow leopards, marmots, and many other animals and birds live there. So, too, do yaks, sheep, goats, and even humans.

Scalps: Many of the descriptions of the Yeti by the Sherpas make particular reference to its high pointed crown. An apparent confirmation of this unusual feature are the three scalps held in monasteries of the Khumbu area—Khumjung, Pangboche, and Namche Bazar. We examined them all in detail and were impressed by their similarity in shape and size and in the color and texture of their hair. The Khumjung scalp is in slightly better repair than the other two, and we were fortunate in being able to take it to the outside world for expert examination. The scientists who saw the scalp in Chicago, Paris, and London agreed that, although it was an interesting and probably ancient relic, it was really a fake—molded from the skin of a serow. It had certainly never held the cunning brain of the elusive Yeti.

Skeletal Hand: In the monastery of Pangboche is the skeleton of a hand which the lamas believe once belonged to a Yeti. Photographs of this hand have been examined in the Western world and the reports given confirm the judgment of my own doctors that this is essentially a human hand, strung together with wire, with the possible inclusion of several animal bones.

Skins: Not a great amount has been previously reported on the Yeti skins which rapidly assumed such an important place in our investigations. The three skins we obtained had all come originally from Tibet, in one case at least quite recently with escaping refugees. It was always fascinating to show one of these skins to a Sherpa, who made no claims to have seen a Yeti, and get the immediate response from man, woman, or child that this undoubtedly was the skin of a Yeti and definitely not a bear.

The skins fit closely the Sherpa's mental picture of the Yeti. With the positive identification of these skins as the blue bear from eastern Tibet we were left with the very strong inference that this bear might well have been the source of much of the Yeti legend.

Sightings of the Yeti: The Thyangboche monastery has the reputation of having been visited more frequently by Yetis than any other area. Careful interrogation of the lamas in this (and many other monasteries) by Desmond, a man who could speak fluently to them without having to operate through a Nepalese or Sherpa interpreter (and who was loved and respected by the Sherpa people), failed to produce a single case of a lama who claimed personally to have seen a Yeti. Even the two old lamas who had lived in Thyangboche since its founding some fifty years before had not seen any Yetis and knew of no other lama in the monastery who had. On the other hand we received many denials of the rather dramatic and lurid stories which had been reported to the world by some Western expeditions.

The Sherpas' Belief in the Yeti: There is no doubt that the Sherpas accept the fact that the Yeti really exists. But then they believe just as confidently that their gods live in comfort on the summit of Mount Everest. We found it quite impossible to divorce the Yeti from the supernatural. To a Sherpa the ability of a Yeti to make himself invisible at will is just as important a part of his description as his probable shape and size. Part

animal, part human, part demon—the Yeti is as calmly and un-
critically accepted as we accept Father Christmas when we are
children.

Pleasant though we felt it would be to believe in the existence of the Yeti, when faced with the universal collapse of the
main evidence in support of this creature the members of my
expedition—doctor, scientists, zoologists, and mountaineers alike
—could not in all conscience view it as more than a fascinating fairy tale, born of the rare and frightening view of strange
animals, molded by superstition, and enthusiastically nurtured
by Western expeditions.

The Physiological Program

The search for the Yeti was not, of course, the sole objective
of our expedition—or indeed the most important one. The thread
which tied the whole expedition together was physiological research into high-altitude acclimatization, and it was in this direction that our major effort was turned. This extensive study of
human functions and behavior at extreme altitudes was the reason the expedition was to be such a long one—nine months or
more—for we wanted long-term results which would not be possible in an ordinary expedition of three and a half months. I
planned to winter a party at a height of over 19,000 feet, something that had never been done before, and finally, as a test for
the party's standard of acclimatization, to attempt to climb Makalu's 27,790 feet without using oxygen equipment. By the end of
the expedition we hoped to know the answer to many questions,
among them:

(a) What is the maximum height at which man can live at
long periods without deterioration?

(b) What are the fundamental physiological changes in the
body during the acclimatization process?

(c) Is it possible to so acclimatize the human body that man
can operate effectively at heights in excess of 27,500 feet without supplementary oxygen?

Dr. Griffith Pugh, the leader of the physiological team, and I
had discussed at some length the ideal conditions we should try to
attain for setting up the physiological tests. Pugh pointed out
that the physiological results would be seriously affected if the

men were living in conditions of extreme hardship and discomfort, as it would be difficult to assess which effects were the result of altitude and which purely resulting from lack of food and the constant battle against low temperatures and miserable living conditions. We resolved, therefore, to overcome this problem which had proved the bugbear of all previous physiological work at high altitudes by constructing two insulated and heated huts. Although these would necessarily be rather cramped in their layout, they would at least supply living and working conditions of modest comfort. As well, we planned to supply as diversified and palatable a diet as was possible under the circumstances.

The choice of a suitable area of operations was not an easy one. We needed a valley where two huts could be established between 17,000 and 20,000 feet. Access to these huts must be moderately safe throughout the year so that we could obtain assistance in case of emergency or carry down any sick person immediately to lower altitudes. It would also be advantageous to have a Sherpa village near at hand with its supply of labor and food. The area would have to be stimulating both mentally and physically to the wintering party and must give them ample opportunity for vigorous exercise. And, finally, the area must have reasonable access to the foot of Makalu—our objective in the final stages of the expedition.

There were many advantages in our operating in the Everest region. It was an area I knew well; there was a large pool of experienced labor available; I knew that some fresh food could be obtained locally; and it was an area of great beauty and interest.

In thinking over the matter I remembered a trip in 1951 with Mr. Eric Shipton. We had just discovered the southern route onto Mount Everest—the route by which the peak was finally climbed in 1953—but now we were spending a couple of weeks exploring the unknown territory to the east of Everest. In an exciting few days we had crossed over a high pass into the grim Hongu Valley and then climbed up onto a steep 20,000-foot pass to the east—to see before us a high-level route leading into the vast trough of the Barun Valley lying at the foot of the enormous massif of Makalu.

On our return Shipton and I were very short of food and decided to attempt a short cut back to our base supplies. To

the south of the imposing spire of Amadablam we could see a
snowy pass, nearly 20,000 feet in height, which must surely lead
in the right direction. Accepting the gamble that the route might
be impossible, we bundled together our last meager supplies of
food and climbed up onto the pass.

Our hearts sank at the view before us. Far below a heavily
crevassed glacier tumbled down into the Mingbo Valley, which
was lined with a fierce array of ice peaks. And from our pass—
as we called it—500 feet of excessively steep ice fluting plunged
down to the snow fields at the head of the glacier.

Our three Sherpas without hesitation rejected this as a route.
But time and food were short, and Shipton and I decided to
make the attempt. Ignoring the protestations of our Sherpas,
we started hacking a stairway with our ice axes down the ice
fluting. It was hard but exhilarating work, and like many problems it became more feasible as we got to grips with it. Halfway down there was a sudden yell, and the next moment the
Sherpa on my rope shot past me like a rocket. I had just finished
cutting a line of steps and my ice axe was embedded in a crack
in the ice as a belay. With a flick of my wrist I threw a loop of
the rope over it and held on grimly—and when the full weight
of the Sherpa's body came on the rope I was just able to hold
the shock. I dragged the Sherpa, somewhat chastened, to safety
and then cut steps downward until we could lower ourselves
over the crevasse at the bottom of the slope and move out onto
the Mingbo snow fields. Without too much difficulty we
forced a twisting route through the crevasses and down the
broken ice of the icefall. A couple of hours after dark we had
struggled far down the valley to the river bed and, exhausted,
slept out in the scrub under a bright moon. Next day we
reached the village of Dingboche and fresh food.

In remembering this trip, and others in the same area, I decided that the Mingbo Valley would fulfill most of our requirements and resolved to put the two huts there—one somewhere near the foot of the icefall, the other at 19,600 feet on
the Amadablam Col itself.

I expected to meet a number of unpredictable factors. Despite the use of huts we would need to be adequately equipped to
operate in very cold temperatures. The extent of our activities
would be largely governed by the somewhat variable weather
of the post-monsoon period. Also, dangerous avalanche snow on

51. *Hillary holding what was said to be a Yeti skin, obtained in the village of Beding. Identified as Blue Bear from Eastern Tibet.*

52. (ABOVE) *Observing a line of Yeti tra[*

53. (ABOVE) *Yeti track with pick ax.*

54. (RIGHT) *Plaster cast of a Yeti footprint.*

55. (LEFT) *Khumjung's Yeti scalp.*

56. (BELOW) *Lama cutting out a mold form from a piece of wood. We used this to shape a softened animal skin into approximate reproductions of the Khumjung scalp.*

57. *Yeti scalp on Hillary's head.*

58. *On return to Khumjung by helicopter with the scalp in its box. Two Sherpas on left are the village's headmen.*

the passes could restrict my party's movements and possibly mean various changes in program. The only thing to do was to wait and see how things turned out but to be sufficiently mobile to make any changes on the spot.

On September 13 I left Kathmandu with Doig, Marlin Perkins, and the main body of sahibs and 160 laden porters, en route to the Rolwaling Valley and the Yeti search.

A day later the major train of 310 porters set off for the Everest area and the Mingbo Valley to build the scientific huts. In charge of this party was Norman Hardie, a Himalayan mountaineer of wide experience and skill, whose greatest feat was the ascent of Kangchenjunga, 28,150 feet—the world's third highest summit. Assisting him were Dr. Jim Milledge, Barry Bishop, and Wally Romanes. All of these men were experienced mountaineers, but only Hardie had been to the Himalayas before. Their task was formidable. Many of the loads were clumsy and uncomfortable, particularly the hut sections and beams, and this would tend to slow down the porters' rate of travel, making for general discontent. Also, the monsoon rains were still in full force. Miserable conditions could be expected on the high passes ahead.

For eleven days they carried across country through monsoon drizzle, climbing over steep ridges and plunging down into deep valleys. They entered Buddhist country on the twelfth day. Because this forecast more rigorous climatic conditions a section of the Hindu coolies began their usual grumbling. Now that they were gaining altitude the ill-clad Nepali porters were beginning to suffer from cold, and the constant rain was depressing their morale. Also they knew they would have to take a high-level route into the Dudh Kosi Valley over a 15,000-foot pass, since the bridges on the usual lower route were invariably washed away during the monsoon.

The straggling caravan climbed to a clearing at 12,000 feet and, with the barometer falling, 160 of the men crowded into three sordid earth-floored huts, recently vacated by yaks, while the remainder made a shanty town outside from the expedition tarpaulins. It rained heavily all night with cold temperatures—obviously snow would be falling on the pass ahead. All the porters were well aware that the 1952 Swiss Everest party had lost two men on this pass in similar conditions. On that occasion over a hundred of the porters had deserted. It had taken the Swiss a week to recruit more labor and continue their journey. Hardie decided to hold the complete party for a day, and in the miserable conditions time passed very slowly. To his consternation it rained heavily again that night. Once more he had to delay moving. By this time coolie food and morale was very low and everyone wanted to go home. The three sordid huts were thick with an atmosphere of wet bodies and smoke, but despite this a gambling octet tossed dice for two days and nights across a bamboo mat, apparently oblivious of the surrounding squalor.

By canvassing the local villages Hardie obtained promises of 180 replacements for the worst of his shivering army. Then began the worst payday he had ever experienced. Nepalese coolies never line up and they always shout. They have surprisingly little imagination when naming their children; Hardie had twelve Lal Bhadurs and eleven Ram Bhadurs on his books. Each of the 180 had to be sorted out, his wages assessed and then be paid, while the other 130 that weren't being paid clamored in the middle of the mob. And still the rain came down while the squalor and discomfort increased.

On the third night the rain stopped. After a dawn conference with his more experienced Sherpas, Hardie decided to push over the pass and not wait for the snow to compact. Romanes and Bishop, with a strong Sherpa group, left early to break the trail, and they were followed shortly by the remaining 130 barefooted Kathmandu men. Milledge and Hardie stayed behind to sign on the 180 new members and to issue them their loads, but they had to wait a long time for some. New recruits absorb astonishing hours in grinding flour for their rations or in taking leave of sweethearts and others. By midday there were still forty depressing loads in the empty camp and the snow-covered pass ahead was again obscured by mist. Hardie sent Milledge off, to keep the only doctor with the main party.

The whole situation filled Hardie with considerable misgivings. Things were mellowed a little by the arrival of the next group, for they had several bottles of arak with them—so newly out of the still that it was quite warm. This added a slightly more cheerful note to the somber surroundings. By 2 P.M. all the loads were moving.

For an hour Hardie stayed with the last group, but it became obvious they would not reach the day's destination or in fact go far enough to get into any trouble. So he issued them cigarettes, gave them firm words on what they would have to do the next day, and then increased his own speed. Before the pass he overhauled forty laden men and women, many already sheltering under rocks and understandably unwilling to make the crossing so late in the day. Hardie wasn't too concerned. They were local people and knew how to handle the conditions.

In driving sleet and with half an hour of daylight remaining he reached the last gully below the pass. Fifty feet from the top he found a boy of fifteen curled up in the snow, whimpering and soaked. He couldn't lift his load, yet he wouldn't desert it. Hardie got him to his feet and in five yards he fell again, so the tough Hardie towed the boy and his load to the summit. There the boy began calling out for someone else and was answered by an even smaller boy, soaked through and crying. Neither was able to cope with the glazed rocks and the awkward loads. A firm hand was needed. Hardie made them pick up their loads and follow him down. Once they had started they were very willing to keep going, for warmth came with movement, and in twenty minutes they were off the snow and in ten minutes more the top scrub was in sight.

When they reached the alpine scrub Hardie deserted his two charges, pushing onward in the dark to see how the other 270 men were situated. Every overhanging rock had occupants, and at every one he was invited to stay for the night. He was very tired by now and once he seriously contemplated stopping. He opened his forty-pound pack to see how things stood for a night out. To his surprise he found there was no food in it. The weight had been mainly money, two thousand cigarettes, camera bag, and a torch. He was wearing shorts and a cotton shirt and inside his pack was only a jersey and climbing trousers with no windproofs. Hardie had been so involved in getting everything moving all day that he hadn't noticed that his Sherpa, Pember Tenzing, taking pity on him, had removed most of his spare clothing and food—and now he was separated from Pember Tenzing.

So on he went and caught up to four young Sherpa women traveling slowly down a boulder track, singing at the tops of their voices. After half an hour they decided to make a bed in the scrub. A few minutes later Hardie heard a shout ahead.

Under a wet rock he found seven men and three women. He gave everyone a cigarette and asked the two most likely looking men who knew the track to come on with him. They were faster than the girls had been, and with the help of his torch and their guidance he reached the camp one and a half hours after dark. It was in a sheltered valley at 12,000 feet, and Hardie sat down to a meal in a dimly lit cave. Behind him gleamed pairs of Sherpa eyes. Continual gossip was punctuated by infectious roars of Sherpa laughter. Hardie had just finished an enormous meal when another torch was seen. Sirdar Dawa Tenzing had no enthusiasm for a night out either and had crossed the pass in the dark, encouraging the stragglers as he came. Fortunately it was a fine night, but it was very cold, and the thought of eighty people scattered over the route gave Hardie little rest.

It dawned a normal monsoon day—high clouds, no wind, mist soon gathering. Hardie waited to check the last men through while the others moved on again. To his enormous relief the roll was complete at 11 A.M. and he was able to set off after the main bunch. Half an hour out he reached the edge of the Lumding Khola, now shrouded in mist.

The altimeter read 12,550 feet. The drop down the wall into the valley is a staggering one, and the track is quite incredible. Halfway down, Hardie's knees were creaking and his toes were skinned and on fire. He changed out of his boots into tennis shoes, which at least transferred the pain elsewhere. At the bottom the altimeter read 8500 feet. It had been a sheer 4000-foot drop. But there is no respite in the heavily forested Lumding Khola gorge—the only place to go is up. For another 3000 feet they struggled up to the ridge on the other side. The long hut beams were terrifying loads for the porters in this rough country, and Hardie knew that some of the men would inevitably be delayed. From the crest of the ridge the thin track dropped down another 2500 feet to the Sherpa village of Tate. And here the day's journey ended for most of the party, although there were still forty loads deep in the gorge behind them.

The following morning Dawa Tenzing stayed with Hardie to help speed up the slower men, trailing behind. Now that they were in a populated area again it was possible to obtain other porters, so they paid off the slowest eight stragglers—and promised to do the same again next day if they had any further trouble. By 11 P.M. that night they were once again a united party.

Two days later the monsoon ended abruptly with a violent downpour. By now the coolies had been paid off, a strong Sherpa team was being recruited, and they were based in the peaceful surroundings of Thyangboche, a village with a view in every direction to gladden the climber's heart, and only twelve miles from the foot of Mount Everest itself.

RECONNOITERING THE MINGBO VALLEY

Over in the Rolwaling I had been greatly concerned about the difficulties Hardie's party must be experiencing as we, too, had been flooded out with continuous rain, and heavy monsoon snow was low on all the hillsides and valleys. It was a considerable relief, therefore, when we made our first contact with Hardie's party on October 2 over our small field radio sets and discovered they had arrived safely at Thyangboche, battered but whole. From this time on I followed the progress of the Mingbo party daily over our radios, and Hardie and I were able to discuss problems and make any necessary decisions on the spot.

Hardie and his group swung into action immediately. For a base storage depot they rented a little house at Chanmitang— only twenty minutes from Thyangboche. For this we had to pay the princely rental of Rs.40 per month ($5). Some ten months previously I had placed an order for large quantities of timber to be used for the framework of the first hut. This was now in a huge pile at Thyangboche. Our builder, Wally Romanes, worked out the various timber requirements and then organized a Sherpa group to cut 6"×4" timber down to 4"×3", check out joints, and pre-cut all rafters, studs, and plates to an exact length. They were still three days' march from the construction site.

It was a major task getting four hundred loads up the Mingbo Valley. Hardie's party struck a foot of soft snow down to low levels, and this taxed their strength to the utmost. It was two weeks before the route was in good order with the loads moving smoothly upward. A site was chosen for the lower hut at 17,500 feet. When enough loads had accumulated, Romanes took over the construction, and in two days the hut frame had risen above its rocky foundation. Despite rather dangerous snow conditions reconnaissance was made of the two passes at the head of the valley—the 19,500-foot South Col and the Amadablam Col to the north. The South Col had enough room for a hut, but the route up to it was menaced by overhanging ice. This left only the Amadablam Col—my original choice. On October 20 Hardie and Bishop flagged the route through the ice cliffs and crevasses to the foot of the Amadablam Col, and the following day the first loads were carried up to a 19,000-foot dump. From now on the loads came through with great regularity.

The final phase of the party's work was harassed by difficulties. The last four hundred feet to the col was up fluted ribs of extreme steepness—too steep, it was felt, for lines of laden Sherpas. I had sent in a light winch to meet this problem (the same type operated by the successful Italian expedition on K2), and this was carried to the top of the face, anchored to a rock on the col, and then used to drag loads up the slope. The winching was exhausting work, and the machinery was incapable of meeting the strains put on it. The party retreated, repaired the winch, tried again. Once again it collapsed.

On October 28 I crossed the Tashi Lapcha Pass from the Rolwaling Valley with the Yeti party. In fine weather we strolled down the lovely Thami Valley, the bright sunshine, sparkling water, and wonderful peaks making me realize anew how lovely the Khumbu area is. Several hours of brisk walking brought us to the large Thami monastery where a very sacred reincarnate lama now resided. We were received with pomp and ceremony and took tea with the lama in the courtyard of the monastery. The whole area was alive with activity, for this was the main gathering point for all the Tibetans who had escaped from their country through the high Nangpa La Pass. There were tents and animals everywhere, and the whole area was decidedly squalid. My old friend and climbing companion, Tenzing Norgay, was born at Thami, but the village had always been a rather grubby and insignificant one, with little in its favor except its magnificent position. We were met here by Norman Hardie, looking very fit after his strenuous activity in the Mingbo Valley, and I spent the evening discussing with him our future plan of operations.

There was a crisp frost next morning as we started down the valley. It is a delightful walk along the Bhote Kosi River, but we were sad to see it spoiled by carcasses of sheep and yaks, dead of starvation. The whole area had been denuded by the flocks and herds of Tibetan refugees. There were vultures circling everywhere. The view as we climbed up over the hill toward the village of Khumjung was breath-taking—mountain after tremendous mountain: Everest, Lhotse, Nuptse, Kangtega, and the terrible Tooth of Amadablam. To the south of Amadablam we could look into the broad entrance of the Mingbo Valley. We descended into the pleasant hollow of Khumjung to be greeted affectionately by many old Sherpa friends.

All the Mingbo party were here to meet us together with Dr. Griffith Pugh, who had arrived from Kathmandu a couple of days before with fifty loads of scientific equipment. The sky was bright with stars and the ground hard with frost, but we talked the evening away, soaking up the warmth from a crackling campfire.

On November 1 we moved to the expedition house at Chanmitang. I was very pleased with this house. Set in a delightful clearing in the forest, it was small but compact with two storage rooms below and two living rooms above. Outside the front door were two tall pine poles draped with prayer flags, while in the main living room was a large prayer wheel that chimed sweetly with each complete revolution. The house was crammed with expedition supplies, so we pitched our tents for sleeping quarters. I arranged with Hardie to travel up the Mingbo Valley as soon as possible to see the progress that had been made to date and to make a decision on the final site for the top hut.

The Two Huts

It was a lovely morning on November 3 as we made our preparations for departure. The usual chaos reigned, and it was 10 o'clock before I left the house behind and set off up the Imja Valley. The crisp clean air and the wonderful views produced a feeling of exhilaration as I plunged down to the sturdy bridge over the foaming Imja Khola. The summit of Everest was sharp against the blue Tibetan sky, and Amadablam was towering over our heads. In brisk time I reached the village of Pangboche and crossed the river again, to climb abruptly up into the Mingbo Valley. The track rose steeply over grassy hillsides; with each gain in height new mountains would swing into view. Soon, behind me, Tawache had risen to guard the mouth of the valley like the blade of a sword. In less than two hours I reached the temporary Base Camp on a grassy shelf at 14,500 feet near the grazing alp of Laparma. I caught up to the other members of the party here and we had a quick lunch. We pushed on again up the Mingbo Valley with vistas opening on every side.

I felt a growing sense of excitement and forged on ahead with only Nevison and Mulgrew hanging on behind. The first 2000 feet was excellent going, mostly over grassy slopes. We made fast time indeed. When we stopped for a few moments to take photographs I made the idle comment to Peter Mulgrew that it would be almost possible to put a little airstrip in the gentle hollow beneath us—never realizing that we would be doing this very thing in a few months' time. We carried on over rough moraine which pushed up in huge heaps and ridges in every direction. The altitude was now starting to tell. Our pace dropped off a little, but we still forced our way on, slipping and stumbling over the loose rocks. Under the warm sun of the previous week the snow had melted off the rocks and all that remained was hard and compacted. In a last surge of effort we drove ourselves up a little gully in the moraine and on to a narrow pass. A hundred feet below us beside a little lake was the green square of a hut with the terminal ice cliffs of a glacier looming above it. We called a welcome to those in residence and a request for cups and cups of tea, then plunged down in a shower of boulders.

I examined the hut at some length and was filled with admiration for the work carried out by Wally Romanes. I had designed this hut in New Zealand with an eye to lightness and simplicity: a framework of local timber covered with a sheath of tightly stretched wire netting; then a layer of tar building paper, and finally an outer skin of heavy green canvas. We had brought in a window, material for a door, and bunks and piping for a stove. But Romanes had built the Green Hut far better than I had ever expected. Using the rough Sherpa timber, he had hammered together a framework as neat and as sturdy as any house at home. The canvas was fitted and battened carefully into place, and the ingenious Romanes had built a fine stove out of rock and cement and the odd pieces of iron sheeting. We were using firewood carried up from the lower valleys for heating and cooking. It was pleasant to escape from the cold and the wind and move into a comfortable bunk in the snug little Green Hut.

I resolved to put a camp on the Amadablam Col without delay, to examine possible hut sites from there. Next morning I set off from the Green Hut with six sahibs and fourteen Sherpas, laden with all the requirements for this camp. The route led up smooth glacier-worn rocks for the first few hundred feet and then entered a long snow trough which penetrated into the heart of the icefall. Hardie had spent much time establishing and marking this route, and an excellent route it proved to be as it wound its way up the ice cliffs and gullies to emerge on a broad crevassed slope above the icefall. Then we climbed slowly up the flagged route to a large dump of hut parts stacked together on the snow at the foot of the steep slopes leading to the Amadablam Col.

I looked up at the col and it brought back memories of my crossing here with Shipton some nine years before. But now the circumstances were very different. Certainly the slope was just as formidable as it had been, but now, zigzagging upward, I could see a line of reliable steps, and stretching from top to bottom was the thin wire of our Himalayan winch. We roped up and with our crampons biting well into the firm snow commenced working our way upward. The higher we got the more satisfied I became. One is always nagged by the thought that memories of a difficult place may grow and develop over the years, but this slope was steep—damn steep—and my memory hadn't been at fault. We emerged over the crest of the 19,600-foot col into the teeth of a bitterly cold wind and hastily donned all our warm clothing. Ahead of us the glacier dropped in relatively easy slopes down into the rugged Hongu Valley. There was snow everywhere. The valley looked cold and wintery.

This was no place for idling! We dumped our loads, and while the majority of the men concentrated on the winch, Hardie and I clambered around and examined tentative hut sites. Soon after our arrival a terrific wind sprang up. I decided we had better pitch our tents before the weather worsened. Getting them up was a fearful struggle in a wind which had now reached gale force. We flung ourselves on the flapping, writhing monsters, pulled them up into place, and then hung on like grim death. Only by piling masses of snow on the tent flaps and lashing them very securely were we able to stop them from disappearing down the valley. It was so cold and miserable outside that we were soon forced to retire to our tents, and Hardie, Gill, Lowe, the six Sherpas, and I spent a most uncomfortable night.

I hardly slept a wink. Lying there, listening to the whipping and cracking of the tent, I wondered whether we could possibly build a hut here under such conditions. And what would happen in the winter if there was an emergency sickness or accident? Could a person be lowered down these flutings if they had four feet of fresh snow on them? Before morning I had quite resolved to abandon the Amadablam Col as a hut site. We would find a more protected and salubrious spot. My decision was made easier by fears expressed by Dr. Pugh back at Khumjung. He thought 19,600 feet might be too high for the wintering hut and that the men would be unable to withstand this height long enough to make the effort worth while.

By morning the wind had subsided and it was fine and clear, but the memory of the night was still very vivid in our minds. I gave the word to pull out. Leaving the others to dismantle the winch and to send back the few loads that had reached the col, Hardie and I descended the fluttings to the Mingbo snow fields. We examined two sites at just over 19,000 feet and finally decided on one of them—a pleasant snow location with excellent access to the Green Hut and safe from any avalanche that might fall from the steep slopes above. By the end of the day everything had been stripped off the col and Hardie and I had commenced shoveling out a platform on a rounded ridge between two snow-filled crevasses. After a full day's work we retreated to the Green Hut for a good meal and a warm night.

The top hut, or the Silver Hut, as we came to call it after its outer coat of aluminum paint, was our answer to the problem of comfortable living and laboratory quarters at high altitude. Originally I had planned to construct another hut similar to the Green Hut, using perhaps a metal framework. However, Dr. Pugh investigated the possibilities of a more advanced type of structure. The Timber Development Association in the United Kingdom became interested, and their chief architect, Mr. Levin, suggested a stressed plywood building with three inches or so of expanded foam plastic insulation. Levin had an active and ingenious mind. I drew out a base plan for a tiny hut with eight sleeping bunks, a cooking stove and table, a laboratory of the minimum dimensions required by Pugh, and a snow-porch entrance. Within a matter of minutes Levin had transformed this into a compact and workable hut of radical but practical design.

The hut was rather like a giant drainpipe, twenty-two feet long and ten feet in diameter. As it had to be carried on the backs of men for nearly two hundred miles, we had strict limitations on the size and weight of individual sections. Levin designed a series of prefabricated curved panels, each fitting into the other like a giant jigsaw puzzle. Large triple-glazed windows were supplied for the laboratory end. There was a light but strong foundation of laminated wooden beams which bolted firmly together. As with all prototypes, we had problems in the early stages of development, and it was only by a concentrated effort toward the end that the hut was finally completed and shipped off to India.

I was determined that the expedition members should have a trial erection of the building back at ordinary levels, for I shuddered to think of anoxic climbers tackling the job for the first time at 19,000 feet, probably in cold and windy conditions. A group of us gathered in London before the expedition and drove down to the builder's factory for the trial. Stacked around in neat piles were our hundred panels and innumerable fittings.

I asked the dour little foreman how long he thought the job would take. His jaundiced eye roved over the mixed bunch of six medicos who made up my party. "I estimate you'll need seventeen hours' working time," he said. "Good heavens," I thought. "Seventeen hours here probably means thirty-four hours at 19,000 feet." Fortunately the foreman had underestimated the skill and resourcefulness of my party. In six hours of vigorous labor we had everything up, and a fine job it looked too. I felt now that we could tackle its erection in the field with much greater confidence.

On the morning of November 6 the whole party of us, sahibs and Sherpas, were away promptly and climbed up the flagged route to the foot of the Amadablam Col. Then we all set to work—making a substantial snow platform, assembling the foundations for the hut, and carrying all the hut sections down from the dump to the hut-site vicinity. There wasn't much room on the little snow rib I'd chosen, but it was the only feasible place which looked completely free from avalanche danger. So we shoveled off the top of the ridge until we were down to really firm snow and had a platform just wide enough to take the foundations of the hut. On this we assembled the plywood beams and carefully leveled them. At the same time we tackled the problem of tying the hut down against the vigorous winds we could expect here. I decided to use a method I had found successful in the Antarctic. A large canvas kit bag was jammed full of snow, the end of a steel wire rope lashed around its middle, and then it was all buried in a hole in the snow. Firmly stamped into position, these bags froze hard to become practically immovable. By the end of the day the foundations were ready and the hut sections were stacked near at hand, awaiting assembly. Tomorrow would be the big day. We could only hope for good weather.

By 10 A.M. next morning we were back on the hut site—it was clear and sunny with only a light cold wind to harass us. We started immediately on the job of assembling the sections, and it was obvious from the start that everything was going well. The trial run immediately proved its worth, for we worked as a team, quietly and confidently tackling problem after problem. As we gained confidence we made firm use of an eight-pound sledge hammer to tightly wedge together section after section—far more efficiently than we had in our trial effort in London. By the end of the day the outside shell was complete and already it made a snug little home. Driven by a feeling of considerable satisfaction at our success, we worked until the last moment—until the wind and cold sent us scurrying off to the Green Hut. We descended into the end of a glorious sunset, stumbling a little as we went, for our eyes were far too busy drinking in the sky and the peaks to worry about our feet.

The hut was completed in the next three weeks—joints sealed; the kerosene heater assembled; the hut well tied down; furniture, beds, and benches installed; the hut wired up for electricity; a wind generator and batteries put into operation. We still could not forecast how much snow would fall during the winter or whether the Silver Hut would be isolated at any stage. As a security measure I concentrated on getting a hundred days of food and fuel up to the hut. The Sherpas had warned us that sometimes the snowfalls could be very heavy, but with the hut well stocked the men inside could live in comfort until it was possible for them safely to break out again.

OUR EYES TURN UPWARD

All the expedition time was not devoted solely to these routine but necessary tasks. My party were all mountaineers, and their eyes inevitably turned to the peaks around. Both Pugh and I believed that it was essential for the success of the physiological program that the mountaineering enthusiasm of the party be maintained at a high pitch—otherwise some of the incentive for living at these uncomfortable heights would be lost.

For some time I had been interested in the feasibility of climbing Lhotse Shar, 27,550 feet. This fine peak—the eastern and lower summit of Lhotse—was still unclimbed and offered an interesting alternative to Makalu as the main expedition objective. However, our physiological program was based on the party getting very high in the latter stages, so I could not justify changing to Lhotse Shar until we had reconnoitered the mountain and were confident of a good route to the summit. The obvious route onto the peak lay up the ridge dividing the Barun and Imja valleys. This was not only a long and formidable climb but had a rather difficult middle section which might take a little overcoming. It was possible to reach the ridge at about 20,000 feet from the Barun glacier, so I asked Norman Hardie to take a small but strong party and carry out a reconnaissance.

Hardie came up with another suggestion. To save the tedious trip from the Mingbo over into the Barun and then up to the head of that glacier, he favored the route being examined from the Imja glacier side, which gave a much more difficult but much shorter approach to the Lhotse Shar ridge. This would also enable him to examine the likelihood of a direct route onto Lhotse Shar from the Imja glacier. I agreed, so Hardie set off with Gill and Romanes and a team of ten experienced Sherpas.

On the third day they put in a Base Camp on the Imja glacier with a full 10,000 feet of the Lhotse ice face above them, while across the valley were the steep slopes leading to the col on the Lhotse Shar ridge.

In a long hard day they carried a camp up a subsidiary ridge onto the face and established themselves in two tents on a sloping snow shelf. Next morning the three sahibs with two experienced Sherpas moved further up the face but discovered to their disappointment that the only feasible route was on never-ending cones of avalanche debris. They were on a spur between two enormous and very active avalanche chutes draining snow and ice from high above—and occasionally their spur came under fire itself. They worked their way upward, being stopped on occasions and having to try elsewhere. The safe route seemed to be running out. Gill led up to the last hopeful *couloir*. They stopped to examine the way ahead. It was steep and badly broken with enormous ice blocks in all directions. It might have been possible for a strong and active summit pair to have forced a way through this maze—and accept the risks in so doing. But the party was barely at 22,000 feet, and a summit attempt would need perhaps three higher camps, and a ton of supplies would have to be carried up these slopes. Hardie decided the face was too dangerous for the establishment of the long line of camps that a summit attempt would require. With reluctance he gave the word to retreat.

They descended once more to the glacier and back to their Base Camp. The only alternative now was to climb the steep ice slopes up onto the Lhotse Shar ridge, and even as they watched a considerable avalanche swept down the side of it. It wasn't a healthy spot, but by keeping a few chains further south the route seemed free from any danger.

In the morning the party split into two. Gill and Sherpa Annullu left early and headed for the island peaks which are over 20,000 feet high and stand in the middle of the Imja Valley. In a long and fast climb they reached the summit of the highest of the group—to get a wonderful view of the Lhotse face plus the pleasure of a first ascent.

Hardie and Romanes with Urkien and Angtemba in support left camp a little later to cross the valley toward the Lhotse Shar ridge. They stopped and rested a few hundred yards short of the avalanche slopes, carefully picking the route ahead of them. Then they moved in with considerable speed, climbing the full face without a rest, keeping away from danger spots as far as possible, and all four of them sharing the lead. In very fast time they reached the 20,000-foot col to be met by a piercing wind. Hardie and Romanes tried to climb farther up the ridge to get a better view of the route ahead, but the wind stopped them from getting very far and they weren't able to learn much that we didn't already know. This same west wind had been blowing mercilessly for weeks. It continued for many more days.

On the return of this party to Mingbo I had no hesitation in abandoning any ideas of asking the Nepalese Government for permission to tackle Lhotse Shar. The route from the Barun is certainly worth a try, but it is long and exposed, and ample supplies of oxygen would be a prime requisite. Lhotse Shar remains a superb objective for a strong, well-equipped party.

Rising near the Silver Hut in an imposing sweep of fluted ice ribs is a fine peak of about 21,000 feet, later called by the party Puma Dablam. Its ease of access was a constant challenge to the building party, and several parties snatched a day off, trying to reach its summit from the Amadablam Col. The ridge proved to be a difficult mixture of rock, ice, and poorly compacted snow, and the first few parties were repulsed by bad weather and sickness. Jim Milledge and Angtsering struck the right conditions and put in a determined effort finally to reach the summit.

Barcham and Gumi Dorji repeated this climb a few days later.

FESTIVAL

For most of the year the monastery of Thyangboche in its splendid position on the crest of a mountain spur breathes an air of peace, quietness, and meditation. But early December brings an amazing transformation, for at the full moon the religious festival of Mani Rimdu is held. From villages throughout the Solu Khumbu district, and from as far away as Kathmandu itself, hundreds of Sherpas stream along the mountain trails to Thyangboche for the three-day celebration.

We had been looking forward to this occasion with as much enthusiasm as our Sherpas, for we were to take an active part in the ceremony by presenting a sacred scarf to the Thyangboche shrine. Several months before joining the expedition Desmond Doig had the opportunity of visiting His Holiness, the Gewa Karmapa Lama, at the Lamasery of Rhumtek in Sikkim. His Holiness, now a refugee from Tibet, is the head of Khajupa, or the Red Hat sect of Buddhism which encompasses most of the eastern Himalayas. Second only to the Dali Lama in importance, he is greatly revered by the peoples of Bhutan, Sikkim, and eastern Nepal.

On learning of our forthcoming expedition, the Gewa Karmapa Lama blessed a large white silk scarf, two feet wide and ten feet long, and presented it to the expedition with the wish that we might be very successful in our scientific and mountaineering endeavors—and with the hope that perhaps a member of the climbing team could place it on the wind-swept summit of Mount Makalu.

Dawa Tenzing, our chief sirdar, and the other Sherpas were delighted when they learned of the sacred scarf. "But it would be better if it were presented to the gompa at Thyangboche instead of left on the summit of Makalu," said the venerable Dawa. "Then it could be seen and enjoyed by all the Sherpas of the area!"

Desmond and I agreed with this practical approach, and so it was that the scarf blessed by the Gewa Karmapa Lama was to be presented by us to the Thyangboche monastery during the festival of Mani Rimdu.

Early in December between three and four hundred Sherpas gathered at the monastery, dressed in their finest regalia. The women were particularly colorful in multihued striped aprons and bright blouses. Their glittering jewelry represented their family wealth, and some wore huge gold earrings and necklaces that flashed in the sun, while others had turquoise, silver, and coral charm boxes suspended around their necks. Knowing that there would be a shortage of food and sleeping accommodation during the celebration, most of the people brought their own food as well as blankets or yak skins for warmth during the cold nights. From the high glaciers and passes of the Everest region came the members of the expedition, determined to see everything they could.

Unfortunately Desmond Doig and I were now on our way to Kathmandu with Khunjo Chumbi and the Yeti scalp, so I had asked Dr. Pugh to act on my behalf in this ceremony and make the actual presentation of the scarf.

The twenty-six-year-old head lama of the Thyangboche monastery, a reincarnation of a former lama, would normally have presided at the festival. He was absent for this year's celebration, having journeyed to Sikkim to confer with his superior, the Gewa Karmapa Lama. His place instead was occupied by a high

Tibetan lama called Dewa Rimpuchi, whose former home had
been the famous Rongbuk monastery on the northern side of
Mount Everest. He had been forced to flee when the Chinese
took over Tibet.

The first day (called Chocksalu) of Mani Rimdu was one of
prayer and meditation. A canopy covering a long dais had been
erected on a broad level area outside the monastery. The Dewa
Rimpuchi sat upon the dais, wearing huge black-rimmed plate-
glass spectacles and flanked by several lesser lamas, while the
throng of Sherpas sat cross-legged on the ground facing him.
Other lamas conducted the rites—praying, chanting, playing
Tibetan drums, horns, and cymbals, burning incense, and making offerings to the gods. Toward dusk the Sherpas, on a signal,
surged forward to be blessed by the head lama. Bowing, each
offered rupees to the monastery and the Dewa Rimpuchi
blessed them—for good health, abundant crops, fine weather,
and freedom from catastrophe. These conditions are vital to the
Sherpas' existence in this rugged environment, and great significance is placed on this yearly blessing.

The last day was devoted wholly to dancing and celebration.
Arriving early, the members of the Wintering Party thrust their
way through a noisy throng to the enclosed stone courtyard where
the dances were in progress. There was a medieval look about the
place, as of an Elizabethan stage: the crowded balcony above on
three sides; the main building behind forming a fourth side with
viewpoints above for the privileged spectators and entrance below for the dancers; and on the courtyard floor itself were the
people—shouting, laughing, eating, jostling, sleeping, drinking.
. . . In the center were the dancers—brilliant in full flowing cos-
tumes, crimson, yellow, green, black, all the colors of the rain-
bow, it seemed. Through the weird rhythms of the lamas, the
throb and crash of drum and cymbal, they danced together,
slowly and gracefully twirling their heavy skirts and swaying
to the beat of the music.

At midday, during an interval, the expedition members accepted an invitation to a lunch of potato and roast yak meat at
the house of Sirdar Dawa Tenzing. It was a pleasant break,
made all the more agreeable by the high standard of the *rakshi*
served. Toward the conclusion of the meal Dawa rose and in his
own inimitably expressive style, with arms waving and spitting
out his few words of battered English, he told the expedition

that today he was going to present the sacred scarf to the monastery. Even then perhaps there was a suspicion that part of
Dawa's fire derived from his excellent *rakshi*. Nevertheless, when
they returned to the dancing it was with the anticipation that
they were to have at least a modest part in the proceedings.
Alas! Their hopes were shattered early. When Dawa Tenzing
stepped forward in the middle of a dance it was obvious that
the timing of the presentation speech was a little unfortunate,
but no one expected the earsplitting outburst from the cymbals
and horns that broke out almost simultaneously. Undaunted, our
sirdar spoke on, but his thunder was now gone; almost un-
heeded, he crossed the courtyard carrying our sacred scarf and
accompanied by Dr. Pugh. A moment later they were all swallowed in the depths of the monastery.

The expedition members returned to Chanmitang for their
evening meal, but not before they had suffered almost more than
they could stand of the aimless wanderings of the local clown
wearing a pink, lipstick-plastered mask ("Mem sahib," gasped
one of the Sherpas, almost paralyzed with laughter). The celebrations were not yet finished; now it was the turn of the Sherpas,
when they might dance through the night. The sahibs lingered
over their meal, and it was late when they set off up the track with
a full moon glowing palely from a frosty sky, severely outlining
the silhouette of the lovely Amadablam. As they drew nearer to
the monastery the sounds of revelry grew louder, but as yet no
light was to be seen. They came into the now familiar courtyard
to an unforgettable sight—a host of shadowy figures eddying
slowly here and there in the moonlight and around them a tight-
linked circle of singing, chanting Sherpas, swaying together in
their strange, rhythmic, stamping style of dance.

The youngest member of our party, Michael Gill, was an
enthusiastic observer. "I had been watching for an hour or so,"
he said, "when I noticed some large coffeepots being handed
around. 'Chang?' I inquired, and indicated in my primitive
Sherpa that I would like a little of this pleasantly alcoholic drink.
Before I knew what was afoot a smiling lad had grasped my
hand firmly in his and was leading me purposefully through the
dancers; out of the courtyard we went, descended a line of steps,
through a maze of narrow alleys, and there was the low-beamed
entrance to his house. Once within its smoke-blackened walls,
I was placed before his fire and, together with the gravely smil-

ing lamas who sat with me in the shadows, my request for chang
was complied with in ample measure.

"But soon I was asking to be led back to the dance. I found
that my sahib companions had left by now, but with the warm
glow of chang dissolving the cold of the evening in a growing
mist of enchantment I cared little. Yet again I pushed my way
into the tumult of the courtyard. Suddenly from among the
surging throng burst the wonderfully smiling face of young Da
Tenzing, my personal Sherpa; throwing an arm about my shoulders, he dragged me into the circle of dancers, and so with one
arm around Da Tenzing and the other around a diminutive
Sherpani I found myself led, unprotesting, into the intricacies of
the dance.

"When I looked at my watch again it was after midnight. I was
unaccountably tired and accepted thankfully Da Tenzing's offer
of a bed in the house where he was staying. With him was his
sister, a handsome Sherpani by the name of Pasang Diki; the
three of us walked to the house in silence, stumbled over the yak
calves below and up the stairs to the room above.

"Pasang Diki laid out a sleeping bag for me, knelt and removed my shoes, and as a final gesture of hospitality she poured
me the customary three bowls of *rakshi*. I fell asleep on a bed
made soft by a cloud of *rakshi* and by the simple devotion of a
people whose friendship one comes to value more than the
attractions of the mountains amid which they live."

11

HIMALAYAN WINTER

By mid-December life in the Mingbo Valley had settled into a
happy routine with the party spread between the Mingbo Base
Camp at 15,000 feet and the Silver Hut at 19,000 feet. For five
and a half months the men worked hard at their common scientific objectives.

The Wintering Party was a strong one. Most of its members were climbers and skiers as well as being physiologists and doctors. The party was composed as follows: Dr. L. G. C. E. Pugh (leader) from the Medical Research Council's Department of Human Physiology, London; Dr. J. S. Milledge (deputy dealer) of Southampton Chest Hospital; Dr. M. P. Ward, Department of Surgery, The London Hospital, London; Dr. J. B. West of the Medical Research Council Respiratory Unit at the British Postgraduate Medical School, London; Dr. S. Lahiri of Presidency College, Calcutta University; M. B. Gill, a medical student from Dunedin University, New Zealand; Captain S. B. Motwani of the Indian Army Medical Corps; Barry Bishop of the National Geographic Society who was responsible for glaciology and meteorology. Walter Romanes from New Zealand was in charge of construction and maintenance. Capt. T. O. Nevison of U. S. Air Force Medical School was also a member of the physiological team but was away from the expedition from January to March for family reasons. Lastly, Rakpa must not be forgotten. Presented as a puppy to the expedition, he was probably the liveliest and best acclimatized of all. He had not, unfortunately, been housetrained. There was one famous occasion at the Silver Hut when he lost a friend by becoming suddenly incontinent on the bunk above Nevison's head and found himself flung with great force through the open door into the rubbish pit outside. But despite these minor crises in his life he remained the most exuberant and energetic inhabitant of the hut.

It was agreed that all would try to join in the Silver Hut for the celebration of Christmas. Pugh and the four other inhabitants of Mingbo arrived up at the Green Hut (17,500 feet) on Christmas Eve. It was not a merry occasion; most of the party were suffering from headaches and fatigue after their long ascent. By next morning, however, recovery was complete and everyone enjoyed the ascent of the icefall and upper snow fields of the Mingbo glacier in the calm, clear air and warm sunshine. As the hut came into view they were greeted with the sound of Christmas carols sung by the five occupants who had come outside to welcome them. The rest of the morning was devoted to skiing. Then came Christmas dinner—soup, roast lamb, and Christmas pudding. This was followed with toasts and more carol singing until it was time to return to the lower hut.

No one seemed to have suffered any ill effects from the height, and even the skiers were reasonably adept. On their return down the glacier they fixed a rope down a treacherous thirty-foot ice cliff for the benefit of those wearing ski boots. The steps they had enlarged and hollowed out in the morning were now full of water—a striking testimony to the power of the Himalayan sun even in midwinter. By the time they reached the Green Hut the sun had gone down and it was intensely cold, so that they were glad to reach shelter.

Food, Drink, and the Comforts of Home

One of the more unpleasant effects of altitude is its impairment of the appetite. The expedition was to be so long in the field that we could not afford the loss of weight and condition that usually results from extended living on a hard-tack diet. We had therefore devoted great care to the selection of food for both the assault phase and the period of high-altitude living. The diet was largely based on ones that had proved successful in the Himalayas and the Antarctic with a number of modifications and additions to ensure greater variety and palatability. We were helped enormously in this by the development of a new type of dehydration process, called "accelerated freeze drying." Based on the evaporation of ice crystals in frozen food when subjected to vacuum, the resultant food reconstitutes with a speed and flavor far superior to the traditional drying methods. To give some idea of the variety in our freeze-dried foods alone, we had for meats: beefsteak, lamb chops, ground beef, cooked chicken, ham mix, beef slices, meat and vegetable stew, shrimp, and cooked beef stew. Among the freeze-dried vegetables were: green beans, carrots, cauliflower, Brussel sprouts, peas, beetroot slices; and in fruit: apples, raspberries, black currants, and plums.

Common expedition burdens are butter gone rancid and melted-down chocolate, a result of taking these foods through the tropics without refrigeration. Fresh bacon, butter, chocolate, and cheese were shipped as refrigerated cargo from New Zealand to Calcutta, kept in cold storage in Calcutta, and then flown direct to Kathmandu. From here on the temperatures were reasonable and all this food kept perfectly. Where possible we purchased local food to supplement and improve our diet. We were able to get modest quantities of eggs, meat (mutton and yak), rice, flour, *tsampa* (precooked barley ground into a fine powder), and potatoes.

The quantities involved in such an expedition as ours were large. We had a thousand pounds of tinned fruit, three hundred and eighty pounds of bacon, eleven hundred pounds of butter, a thousand pounds of chocolate, three thousand pounds of sugar. We had to feed our Sherpas as well as ourselves, and although in general we purchased local food for their requirements, we also supplied them with freeze-dried meats, butter, dried milk, chocolate, tea, and sugar.

For use high on the mountain a well-balanced assault ration was devised. This was all vacuum packed in two man-day quantities so that each man received the following daily ration:

4 ozs. stew, freeze dried
1½ ozs. fruit, freeze dried
2 ozs. instant Quaker Oats
2 ozs. dried milk, skim, instant
1 oz. butter
9 ozs. sugar
3 ozs. biscuits
½ oz. soup
1 oz. cheese
1 oz. jam
1 oz. sweets
1 oz. raisins
2 ozs. glucose lemon drink powder
½ oz. tea
3 ozs. chocolate, milk
¼ oz. salt
10 sheets toilet paper
1 book matches
1 razor blade, stiff-backed for cutting wrappings etc.

I spent December in America and Europe with Khunjo Chumbi and the Yeti scalp, then arrived back at Mingbo Camp on January 5, this time by helicopter, after having returned the scalp to the village of Khumjung. I was anxious to check on the progress of the wintering party and to see that all was well with them. Somewhat to my surprise (for every expedition leader is quite convinced that all will collapse in his absence) I found that everything was progressing admirably. Mingbo Camp was now quite an extensive one. The tents were pitched in the snow on a charming yak pasture nestling among great moraine humps, and the level ground was divided into small enclosures by crude stone walls. There were several stone huts here, used by the Sherpas for shelter in the summer. These had been hired by the expedition and transformed into storage rooms and a mess hut.

In my absence the mess hut had been made reasonably comfortable. Plastic sheeting had been added to the roof of juniper boughs and flat stones to keep out melting snow, a skylight put in to admit light, the chinks in the wall stuffed with mud, and the smoke-blackened inner walls brightened with a pale gray wash of the kind used for painting Buddhist shrines. The furniture consisted of a table built around the central roof pole, yak skins on the floor, and collapsible aluminum-and-canvas chairs. With a warm fire glowing in the sheet-iron stove the hut was snug and cosy even in the midst of a blizzard.

The laboratory had been adapted by Wally Romanes from one of the sixteen-man Arctic dome tents erected on two-foot stone walls to give added head room. Romanes had fitted the tent with two excellent laboratory benches. During the day when the sun provided the necessary warmth and light the conditions for working were perfectly satisfactory.

Water was in rather short supply. In November we had constructed several dams on a little stream close to camp and had stored a certain amount of water there, but now everything was frozen solid and the snow lying around in drifts was too dirty to be used for melting. As a result frequent trips had to be made 500 feet down to the Mingbo River and Sherpas were detailed to this every day. The problem of bathing was overcome by the use of a *sauna* or Finnish bath. This had been introduced, as Desmond has written, early in the expedition by Tom Nevison at a lower camp and had grown from the simple pile of stones surrounded by plastic sheeting to a fine stone structure complete with wooden benches and a central pyramid of large round stones under which the fire was lit.

The procedure for taking a bath was as follows. Three or four hours beforehand the fire was kindled and the pyramid of stones brought to an intense heat. The fire was then extinguished; the bathers stripped and entered the *sauna* carrying mugs of cold water. They sat around on benches and poured the water in driblets over the hot stones, generating vast quantities of steam. It soon became very hot and sweat began to pour from the body so freely that it required but a little extra water to allow one

to soap down and wash off the accumulated dirt of the past
week. After about an hour of this treatment the bathers would
emerge into the cold crisp air, rub themselves down with towels,
and put on their clothes again, to feel wonderfully refreshed.

TESTING IN WINTER WEATHER

I left Mingbo confident that the scientific program was in
good hands and that much of value would result from it.

After my departure the party entered a period of winter
storms. Dr. Pugh found that working at the lower camp became
increasingly difficult because of the cold and the buffeting
winds. In view of deteriorating conditions he decided to move
the majority of the party up to the Silver Hut where they were
completely independent of weather conditions, at least as far as
the scientific work was concerned. The whole party was now
well acclimatized. The route between the Silver Hut and the
Mingbo seemed likely to remain open; any man who found the
altitude too much for him could always return and carry on his
work at Base Camp. In practice, those who were occupying the
Silver Hut found it so comfortable that they showed little inclination to return to more primitive conditions lower down, and
the hut remained full for the next three months.

Life at 19,000 feet quickly developed into a comfortable routine. The hut was sited on the edge of a roomy snow field perhaps one mile long and a quarter mile wide, leading gently
down to a broken area and a relatively inactive icefall. This
expanse of snow lay on three sides of the hut; on the fourth an
ice cliff dropped sharply away to a group of bluffs three hundred
feet high, at the foot of which lay another part of the complex
Mingbo glacier system. Beside the hut was a shallow gully—a
partially snow-filled crevasse. The walls of this gave scope for
the digging of snow caves for various purposes, and there was
shelter for tents both for laboratory use and for the members
who preferred the extra privacy of sleeping outside.

Inside the hut was divided into laboratory space at one end
and eight bunks at the other. A large furnacelike kerosene stove
formed the dividing line. Although the stove did not always
function perfectly, it was undoubtedly successful in its prime

59. (ABOVE) *Tibetan lama's idea of the Yeti—obviously it is the The-Mo, or the Tibetan Blue Bear.*

60. *Tibetan impression of the Serow Yeti.*

61. *Tsheringma, the consort of Khumbila.*

62. *Khumbila, god of the Solo Khumbo Sherpas.*

63. *Yeti drawn by a famous Tibetan artist.*

task of heating the hut; indeed, the tropical atmosphere sometimes woke the sleepers up in the middle of the night. Light
shoes, pajama trousers, and string singlet were usually the most
practical working ensemble.

Electricity was essential for most of the laboratory equipment
and came from two twelve-volt banks of nickel accumulators
charged from the wind generator, or alternatively in the wind-
less periods from a gasoline motor. These also gave the party
the inestimable luxury of electric lighting. Cooking and clean-
ing were done by two or three permanently stationed Sherpas.
At first these men cooked in the hut but later shifted to a big
dome tent outside, when room became more scarce and when
it was found that the primus stoves were giving rise to alarmingly
high concentrations of the poisonous gas, carbon monoxide.

The Silver Hut was an extraordinarily well-equipped laboratory, most of the apparatus being the best obtainable and with a
total value of many thousands of dollars. Because of practical
difficulties, experiments were made not on a moving climber but
on a subject working inside the hut on a stationary bicycle. By
applying friction to the wheel, each victim could be made to
perform an accurately measured amount of work while samples
were being taken and measurements made. For instance, while
working at a rate equivalent to steady climbing up a snow slope,
the subject breathed through a valve into a bag collecting his
expired air; blood samples were taken from a hand vein for gas
analysis; his pulse was counted, as were the number of his
respirations per minute and the output of the heart per minute;
his blood pressure was measured together with the diffusing
properties of the lungs, and so on. The same experiment could
be exactly repeated at monthly intervals and the extent of
changes thus measured. Numerous other types of experiments
were performed, covering most of the principal functions of the
body—more than enough to keep the scientists fully occupied
throughout their stay.

At the end of the day, as the incredible eastern faces of
Amadablam were falling into shadow, the party would take to
their skis and glide swiftly down the névé into the icefall below,
winding between crevasse and cliff to an airy platform above
the terminal ice face. And in the evening after a good meal,
mellowed perhaps by a taste of whisky sent in by expedition

friends in Kathmandu, they would sit or lie on their bunks, reading, writing, and talking about faraway places.

Barry Bishop, the expedition glaciologist, ably assisted by Wally Romanes, carried out a study of the movement of the Mingbo glacier, and the balance between nourishment of the glacier by snowfall, avalanche, and wind deposition, and its ablation by melting and evaporation. Valuable information about the recent climatic history of the region was obtained by studying stratification of the glacial snow and ice by means of pits and borings. A cross section of the glacier was revealed in the walls of some of the immense crevasses; it was possible to identify seasonal stratification reminiscent of the rings of a tree. Meteorological readings were also made thrice daily throughout the winter. Bishop did a survey of the entire Mingbo Valley for map-making and glaciological purposes.

It wasn't possible to be long in the Khumbu area without becoming conscious of the plight of the Tibetan refugees, most of whom had only escaped with difficulty from the Chinese invaders of their country. The International Red Cross was anxious to help these people and had obtained a small aircraft for the job—a Pilatus Porter with an outstanding high-altitude performance and the ability to operate off tiny airstrips. They were anxious to establish a landing strip in the Khumbu region and asked my opinion on a suitable area. I remembered the long slope in the little valley above Mingbo—the only possible place I could think of—and we decided to co-operate on building a strip there. The Red Cross wanted the refugees to do the labor— at a modest wage because they were also to receive much aid with food supplies—but I knew this would cause considerable resentment among the Sherpas, who were seeking work, too, and whose economy had been impaired by the flood of refugees and the cessation of trade with Tibet. I suggested instead that my expedition should build the strip, using Sherpas for the purpose at ordinary rates of pay, and that in return the Red Cross plane could give us assistance with the transport of our personnel and equipment.

Dr. Pugh put a team of men to leveling the site at 15,500 feet, chopping off the frozen clumps of snow grass, filling in the worst of the holes, and rolling away the large boulders. Snow sometimes restricted their activity, but it rarely lay for long once the sun was shining again. When the strip had been cleared to four hundred yards the first aircraft landing was made—only to damage its tail wheel on a rock and make an unscheduled visit of some days while being made airworthy again. Work on the strip continued for some months (until well after my return to the Mingbo), and we finally enlarged it to five hundred yards and generally improved it.

At the take-off end were two huge boulders weighing possibly twenty tons each, standing six feet above the ground. We had no explosives and the boulders were singularly unresponsive to the blows of a sledge hammer. The problem was finally solved in a highly ingenious fashion by our Sherpas. They dug enormous craters beside each boulder, then used long heavy poles as levers to tip the boulders out of the way into them. Altogether we paid out Rs.7000 ($900) for the labor used in building this strip, which possibly made it one of the cheapest as well as the highest airstrip in the world. At no stage would the airstrip have been approved by Civil Aviation Authorities, but due to the skill and experience of Captain Schrieber, the Red Cross pilot, large quantities of refugee food were transported safely to it and we in turn were helped considerably with the rapid freighting of personnel, scientific equipment, and later a whole building.

In general the winter weather was far less arduous than we had expected. Temperatures were fairly cold and there were frequent strong winds but, apart from short periods of storm, clouds were a rarity and the sun shone down day after day from a clear blue sky. This coincided with my experience in an Antarctic winter when, despite cold temperatures and wind, the weather proved more stable than at any other time of the year. Hardly more than a foot of snow fell during these months. It became clear that the Himalayan glaciers, in this region at least, were fed more by the wet monsoon snows than the cold powder snow of winter.

All in all, the wintering period was the most profitable and productive of the expedition—certainly as far as the scientific work was concerned. Firmly established and supplied, the scientists were able to concentrate on their research tasks without being constantly sidetracked by other temptations.

12

THE "TERRIBLE TOOTH"
OF AMADABLAM

There must be few walks in the world more wonderful than the track from Namche Bazar to Thyangboche. The rivers foam through great gorges far below; the hillsides are clothed in forest, broken only here and there by a sheer rock face, a sharp crag, or a steep mountain meadow; and above everything tower the incredible peaks of the Khumbu region—mighty ice-fluted faces, terrific rock buttresses, and razor-sharp jagged ice ridges soaring up to impossible summits.

Kangtega, Taweche, Tamserku, and Amadablam—their names conjure up a vision of climbing so difficult that one is tempted to call it impossible. For surely even man, incredibly stubborn and determined though he may be, must be stopped by these terrible ice-encrusted walls and airy buttresses?

Most spectacular of the lot is Amadablam: a colossal rock and ice monolith shaped like a great tooth. Its first impact on the senses is disbelief. "It isn't true! It can't possibly exist!" was the reaction of one member of our party when we first gazed up at the mountain in 1951, and even after years of photographs in every mountaineering publication it is still a shock when you first see the mountain for yourself.

Ama is mother in the Sherpa language, *dablang* a locket worn around the neck; wherever one goes in Khumbu she may be seen, the delicate rock ridges that are her arms extended as if to embrace the diminutive villages and pastures lying at her feet, while on her bosom is a gleaming *dablang* of ice. Every expedition in the area has looked at the peak with kindling eye, but few have had the temerity to invade her virgin slopes. The

Sherpas told us of a small reconnaissance party in 1955 which had started on the rocks of the south (Mingbo) ridge, and in 1958 Cunningham, a member of Alf Gregory's English party, had put in two camps on the same ridge and reached 19,500 feet before turning back at an overhang.

The most determined attempt, in 1959, ended in tragedy. Harris and Fraser, two of Britain's finest climbers, were seen at a height of 21,000 feet on the north ridge, reached after many days of exceptionally difficult climbing. They disappeared into the clouds and were never seen again.

Our camps in the Mingbo Valley lay on the south side of the mountain with the Mingbo ridge dropping down into the high pastures and moraines between the Base Camp at 15,000 feet and the Silver Hut at 19,000 feet. Inevitably our eyes turned upward onto Amadablam, searching rather hopelessly for some possible niche in its armor. And as the wintering party gained familiarity with the mountain they came to the conclusion that the Mingbo ridge offered a possible route to the summit.

Below 19,000 feet this ridge is merely a few easy slabs showing through a broad sweep of scree. Above this height there is a dramatic change; the jagged blade of the ridge proper is abruptly upthrust from the surrounding slopes to rise in a series of mighty steps to the great ice bulge at the foot of the final airy snow slope. The two most notable of these rises were called the first and second steps and constituted the most obvious difficulty on the route. At the foot of the first step was "the Gap," a relatively level section which might provide a camp site, always a difficulty on such a steep mountain. Below this the general angle of the ridge lessened, but the crest looked of so tenuous a nature that its length might be an insuperable barrier to the carrying of loads.

The wintering party made every effort to maintain their fitness during their life at 19,000 feet, but their scientific program was a full one and little time could be spared for mountaineering. Ward and Gill took a day off to perform some high-standard icework on a spectacular peak to the south of the Silver Hut; and a strong group carried skis onto the Amadablam Col and skied down the Hongu Valley and back over the southern col into the Mingbo. Still Amadablam became an ever-present challenge to the climbers every time they raised their eyes, and interest in examining it more closely rose to a high pitch. By mid-February the scientific program was well in hand and Dr. Pugh agreed that time could be spared for a closer look at the mountain; Michael Ward was to lead the four-man party. Wally Romanes and Pember Tenzing set out on a reconnaissance on February 18, carrying materials for a light camp, supplies for two days, and a radio which was used to maintain contact with the Silver Hut throughout the following month. Through the big telescope at the Silver Hut the other members of the party watched their progress with interest. Camp I became visible as a bright yellow speck on the boulder-strewn slopes at 19,000 feet, and the following day two tiny figures climbed slowly upward, silhouetted against the vast luminous background of sky and mountain beyond them. From the steadiness of their progress the observers judged that the lower rocks at least were not too excessively difficult. Romanes gave their story on the radio that night. At 19,500 feet they had been brought to an abrupt halt by an eighty-foot wall guarded by an overhang, with no possibility of sidling past it—probably the highest point reached by Cunningham three years earlier. Romanes reported that there was a perfect site for Camp II at the foot of this pitch. Altogether it had been an encouraging start.

Enthusiasm gathered momentum at the Silver Hut and that night the snow cave was emptied of its stores of climbing equipment: *pitons* (steel spikes) were sorted, rope ladders checked over, and coils of manila rope disentangled. To Mike Ward and Barry Bishop fell the task of establishing Camp II and starting the assault on the overhangs above. Several more Sherpas were brought in to carry up Camp II, although as yet none of them were to sleep there. A well-laden party set off next day under a brilliant and cloudless sky, a blessing that the expedition was to enjoy every day in the month to follow.

Camp II was superbly sited. After an hour or so of strenuous hauling up the cracks, chimneys, and slabs of the lower ridge a broad ledge led out on the Silver Hut side. Here, fortuitously clinging to the side of the ridge like a giant limpet, was a bulge of ice presenting a roomy ledge which held all their tents, nestling into a warm shallow cirque in the rock behind. And looming over their heads was the wall that formed the next part of the route. Rappelling (descending on a double rope) down this later became routine, but the site never became less than spectacular. In the late-afternoon sun a figure would appear on the

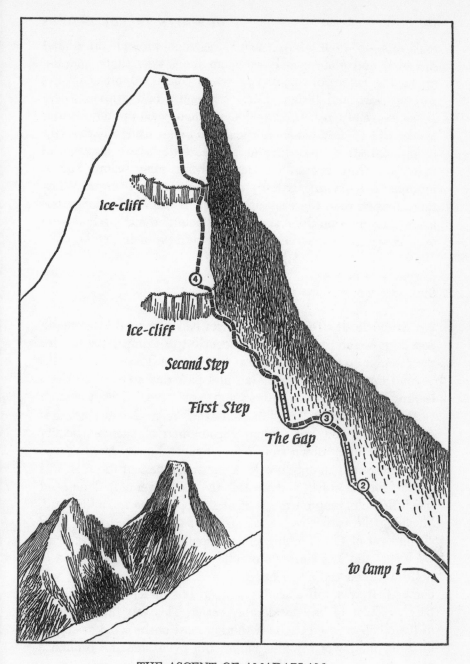

Ice-cliff

Ice-cliff

Second Step

First Step

The Gap

④

③

②

to Camp 1 →

THE ASCENT OF AMADABLAM

"Most spectacular . . . is Amadablam: a colossal rock and ice monolith shaped like a great tooth. Its first impact on the senses is disbelief . . . every expedition in the area has looked at the peak with kindling eye, but few have had the temerity to invade her virgin slopes." Camps were placed on the south side of the mountain with the Mingbo ridge dropping down into the high pastures between Base Camp at 15,000 and Silver Hut at 19,000 feet.

rock outcrop high above, wind the rope around thigh and shoulder, and glide swiftly down to the lower ledges and the camp. The ascent of this section was a considerable feat on the part of Ward and Bishop. For a day and a half, with the help of some twenty *pitons*, they fought their way up the slender cracks and smooth slabs. Artificial climbing, using "hardware," is an exhausting procedure at this altitude where a powerful muscular effort cannot be sustained for long before one is brought to a panting halt by acute respiratory distress. When they stepped onto the easy upper section and fixed a long rope ladder into position the first major obstacle of the climb had been overcome. They were free to tackle the next problem.

STRAIGHT UP

Meanwhile, at Green Hut, Romanes had recovered his strength and he now returned as a third occupant of Camp II, ready for the attempt on the first step next day. Half a dozen rope lengths beyond the ladder was the Gap and past this a steep ice slope leading to the foot of the first step, now revealed as a smooth vertical wall for its first hundred feet. Vertical walls are frequently described but seldom encountered of such verticality that a rope hung down from above dangles freely—but this one stood the test. The only break in the smoothness of the rock was a wide central crack, and up this the party went. It demanded much fine climbing on the part of Bishop, Romanes, and Ward, involving the extensive use of *etriers*, *pitons*, paired ropes, and all the rest of the climbing paraphernalia. After two days' hard work the step was surmounted and the second ladder placed in position. Then the three hundred feet of rock beyond this was climbed. It was still alarmingly steep but far enough from the perpendicular to be considerably easier. This was the only part of the climb exposed to the withering blast of the wind sweeping up from the lower Mingbo Valley, but even here the brilliance of the sun was always there to temper the winter chill.

When the successful party returned to Camp II that evening they found Mike Gill there. "I arrived at Camp II," he said, "tremendously impressed by what I could see of the upper part of the mountain and by the awe-inspiring pitches already overcome by the others. Between us and the great ice 'dablang' where we were expecting to place our final camp there remained only the second step. Romanes still seemed as fit as ever and was keen to carry on with me the next day.

"Beyond the highest point of the previous day we encountered some curiously hollow and rotten ice, up which we carved a precarious collection of steps. Then we halted to consider the alternatives: there was a fine steep buttress immediately above, fashioned of rock which at home might have delighted any climber but which here, at 20,000 feet, was obviously a two-day job; the second possibility lay at the left up and across a rotten gully nostalgically reminding me of the New Zealand Southern Alps. Dangerous though it was, we had little option but to take the gully.

"Gingerly we stepped across from one tottering boulder to the next, watching with interest as the looser rocks bounded over the precipice where the gully terminated. Time ran out soon after reaching a snow rib on the other side, but we could now see our way clear to the ridge above and the second step was no longer a problem.

"Ward, Bishop, and Romanes felt that by now they were due to be retired to Green Hut for a rest. I was loathe to join them myself, having taken a liking to Camp II and a considerable dislike to the lengthy reaches of rubble below. So far we had managed at Camp II without Sherpas, but it seemed that we could well use them now—the thought of carrying Camp III entirely on our own shoulders being apt to cause despondency even among the most independent of us. Pember Tenzing and Gumi Dorji eventually came up, a cheerful pair, Pember Tenzing in particular, being much given to singing. They lost much of their good cheer when they looked more closely at the ladder hanging ominously over the camp and realized that they, too, were expected to climb this. Both shook their heads and agreed emphatically that it was a very bad route. Gumi fortunately proved to be fairly adaptable and went up with some speed, and finally the pale, sweating, but grimly determined face of Pember Tenzing also appeared at the top of the ladder; we could be sure of their assistance as far as the Gap at least.

"The others returned after four days, well rested and ready to launch the final assault. Fundamentally the plan must be to establish a well-stocked camp on the 'dablang,' but the details gave rise to lengthy discussions: tents or snow cave, two climbers or four for the summit, Sherpas or no Sherpas, how many days from high camp to the summit, and so on. Eventually we postponed major decisions and decided to establish Camp III in the Gap; this admittedly left us only two hundred feet higher, but in time this had been costing us two hours each day.

"Camp III was another camp that easily encouraged indolence—three rock platforms gathering all the warmth of the sun; we could look down on the Silver Hut, now well below us, and see the occasional black dot moving on the glacier, the figure of a Sherpa going up from Green Hut or the slower movement of a sahib, and often the swift, usually graceful, descent of a skier.

"It was now March 8, nearly three weeks after Romanes' reconnaissance. The route to Camp IV had still to be completed, and this we did in the following two days. Another day was spent carrying up sixty pounds of food and equipment, using sahibs only for the porterage, to the Sherpas' great relief. On the eleventh the summit assault began.

"It was a day I would forget if I could, a day of unremitting struggle against what Tilman calls 'mountaineer's foot': reluctance to put one in front of the other. Beyond the second step the ridge was of easy rock and strangely wind-sculptured snow leading via a ten-foot ice wall to a broad open snow ledge that was to be our camp. We had not carried tents, partly because the snow had looked suitable for caving and partly because we couldn't have carried the extra forty pounds anyway. Our first project, an igloo, gave us little joy; even the optimist could hardly see in these poor tottering walls the graceful dome we had imagined; a snow cave it must be. The compensation for the exhausting one-man bouts of digging that continued through the few remaining hours of daylight and far into the night was that one could sit back, resting with a clear conscience, and contemplate the scene in peace, as fine a mountain camp site as I have known. We were looking from a new angle at the long-familiar sky line of peaks: the awful precipices of Kangtega, the spires of Menlungtse where the Sherpas say the Yetis live, the massive Dongiragutao rising north of the Tesi Lapcha, Karyolung, and Numbur, whose ridges we used to see from Silver Hut as they caught the last rays of the setting sun. We saw the darkness gather around us without dismay, for the sky was clear and the wind not troubling us; if there be gods on Amadablam they were for us, it seemed. We prepared a substantial meal and finally, after midnight, fell into a deep sleep of exhaustion.

"The following day found us with little inclination to stir early. The summit attempt could wait a day, leaving us time to prepare the lower part of the route, improve the cave, and most important, rest and recover our strength. The final pyramid rose directly before us; the Mingbo ridge now ceased to be distinct and became merely the corner between two faces, the one a sheer rock wall facing Silver Hut, the other of gentler aspect, the snow face one sees in the view from Khumjung or Thyangboche. Halfway up a line of ice cliffs stretched across, menacing the whole lower face except the extreme right-hand edge. Above this only lack of time could keep us from the summit, we thought. On this first day at Camp IV Romanes and Ward, the fittest pair, put in some splendid work on the lower section, cutting steps, fixing a rope, and so putting us in a strong position for the summit."

"I Will Die"

"We were away before 8 A.M. on the thirteenth, our summit day. Progress was steady over moderately difficult ground: a few patches of ice, a few awkward moves on the rock, all of it steep. At the point where the ice cliffs seemingly blocked our way, an alarmingly exposed strip of rock allowed us to slip past and through to the open snow face beyond. This was about the halfway mark, the point reached yesterday.

"The face above was scalloped out in huge flutings and it was up the most prominent of these that we proposed to climb. At first we struck ice, but this soon gave way to crisp snow as we drew up to a rock outcrop standing prominently on our fluting. Here we rested; it was 12:30 P.M.; two thirds of the day's climb was below us, and we were separated from the summit only by an easy snow rib. With mounting elation we climbed on as rapidly as the thin air would allow us, scraping and kicking, rope length after rope length. At 2:30 P.M. we stepped onto the summit, not the blade of ice we had imagined, but a broad plateau split by a narrow crevasse. Directly ahead loomed the colossus of Everest, no longer squatting behind the Lhotse-Nuptse wall, but for the first time massively dominating the whole fantastic landscape.

"To its right stood Makalu, gracefully proportioned despite its bulk; and in between a vista of rolling brown hills stretched to the horizon where a shaft of light through the clouds played on the snows of a range far inside Tibet.

"Before dropping off back down the Mingbo face we peered down the north ridge on which Harris and Fraser had made their last climb. We were appalled at the steepness of the final ice ridge and the ferocious severity of the knife-edge rock falling away below it. Why had they chosen this route, we wondered. . . .

"The descent may be passed over quickly; we moved singly, the tedium relieved only by anxiety and relief as the more difficult pitches were approached and passed. It was a relief, too, to rejoin the Sherpas at III; they beamed happily at us, as pleased as we were, and plied us with mugs of hot syrupy tea. 'Shabash [Well done]! Very good summit, sahibs.' Between III and II Romanes engineered an overhead ropeway which took our loads down in quick time, and at II we were met by two Sherpas from Green Hut. The sahibs shouldered forty pounds while the Sherpas took sixty to eighty pounds each rather than make a return trip the following day. The last of our difficulties was behind us; the pressure was off, and that evening we would be relaxing at Mingbo.

"But it was not to be. Two rope lengths down the ridge we found the Sherpas supporting Gumi Dorji, in pain and terribly afraid. 'Broken, sahib—I will die. . . .' We looked and saw one leg hanging uselessly from a transverse fracture halfway up the shin; he had stood on a loose rock which gave way beneath the weight of his too-heavy pack, and in a fall of ten feet his leg had snapped.

"God! Why did this have to happen now when in an hour we would have been off the mountain? How on earth would we get him down the chaotic tangle of cracks, chimneys, and gullies that barred our way below? Before they had been easy, but with an injured man on our hands they suddenly looked impossibly difficult.

"No use brooding on the change of our luck anyway; we must act somehow, devise some sort of plan. Ward splinted the leg with an ice ax and pieces of cardboard food box and gave a morphine injection. Reluctantly we admitted that the Sherpas would not be able to carry Gumi Dorji over the rock below for they found it difficult even with an ordinary load. This would have to be a sahib job.

"We devised a system whereby Ward and I alternated carrying and assisting while Romanes maneuvered himself into position above so that the belay was always as near to giving vertical support as possible. Meanwhile Bishop supervised the Sherpas, carrying down essential loads. Progress was pitifully slow; we needed the strength of a Sherpa with the ability of an experienced rock climber, a combination not found among our porters. After four hours' determined effort we were still only halfway down and an ominous sky had closed in, bringing snow. Anxiously we looked around for the suggestion of a spot level enough for a tent and eventually spied a debris-covered ledge a hundred feet down, which would yield one platform; further below we could probably construct another in a small gully half-choked with rubble. In the fading light, with snow silently covering the rocks, we built a makeshift camp and settled down for a weary night, short of food and with no fuel.

"Although the morning dawned clear we could not move early because of the snow, which had not melted off the rocks sufficiently until near midday. We started badly with a difficult move, pendulum fashion across steep smooth slabs, but once the ridge had been regained we moved more rapidly. At last the worst was behind us and a Sherpa could take over. In the meantime Silver Hut had been informed by radio of our troubles and food, fuel, and more porters had been dispatched. But again the clouds descended on us, snow fell, making carrying difficult over the boulder-strewn slopes, and we were obliged to scratch out another bleak temporary camp.

"The next day was our last on Amadablam. Again the sun rose in a cloudless sky, the snow soon thawed, and we knew we would reach Mingbo Camp that day. It was March 18, exactly a month from the first day of the reconnaissance."

13

ACROSS THE HONGU

I returned to Kathmandu in February 1961 with large quantities of supplies for the restocking of the Mingbo Valley and the mounting of the assault on Mount Makalu. I had two new additions to our climbing team, Leigh Ortenburger from California and John Harrison from New Zealand. These men were both experienced mountaineers with fine records in the Andes and in the Himalayas. Their inclusion followed my policy of bringing in new and vigorous blood in case the long period of altitude was taking its toll on the others in the party. I was interested to see how they would perform in comparison to the more acclimatized men.

There were six other temporary additions to the team—the wives of some of the party. The Lady Leader, as we facetiously called her, was my wife Louise, and she had with her June Mulgrew, Irene Ortenburger, Betty Milledge, Lila Bishop, and Gita Bannerjee. They were to walk over the 180-mile route to our Mingbo Base Camp and then return by aircraft.

Our rushed period in Kathmandu coincided with the state visit of Queen Elizabeth and the Duke of Edinburgh. Tremendous preparations were made for their arrival—streets relaid, buildings painted, columns and bunting erected, and welcoming slogans written everywhere. We took time off from the never ending task of making up coolie loads to perch on the high wall of our hotel compound and watch the colorful royal parade going by in open-horse carriages with an imposing escort of mounted troops in brilliant red uniforms.

My wife and I were fortunate enough to attend the King's Banquet in the Singha Durbar. This is a beautiful banquet hall, lined with great mirrors and lit by huge crystal chandeliers. In the center of the room was an illuminated fountain, at one moment shooting streams of water magnificently toward the high roof and at the next drooping sadly toward the floor. This display was not, we discovered, by design but due to the Kathmandu water system, whose spasmodic performance was rather notorious. The colorful uniforms, beautiful dresses, the superb food and wines made it a magnificent occasion, and it all seemed very far removed from the simple tents on the trail which would be our homes in a few days' time.

On March 2 we drove to the end of the road at the village of Banepa, issued our loads to two hundred coolies, and then sent them on their way. Together with fourteen or so of our permanent Sherpas and a dozen of us, we had a total strength of 230—a large but not cumbersome group for this well-established route.

The journey into Thyangboche was a reward. Our Sherpas reveled in the presence of the mem-sahibs and went to tremendous trouble to make the walk a pleasant one. We were wakened each morning at 6 A.M. with a cup of tea and some biscuits. Yet any tendency to linger in our sleeping bags was removed by the sounds of activity around the camp and the shaking of our tents as the Sherpas started pulling them down around our ears. We were always away before 7 A.M., walking in the cool of the morning when the world was fresh and shining. This was an old familiar route to me, but now I was seeing it through the eyes of the newcomers, enjoying its varied charm as much as I had ever done. We were constantly climbing or descending over great mountain ridges, crossing tumbling streams, and exclaiming at superb views of the snow-clad Himalayan giants. We usually camped by midafternoon in some pleasant corner and could relax in the sun, reading and writing, or just snooze in our tents.

On several occasions our Sherpas entertained us in the evenings with their dancing and songs. It was cold at night for the winter was barely behind us, but we gathered around glowing campfires while the Sherpas stamped and swayed and sang through Tibetan dance after Tibetan dance. They would continue far into the night. After a couple of hours of this we preferred to creep off to our sleeping bags, to sleep without dreaming until wakened in the chill morning with the friendly cry of "Char hai, sahib [Tea here, sir]!"

But it was the flowers that really made our days so won-

derful. The crimson rhododendrons were in full bloom; our path
clung to hillsides which were a blaze of color in every direction. And as we climbed up to each pass or saddle the air
would be heavy with the scent of daphne and the grassy sward
hidden by a thick carpet of primulas. The magnolias were just
coming into bloom, and in every shady spot and on every second tree, it seemed, were clusters of graceful orchids.

We reached our house at Chanmitang on March 18, to be
greeted by the victorious Amadablam team and the other members of the party. We spent a day here sorting out our gear and
paying off the coolies. The same day the Pilatus Porter flew Dr.
Pugh and the injured Gumi Dorji out to Kathmandu. On March
20 we moved up to our 15,000-foot Mingbo Base Camp and I
started the ball rolling for the final major stage of the expedition
—the Makalu assault.

More Sherpas were signed on and equipped; food and equipment were sorted out into loads, and large supplies of local food
were obtained.

EMERGENCY RETURN TO KATHMANDU

Our approach to Makalu was to be an unusual one. All previous expeditions to this mountain had brought their main supplies along the great Arun River over a snowy 15,000-foot pass
and into the deep Barun Valley which drains the west side of
Makalu. This was the route pioneered by Shipton, Lowe, and
myself in 1952. It wasn't a particularly easy approach and it had
the disadvantage that it was sometimes hard to obtain men to
carry loads over it. As we were operating in the Mingbo Valley,
it was easier to use this as a base of operations. But from
Mingbo to the Barun by the low-level route involved at least
sixteen days of traveling over rough and sparsely populated
country with limited possibilities of obtaining food for large
numbers of men. Instead of using this route, therefore, I planned
to use a high-level approach.

By going from the Mingbo over the 19,600-foot Amadablam
Col, then across the Hongu glacier, over 20,000-foot passes on
either side of the high Barun Plateau, and finally down to the
Barun glacier, we could cover the distance in three or four days.
It was a formidable route over which to take two hundred

loads of sixty pounds each, and my heart almost failed me when I thought of the consequences of a heavy fall of snow on these steep passes. The danger of avalanches could then immobilize the party—but this was a risk we would have to take. I resolved to stick to the high-level route.

On March 22 we were making preparations for our move up the Mingbo Valley when the Pilatus Porter arrived back with Griff Pugh on board. We were all up at the strip to greet the plane as most of the wives were returning to Kathmandu on it. Pugh climbed out—a rather cheerful and astonishing sight in his favorite padded red underwear—but it was immediately clear that something was worrying him. "I think you'd better go back to Kathmandu on this flight, Ed. The Nepalese Government is getting rather sticky about the Amadablam climb, and it may require some official explanation."

This was an unexpected blow to my plans, for I was just on the verge of launching the main thrust across to the Hongu. What should I do? A moment's reflection and I realized I would have to return to Kathmandu and attempt to clear the matter up. In a few hasty seconds I tried to give Pugh details of what I wanted done. Then I snatched my satchel of papers and leaped aboard the plane.

We were loaded to the maximum. Captain Schrieber started up the motor and revved it fiercely. We were held firm by two large rocks under the wheels, for the brakes were insufficient on this steep slope. Now the engine was warm, the large rocks were removed, and we rolled forward onto two smaller ones. The motor was given full throttle and the plane shuddered with power as the wheels inched over the small rocks and then rolled suddenly down the other side. The motor blaring like a demon, we surged into our take-off run. . . .

To my startled eyes the short strip ahead seemed quite inadequate for our needs and the hill at the end loomed up with frightening rapidity. At the last moment Captain Schrieber pulled back on the stick and we lifted sluggishly off the ground. Next moment he had tipped us over onto one wing to dodge the hill and we were slipping through the gully to the left, to be precipitated out into free air as the river valley dropped sharply away beneath us. With a sigh of relief I unclenched my hands as we soared high over Thyangboche and set course for Kathmandu.

I was met at the airport by Desmond Doig and paused only
long enough for a quick bath and a change. Then we drove to
the British Embassy to find out the position. My jaw dropped
as I read the following letter sent to the Embassy:

March 21st, 1961.

I understand that the party under Sir Edmund Hillary which was
permitted to carry on some scientific research in a specific area and
later to make an attempt on Makalu has climbed without authority
another peak called Amadablam. As you know, permission is granted
to the teams on the definite understanding that all the mountaineering
regulations of the Government will be observed strictly, and these
regulations provide among other things that a team shall restrict
itself to the route, the area, and the peak specified.

It is regrettable that a party led by so experienced a mountaineer
as Sir Hillary should have disregarded the rules. As His Majesty's
Government believe that for the proper development of international
mountaineering in Nepal it is necessary that the regulations are
observed strictly, they feel compelled, though reluctantly, to withdraw the permission granted to it to make an assault on Makalu in
March–June, 1961.

Yours sincerely,
N. M. SINGH
Officiating Chief of Protocol

The uncompromising nature of this letter made me realize
that the situation was far more serious than I had supposed. In
fact, if I accepted this letter at its face value I would withdraw
my expedition immediately with disastrous consequences to our
scientific program. This I had no intention of doing. I planned
to fight this decision in every way possible.

The problem was not an easy one. Amadablam forms the
northern boundary of the Mingbo Valley, and we were therefore
quite justified in operating on its slopes and ridges. But we did
not have specific permission to attempt the summit. I had been
most anxious for the wintering party to keep fit and active during their sojourn at high altitudes so had quite happily given
them permission to reconnoiter the mountain—not believing for
one moment that they would actually reach the summit during
the winter months. I had been proved wrong and now was suffering the consequences. The Nepalese Government, unlike any
other mountaineering country, charges a substantial peak fee

for the pleasure of attempting one of its mountains and is most anxious not to lose this profitable source of income.

But our expedition had been able to do much for Nepal and had also brought more foreign exchange into the country than any previous expedition, so I hoped that I might be able to reduce the very harsh instruction of the official letter into a more modest reprimand in the form of a fine or something of this nature.

Our path toward this objective was stony and uphill. A visit to the Foreign Secretary produced nothing but a few cold expressions of regret and then a tongue-lashing about the principles of international mountaineering. For several days we were given the "treatment" by the Foreign Office—sent from room to room, asked to phone up again and again without result—and generally had a most depressing time. I was feeling so desperate on the evening of March 26 when we had a radio circuit with Mingbo that I asked them to pay off some of our more junior Sherpas rather than keep them all on unprofitably, awaiting a decision.

The news from Mingbo was a little startling. John Harrison and Bhanu Bannerjee had arrived at Namche Bazar with the last sixty loads of supplies on the way to the Mingbo and had been detained by the captain in charge of the check post there. Wally Romanes had gone down to see if he could get them released, but nothing had since been heard of him. It was a fair surmise that he had been detained as well. The rest of the party didn't know what to do. They were very concerned about the three men but didn't like to send anyone else down to investigate in case they, too, were incarcerated.

Doig and I rushed off to see the British and Indian ambassadors, and they promised to take the matter up with the Chief Minister. Next afternoon I was greatly relieved to hear that the men had been released and that in fact the check-post captain had acted rather precipitously on his own initiative.

From then on things took a decided turn for the better. The Chief Minister, Dr. Giri, proved most co-operative, although by March 28—a week since I had arrived—we still didn't have a final decision. I was very worried about the week's delay in my Makalu plans and decided, as things were looking more hopeful, to take a risk and sign on the discharged Sherpas again. In due course on March 30 I received another letter from the Nepal Government:

March 30, 1961.

My DEAR SIR HILLARY,

In view of the unqualified apology submitted in your letter dated March 23, 1961, and in consideration of the undertaking given therein that no such incident would occur in future, His Majesty's Government of Nepal have been pleased to give a sympathetic consideration on the subject and, as a special case and without creating any precedent whatsoever, to permit the party to continue and complete the scientific study in the Makalu range, including an attempt on the peak, up to the end of May 1961.

His Majesty's Government of Nepal have decided to impose a fine of Rs.800/- ($105) on the party for having climbed Amadablam, a virgin peak, without the sanction of the Government, in addition to royalty amount of Rs.3200/- ($422) N.C. for Amadablam.

You will have to take with you a new Liaison Officer in place of Mr. Rana.

Yours sincerely,
Y. N. KHANAL
Foreign Secretary.

We could now get moving again, but nine valuable days had been lost. I told Mingbo to go full steam ahead and move all supplies up to the Green and Silver Huts. I kept in touch with them over the radio, fretting at the delay at getting back there myself. On April 2 a group of climbers tackled the fluted slopes leading to the Amadablam Col.

Large safe steps were cut in the ice and *pitons* driven firmly in as tie-down points for a long fixed rope. The next day, despite heavy snow overnight and continual snow flurries and cloud, they carried on with the job in decidedly unpleasant conditions. In the afternoon the crest of the col was reached and the last of the six hundred feet of fixed rope securely tied into place. On April 4 sixty-three loads were carried up to the top while Romanes and Ortenburger took a party of Sherpas, plus camping equipment, and crossed over into the Hongu Valley to look for a suitable relaying camp site and to examine the route forward to the west col.

It was April 5 before the plane could be spared to fly us into

Mingbo from Kathmandu. It was a far from perfect day, with heavy clouds along the mountains, but Doig, Mr. Rai (the new Nepalese liaison officer), and I were very happy to be on the move at last. Captain Schrieber started up the motor and went through his check routines—only to find that one of the magnetos was faulty.

Resigned now to continual delays, we clambered out of the plane and left it to the captain and his mechanic. For two hours we watched the clouds building up over the hills. Finally Captain Schrieber signaled that he was ready to go. We hastily clambered aboard and were soon airborne over the Kathmandu Valley. Ducking and diving through the clouds, we worked our way to the east, now and then catching glimpses of great snow-clad peaks to the north of us.

Our chances of getting into the Mingbo looked hopeless, but Captain Schrieber refused to give up. We were flying at 16,000 feet. Recognizing the bulk of Kwangde on our port side, he banked left around it up the cloudy valley of the Dudh Kosi. Everest and Amadablam were quite hidden, as were all the high peaks, but we could see a possible break in the clouds over Thyangboche and the captain confidently headed in. We circled down through the hole in expert fashion and, surrounded by great mountain walls wreathed in mist and cloud, we swung into the Mingbo Valley toward our airstrip. Soon the bright yellow and red tents of Mingbo Camp were beneath us and we were coming in over the hills toward the end of the strip—still operating on maximum power as conditions here were very windy.

We were a few hundred yards from touchdown and fully committed to land when a tremendous gust of wind came from behind and threw us toward the field with startling velocity. We hit with a crash and I prayed for a robust landing gear; then we were wheeling diagonally across the strip at tremendous speed and only a few seconds away from the jagged rocks ahead on the left. Somehow Captain Schrieber managed to swing the aircraft back onto the line of the airstrip, and we rolled furiously up the hill to the far end. We all scrambled out somewhat shaken, mightily relieved to be safely down. Captain Schrieber shook his head and spoke in his guttural Swiss accents. "Mingbo is not for a beginner." We heartily agreed with him.

A WALK ON THE MOUNTAINS

It was good to be back and getting on with the job. Peter
Mulgrew had come down from the Silver Hut to put me in the
picture once more, and I was pleased at the progress made
while I was away. But we were still well behind schedule. I
became determined to make up this time between Mingbo and
the foot of Makalu. I decided to move up the Mingbo through
the various camps, sorting out gear as I went and sending all our
requirements on into the Hongu.

Our small field radio sets were working very satisfactorily,
enabling us to keep in close touch with each other. These radios
had been specially designed for the expedition to meet three
specifications: a weight of less than ten pounds; economy in
operation; and a range of at least twenty miles from valley to
valley (which automatically ruled out the ordinary H.F.
walkie-talkie which only works effectively in line-of-sight operation). It would be untrue to say that our one-watt transmitters
beamed across country like a kilowatt giant, but they did enable me to keep in constant touch with all the parties. We had
effective contact between the Silver Hut and the camps on
Makalu across two great mountain ranges.

The weather continued rather unsettled with much cloud on
the peaks and periods of snow each afternoon—even as low down
as the Mingbo Camp. But it was never bad enough to keep us
from working.

On April 6 Romanes and Annullu climbed the west col,
20,300 feet, and started fixing it with ropes. They found it a
long day from the Hongu Camp for laden men but not an impossible one. The following day John Harrison (who was showing astonishingly rapid acclimatization) crossed to the Hongu
with thirty-eight Sherpas and started the relaying of loads from
there.

During the day at Base Camp the folder containing all my
immediate plans and supply lists disappeared. I had only put it
down for a few moments to do something else, and on my
return it was gone. I knew our movements were being checked.
Several of our less likable men were sending off regular reports
about us, but this was carrying things rather far.

In common with all foreign expeditions to Nepal we had been having a lot of trouble with the representatives of the Himalayan Society. This society had been organized by the Nepal Government with worth-while objectives—to protect and help the Sherpas and also to assist expeditions by supplying them with reliable staffs and arranging for porters, etc. Unfortunately the worthy purposes of the society were being sidetracked in its administration. It was being used as an opportunity to exploit both the Sherpas and the expeditions and was a constant source of irritation to everyone. I had complained to the Government about the running of the society and as a result was not held in too favorable a light by those who were exploiting it. At the conclusion of the expedition I discussed the whole matter with the Chief Minister, Dr. Giri, and he assured me that an inquiry into the affairs of the society was already under way and that he was determined to ensure that it pursued its original goals.

Despite an intensive search the folder was never located. Fortunately I could reproduce most of the information from memory, so it caused me more hard work than embarrassment.

On April 9 Mulgrew and I completed the work at Base Camp and moved up the valley to Green Hut. We covered the distance in two and a quarter hours, which was fast traveling, but after my fortnight's sojourn in Kathmandu I felt lethargic and unacclimatized and had to drive myself every inch of the way. The Green Hut was cosy and warm. Pugh had come down to meet me. We spent the afternoon and evening in pleasant discussion, covering the progress of the work to date and the scientific work it was hoped to do on Makalu. I was anxious for Pugh to cross to the Barun if possible and supervise the scientific work there, but his long period at high altitudes was undoubtedly affecting him (he was a good deal older than the rest of us) and he doubted if it would be wise for him to attempt the journey.

By April 11 I had completed checking the supplies at the Green and Silver Huts and made preparations to move on over to the Hongu Valley. It took us less than an hour to climb up through the ice cliffs to the Silver Hut, and we were soon drinking a cup of hot coffee with the scientists. Despite the cramped confusion of the hut there was an air of purposefulness about the place. Clothing and sleeping bags were strewn over the eight bunks; batteries and wire seemed everywhere; scientific books

and pieces of equipment were mixed up with *piton* hammers
and *karabiners*. In the laboratory end of the hut—ten feet square
—there was a profusion of delicate equipment on every bench
and ledge. The floor itself was completely dominated by the
"torture machine," the stationary bicycle with its innumerable
attachments and recording equipment.

I was interested to hear of tests the physiologists had made
on one of our stronger Sherpas. Despite this man's lack of experience on a bicycle he quickly adapted himself to our machine and was able to demonstrate an astonishing work output.
The sahibs were generally larger and stronger than the Sherpas
but, coming from homes near sea level, they were operating at
barely 50 per cent efficiency at 19,000 feet. On the other hand,
Da Tenzing II showed that a Sherpa, strengthened by generations of living at heights above 12,000 feet, lost little of his efficiency at 19,000 feet and could still produce an almost sea-
level performance.

At 11 A.M. Mulgrew and I said good-by to the physiologists,
put on our crampons, and walked up the easy snow slope to
the foot of the Amadablam Col. Grasping the end of the fixed
rope, using it as a handrail and lifeline, we carefully crossed the
deteriorating snow bridge over the giant Bergschrund and then
commenced climbing up the steps in the ice. The steps and
rope had been well done. They gave a great deal more security
to the climb, but the slope was still just as steep and the impression of exposure in the top portion very impressive. Soon the
Silver Hut was far below us and we grunted our way over the
19,600-foot col with lungs laboring and hearts pumping furiously.

We were just in time to meet a group of Sherpas who had
come up from the Hongu Camp to get loads. With them we
plunged back down a subsidiary glacier, descending several
steepish slopes, and then wended our way through an area of
ice hummocks to a frozen lake at the terminal face. We all
rested here in the sun, but a bitter wind wouldn't let us linger for
long, so we carried on over the ice of the lake, scrambled down
some great moraine walls, and finally reached the Hongu Camp
site in a moraine hollow at 17,600 feet.

This had become quite a little town. We had asked the
Sherpas to construct two rock-walled houses, and they had

64. *Lake camp in the Rolwaling Valley at 16,000 feet.*

65. *Climbing up toward the Tashi Lapcha Pass (on the right of the peak in the background).*

66. (LEFT) *The last slopes toward the Makalu Col.* 67. (BELOW) *Men approaching last steep slopes leading to Makalu Col—Camp IV in the distance.*

68. (TOP) *The Mingbo Glacier between the Green Hut and the Silver Hut.* 69. (BOTTOM)
*Camp III on Makalu at 21,200 feet. The peak in the background is the unclimbed Cham-
lang, 24,000 feet.*

roofed them in with canvas tarpaulins. These proved admirable
for cooking, storage, and sleeping. And there were a dozen or
more brightly colored tents, pitched on every available flat piece
of shingle. A small stream from the melting snow meandered
through the camp, and above us an unstable cliff ejected bar-
rages of stones and boulders every half hour or so. I now had a
formidable team assembled here—forty-nine top-class Sherpas
with six sahibs. Over the next few days we worked like demons,
moving the loads across the valley.

On April 14 Romanes, Harrison, Ortenburger, and Nevison
left with forty-seven laden Sherpas for the west col—the second
major obstacle on the way to Makalu. I wanted the four sahibs
to camp there and then establish the onward route across the
Barun Plateau and over the final obstacle, the east col. Peter
Mulgrew and I walked a thousand feet up above the camp and
photographed the progress of the carrying party with telephoto
lenses. As we watched them moving like a trail of black ants
over the snow field toward the foot of the pass, I had time to
dwell on the problems ahead of us and to grumble to myself
about my lack of fitness. I was still able to get around the country without too much difficulty, but I didn't have the punch
and drive at 19,000 and 20,000 feet that I'd shown even at an
earlier stage in the expedition. It was hard to pick up the fortnight's loss of fitness in Kathmandu.

The Sherpas arrived back in the Hongu Camp at 3 P.M.,
having done the round trip in just over seven hours, which was
very good time indeed. There were now eighty-eight loads on
the plateau. Our Sherpas were the strongest group I'd ever seen
together, and there was hardly a weak link among them. They
were doing a great job for us and we made every effort to keep
them well fed and happy. Their daily ration was:

1½ lbs. of rice or *tsampa*
2 ozs. sugar
1 oz. milk powder
2½ oz. meat bar
2 ozs. chocolate
1 oz. biscuits
1 oz. potato powder
2 ozs. butter
Tea, chillies, salt.

This was supplemented by fresh meat and dried vegetables whenever possible. Before leaving Mingbo I had bought a yak, and this had been slaughtered at the Green Hut. Most of this meat had been brought over into the Hongu and was greatly appreciated by the Sherpas. The sahib food was basically similar except for more variety. It was always necessary to tempt the wishy-washy sahib appetites which were far more affected by altitude than those of our robust Sherpas. Even so the Sherpas generally ate better and kept stronger than we did.

On April 15 Mulgrew and I crossed from the Hongu Camp back over the Amadablam Col to the Silver Hut for a long and useful talk with Pugh and the scientific party. They were now bringing to a close their experiments in the Silver Hut and were all keen to get over into the Barun and onto the mountain. Mulgrew and I said good-by in midafternoon and climbed up onto the Amadablam Col in overcast and bitter weather. There was no incentive to linger in these miserable conditions. We raced down the glacier and back to the Hongu Camp. We were glad to crawl into our tents, accepting a mug of hot tea from a friendly Sherpa hand. At 6 P.M. we had a radio schedule with the advance party up on the west col. They reported a successful day's reconnaissance. They had succeeded in crossing the final 20,000-foot pass—the east col—and they had carried on for an hour and a half toward the Barun glacier before turning back.

It snowed heavily that night, and there were snow showers and a gusty wind in the morning. Despite this, Mulgrew and forty-five Sherpas carried loads to the west col—and were glad to get back to camp after a rigorous trip. We had imbued the Sherpas with our sense of urgency. Although I gave them rest days when I felt they needed them, I was loath to waste a working day even if the weather was rather unpleasant.

CAMP I: ON THE WAY TO THE CLOUDS

April 17 was another important day in the expedition. It was a lovely morning with only a light skiff of snow on the ground. Although we started breaking camp at 6 A.M., there was a very cheerful atmosphere about the place. Our objective was to establish Camp I in the Barun Valley, and we were loaded and off by 8 A.M. In the crisp, sharp air we clambered up long troughs in the moraine, crossed some frozen glacial lakes, then climbed along a narrow gully where a towering ice wall had shrunk away from the cliff face. After several hours of hard work we emerged onto an extensive snow field and made our way slowly up this to the foot of the west col.

The mixed rock and ice slopes above were long and steep, but a cleverly attached series of fixed ropes helped our speed and security. First we traversed over a steep ice slope to the foot of a rocky rib and then zigzagged our way upward. A bitter wind was blowing and I found it cold and hard work. As we crept toward the crest of the pass the impression of exposure, of a terrific drop beneath, was overwhelming, but the presence of the fixed rope gave even the laden Sherpas the confidence to push on upward as hard as their aching muscles and gasping lungs would let them. I was glad to stagger over the top of the 20,300-foot west col and drop down into the tent of the reconnaissance party soon after midday. Half an hour later all forty-five Sherpas were up the ridge and the pile of supplies beside the tent had grown considerably.

The weather was looking decidedly bad and we had a long way to go. At one o'clock Mulgrew and I set off again with thirty of our best Sherpas.

We wound our way through a series of crevasses and descended into the middle of a wide snow plateau, most of which was over 20,000 feet high. Widely spaced flags had been placed by the reconnaissance party, and we followed quite safely along from one to another of these, seeing only a few crevasses—and mostly small ones. A very strong wind and drifting snow were now starting to annoy us, and I feared we might strike very unpleasant conditions on our descent of the east col.

We were halfway across the plateau before Mulgrew shouted that we'd left our radio back on the west col. Grumbling at our forgetfulness, I delegated two strong Sherpas to drop their loads and race back for the offending object. As punishment Mulgrew and I each added a tent from their loads to our own packs; then we carried on.

I was roped to a group of our strongest Sherpas and had been breaking trail in the soft snow all the way across the plateau. When we started up the slopes toward the crest of the east col my extra load started to tell and I was glad to hand over the lead to Mingmatsering, who went off like a rocket. He was much too fast for me despite his sixty-pound load, so I un-roped and let him go with the other Sherpas keeping grimly behind and a stubborn and panting Mulgrew, clinging onto the end of the rope. I took a moment to get back my breath. Then, feeling decidedly ancient, I tied on to the next group of solid but less dashing Sherpas. Zigzagging among the crevasses, we climbed the relatively easy slopes toward the east col and braced ourselves in the wind to dwell on the tremendous view ahead of us.

Below us a steep little glacier plunged abruptly down into the vast trough of the Barun Valley. Above, filling the whole of the horizon, was the great bulk of Makalu—its tremendous rock faces and ridges encrusted with ice and sweeping up to the sharp summit at nearly 28,000 feet. From the top trailed a long plume of snow, fair indication of the strong wind that must be blowing up there and an ominous sight to the mountaineer.

Things were getting decidedly rough on the east col! With a lashing wind behind, we started down in a cloud of snow. We were descending a long slope, covered with loose rocks and dropping over high bluffs far below. The rocks were often cov-ered with a film of ice, making them slippery and difficult. We were thankful for a fixed rope put in by the reconnaissance party, but this soon ran out and it became quite a job to cling to the slope in the fierce wind. The Sherpas with their heavy loads didn't like it at all. I resolved to get the slope roped from top to bottom as soon as possible.

We had descended a few hundred feet when a Sherpa in front of me picked up a loose rock weighing about five pounds to throw it out of the way. His intention was well meaning, but his execution was a little halfhearted. The rock bounced off a large boulder and then, gathering way, flew down toward Peter Mulgrew, fifty feet below. To my horror I saw the rock glance off his head. He slumped down out of sight, and I ex-pected next moment to see him rolling down the slope and over the bluffs.

With a burst of energy I shot furiously down the slope, calling to some Sherpas nearby to hold onto him. I arrived to find him dazed and bloody but still safe—by good chance he was grasping a good handhold at the time the rock struck him and he had hung on grimly. All the blood came from a modest two-inch cut on his skull, and already Mulgrew was asking to be left alone to get down under his own steam. Ignoring his protests, I tied him onto the end of my rope, and the Sherpas and I watched him carefully all the way down the remainder of the slope.

First we edged our way over a wicked traverse where loose snow was very unstably perched on the slabby rocks. This brought us out thirty feet above a steep snow slope which plunged down several hundred feet to the glacier below. It was obviously the way to go, but it was no easy route. Climbing carefully and cautiously, harassed by fierce gusts of wind, we edged our way down the steep little rock face, finding the holds slick with fresh snow. It was a relief to step off the rock onto the snow slope and slam in an ice ax for a good firm belay.

We stayed here for some time, helping the laden Sherpas over this more difficult pitch. Then I thrust an ice ax up to its head in the slope and tied to it a 120-foot climbing rope. Down this lifeline went the Sherpas in a series of jerks and slides which took them to the bottom, breathless but safe.

Our route now led through large chunks of ice which had recently fallen from the hanging glacier above. We didn't waste any time over this section. It was still snowing at 4 P.M. as we turned off the glacier ice and started descending over rough moraine on the left of the valley. The boulders were large and loose and with their fresh covering of snow decidedly slippery. We lurched our way downward with frequent falls and by 5 P.M. we were five or six hundred feet above the Barun glacier, looking hard for a camp site.

The Barun glacier here is a huge waste of moraine heaps, incredibly dry and barren, and with only the odd tongue of glacier ice thrusting fifty or sixty feet above the rock. For an hour and a half I struggled around, searching for a camp site, but was unable to find the slightest trace of water. Darkness was coming on and I felt very tired indeed. I crawled on down over rocks and shingle, searching now rather desperately but without success, and finally reached the Barun glacier itself. There was water here but room for only a couple of tents—a miserable prospect for thirty tired men. Safest move would be to camp here as best we could and then try and find a better place in the morning. The Sherpas were far above on the side of the valley, so I called to them and indicated vigorously by waving that they should come down and join me. Reluctantly they picked up their loads and worked their way over the face of a tremendous moraine wall.

They were still four hundred feet above me when they disappeared from view and I didn't see them for some time. Then two appeared without their loads and started calling down. It took me a long time to hear what they were saying, but finally it penetrated: "*Acha* camp! *Acha* camp [Good camp]!" With my last bit of energy I climbed up slowly to join them. It was almost too good to be true—a lateral trough behind the moraine wall high above the glacier. It was free from rock fall; there was enough room to pitch our tents; and most important of all, a modest little stream ran vigorously down from a huge mass of ice above us. Without hesitation I gave the word to pitch the tents and proclaimed that this would indeed be our Camp I for Makalu. It had been a hard day, and Sherpas and sahibs alike were soon into their sleeping bags.

Preparations for Attack

The establishment of Camp I ushered in a period of great activity with the relaying program. Despite strong, cold winds and frequent snowfalls we kept the loads moving. The supplies grew steadily. On April 19 Mulgrew and I left Camp I with a group of Sherpas in four inches of fresh snow. Two hours of strenuous plugging brought us to the foot of the east col where Romanes and Ortenburger were extending the fixed ropes. We climbed the east col, crossed over the Barun Plateau, and reached the dump on the west col at 11 A.M. At noon I had a radio schedule with the other camps. We received an urgent message which demanded my presence back in the Mingbo. With a stout companion in my personal Sherpa, Mingmatsering, I descended the steep slopes of the west col, made more difficult by a thin blanket of snow from a recent storm, and then tramped wearily down to the Hongu Camp. Next morning Mingma and I crossed the Amadablam Col to the Silver Hut to spend the day in talks and general planning. On April 21 I rushed down to the Green Hut for a long talk with Desmond Doig, then climbed back up to the Silver Hut and drafted out a number of cables to be sent off on the radio circuit to Kathmandu. Late in the afternoon Mingma and I climbed back up to the Amadablam Col and were blown along by a chill wind and flurries of snow down to the Hongu Camp.

In these three days Mingma and I had covered a lot of high country and I was feeling badly in need of a rest. However, we had another long day in front of us.

I reorganized the final loads at the Hongu Camp—leaving substantial reserves in one of the rock huts—and then loaded up all the Sherpas and got them on their way toward the west col. After checking the camp I set off behind them, accompanied by two of the wintering party, Jim Milledge and John West. These two were in fine form and seemed capable of going faster than I found comfortable. I hoped this was less a reflection on my condition than an indication of how fit the members of the wintering party were going to be high on the mountain. At 19,000 feet we stopped for a rest on a bare rocky spur. It was a fine viewpoint with tremendous peaks thrusting up in every direction. The Sherpas were all in a cheerful mood and making very good time with their heavy loads. Pembertarkay, an enormously powerful man with a spirit as strong and vigorous as his body, came across to me and felt the weight of my twenty-pound pack. He strolled off with it in his hand. It was a few moments before I realized that he was adding it to his own sixty pounds, making it an eighty-pound load. I knew he would still reach the west col with the leading group, but my pride wouldn't allow it and I took my modest twenty pounds back again—with a deep feeling of appreciation for his kindness.

We reached the west col soon after 11 A.M. and I concentrated on a final sorting of all the loads at the dump. Some of the loads from the Hongu I left in the dump and issued others that were urgently required at Camp I. I noted that Phudorje—an experienced climber, but a man we were all starting to regard as being a little too clever for his own good—had a bulky pack. As I watched, his pack fell over on the snow. He leaned down casually and tipped it up again with a minimum of effort. A sixty-pound pack is not easily moved, so I strolled over to investigate. His load weighed about fifteen pounds and contained only a couple of sleeping bags, well fluffed up to give an impression of size. Somewhat indignant, I then checked every one of the forty-five Sherpas' loads and found only one other man carrying less than his fair share. From then on Phudorje and his fellow bludger carried substantial loads on all occasions.

Milledge and West set off for the west col on skis, and we watched with envy as they slid effortlessly down through the crevasses and across the floor of the plateau. We caught up with them on the east col and descended the steep slopes together. The fixed ropes now went all the way down the rocks. We slid along them with much greater ease and safety. When we reached the snow again our skiers were off like rockets, zigzagging through chunks of avalanche ice, slithering over small crevasses, and reaching the moraine traverse a thousand feet below us in a few short moments. We plunged down in more mundane fashion and had our revenge as we passed them among the moraine boulders, struggling with their cumbersome skis. We arrived at Camp I in the midst of a vigorous dust storm.

In my absence the site had been expanded considerably, and now it was a thriving community with three rock huts and many tents. Our arrival brought the total inhabitants up to fifty-five.

On April 25 the last thirty-seven loads came down from the west col and brought to a conclusion this important phase of the expedition. All the supplies for the attack on Makalu were now at the foot of the mountain. The dangers of the Hongu route had been overcome with the judicious use of fixed ropes, and by an immense effort our tough Sherpas had brought us up to schedule and put the lost days spent in Kathmandu behind us. We could now devote ourselves to the assault—opposed by the forces of the mountain and the weather but not, thank goodness, harassed by shortage of time as well.

14

TO THE MAKALU COL

"Among all the mountains I have seen, and, if we may judge by photographs, all that ever have been seen, Makalu is incomparable for its spectacular and rugged grandeur."

In these words George Leigh Mallory—later to die close to the summit of Everest—recorded his impressions of Makalu. It is a superb mountain, viewed from any direction, and perhaps it is a little surprising that no one had made any particular effort to investigate the peak before 1952. In that year a small party of us under the leadership of Eric Shipton made the first crossing into the Barun glacier which drains the great western face of Makalu. We were operating in the early days of the monsoon, and the summit of the mountain looked even more impregnable when seen through writhing mist and cloud. From the head of the Barun glacier we could look back at Makalu and noted a possible route up a steep ice shelf which clung like a limpet below the Makalu Col—a 24,300-foot saddle between Makalu, 27,790 feet, and its northern outlier, Makalu II, 25,120 feet. The following year I was able to look down from the summit of Everest and confirm my belief that the Makalu Col route was the way to tackle this great mountain.

I returned to the Barun in 1954 with a New Zealand Alpine Club expedition but not, alas, to Makalu. A Californian expedition had obtained prior permission for this peak, and they tried to force a route up the fantastically difficult southeast ridge, reaching a height of nearly 23,000 feet before grinding to a halt. I was still convinced that the obvious route to the summit was from the north. The Californians were fully committed to their route and did not wish to change, but their leader, Will Siri, generously suggested that our party should reconnoiter the

Makalu Col if we felt so inclined. From a camp on the Barun glacier we established Camps II, III, and IV up the small glacier draining to the southwest from Makalu II. Camp IV was at 22,000 feet, and from here we forced a route up a long steep ice and snow *couloir* onto a sloping ice shelf at 23,000 feet —only 1300 feet below the Makalu Col.

We were operating without oxygen, but the party was fit and strong. A group of us moved into Camp IV, planning to put in Camp V on the ice shelf next day—and then on to the col. But it was not to be! I had broken three ribs in a crevasse rescue some two weeks before, and this seemed to have bruised a lung and restricted my breathing. During the night I became very ill and had to be evacuated to the thicker air at Camp I with considerable urgency. Here I quickly recovered, but as time was now getting short for the main expedition program, I had to withdraw the reconnaissance from the Makalu Col at this interesting stage and send them off instead to the successful first ascents of Baruntse, 23,688 feet, and Nau Lekh, 21,422 feet.

In the post-monsoon period of 1954 a strong French party under the leadership of Jean Franco entered the Barun Valley and moved up our route to Camp III. They were a well-equipped expedition with large supplies of oxygen and they established Camp IV on the ice shelf at 23,000 feet, then surmounted the rock and snow cliffs above to reach the Makalu Col for the first time. From Camp V on the col, and despite extreme cold and strong winds, they climbed Makalu II and Chomo Lonzo, 25,640 feet. These peaks gave the French a fine view toward the summit of Makalu itself.

Jean Franco returned to Makalu in the spring of 1955 with probably the finest group of climbers that has been assembled in the Himalayas. In highly efficient fashion, and using large supplies of oxygen, they worked their way steadily up the mountain. They were favored with an extraordinary period of fine weather and carried on to achieve a unique success—all nine members of the assault party ultimately reached the summit during an assault period of three days.

We also hoped to reach the summit of this fine peak, but we had other objectives as well. We planned to carry out a scientific program not only at Camp III, 21,000 feet, but also on the Makalu Col, 24,300 feet. Even above this we wanted to keep the research going with the final hope that we could collect alveolar air samples on the summit itself. And whereas the French had used oxygen in their assault, we would try to get up without it. This would be the final test of our long-term acclimatization program and also enable the performances of our assault parties at extreme altitudes to be equated with the extensive observations taken on them at the Silver Hut and elsewhere. We had ample supplies of oxygen for medical purposes and for possible rescue operations, but I believed that our assault parties could reach the summit of the mountain without it.

THE TREACHERY OF MEMORY

Now that Camp I was fully stocked, I devoted a day to reorganization and preparations for the move up the mountain. Extra clothing and high-altitude equipment were issued to the twenty-seven best Sherpas to prepare them for the carrying to the highest camps, and 120 loads of assault food and gear were made ready for the lift to Camps II and III. I had decided to split the party into two groups. Ward, Milledge, West, Gill, and Romanes had spent a great deal of time above 19,000 feet as members of the wintering party, so I now sent these men down the Barun Valley for a short rest at lower altitudes—planning to bring them back into the attack above 23,000 feet. I was hopeful of a fine performance from Ward, Gill, and Romanes, who had done so well on Amadablam and seemed to be very fit. The fourth member of the Amadablam party, Barry Bishop, was still back at the Silver Hut, finishing off his radiation measurements, but as he had recently had a minor operation it was doubtful for health reasons if he would get across to help us. The five remaining members of the assault party were Harrison, Mulgrew, Nevison, Ortenburger, and myself, and we would concentrate initially on putting in the lower camps and establishing an effective route as far as 23,000 feet.

On April 26 we started the carrying of loads up the mountain. Four sahibs and two Sherpas established Camp II at 19,500 feet and commenced work on the route ahead. Two days later we dismantled most of the tents at Camp I and set off with the final forty loads. We plunged down several hundred feet of moraine to the floor of the Barun glacier and then followed a well-established but tedious route over huge heaps of moraine to the far side. After a brief rest here we shouldered our loads once more and climbed steeply up the terminal face of the subsidiary glacier which finally leads to the foot of the Makalu Col.

I pushed on here, jumping from boulder to boulder up an easy ascent, but keeping an alert eye cocked on the crumbling cliffs above with their frequent cannonades of small rocks. Ahead of me the whole Nor-west cirque was filled with a complex of glaciers. The route was by no means obvious as the way ahead was blocked by a steep conglomeration of tall ice pinnacles. Confident in my memory of seven years before, I struck up a steep gully. It didn't seem quite as I remembered it. Half an hour later, to my intense chagrin, I had to admit that I was on the wrong route. It took some vigorous step cutting to extricate myself from this predicament and rejoin the grinning Sherpas below. Much subdued, I was happy to follow their trickly little route around to the right. The hidden ice gully opened out before us. I rushed on again, seeking to hide my red face in a burst of energy.

The way led steeply up between ice pinnacles, but a scattering of shingle in the floor of the ice gully gave an excellent foothold. I made a rapid gain in height. Then the pinnacles became taller and more menacing, and I was forced to the right toward an evil little trench where the ice had drawn away from its retaining rock. High above leered bulbous and broken tongues of ice, and the quarter-ton chunks littering the trench showed that this could be an unhealthy place to linger. Wasting no time, I kept close under the rock wall in the faint hope of gaining some small protection from falling ice in its modest overhang. It was a relief to get clear of this menaced section and start scrambling up firm and easy rock in a steep gully.

Scattered here and there were weathered pieces of wood and rusted tins—indication that I must be approaching the old French camp site. A few moments later I heard a hearty yell and looked above me to see a waving figure standing on the crest of a great rock tower. Another ten minutes of vigorous work and the gully led me in back of the tower and gave easy access up onto its broad summit. Here, among the piles of rock, small flat areas had been cleared and the tents of Camp II were pitched. The warm red rock and the magnificent outlook made this the most popular camp on Makalu.

My first night at Camp II was a cold one, although I was snug enough in my sleeping bags. The morning was clear and bright, but there was a high wind up top and we could see clouds of snow being driven off the summit of the mountain. From the Makalu Col came a dull roar like the distant sound of breakers on the shore. The sun didn't reach us until 8 o'clock, and it was an hour after this before we had thawed out and started on our way. The route led along a rib of snow on the edge of the glacier, then up a steep loose-rock gully to the foot of an ice wall. Up this went steps and a fixed rope, put in the previous day. Here we strapped on our crampons and roped up.

I led off up the glacier, retesting the bridges over the crevasses and putting in extra marker flags. In a couple of hours we were approaching 21,000 feet. The great rock face of Makalu II was towering above our heads. Rocks embedded in the snow warned us we would have to take care in our selection of a camp site. I examined several alternatives before finally deciding on a gentle ridge between two large crevasses. In front of us the snow slope dropped away rather abruptly, but there was plenty of room to excavate ledges for tents and we were completely protected from any sort of avalanche.

Cheerful shouts indicated that the laden men were climbing up to join us. I grabbed a large shovel and quickly shaped up a terrace. The Sherpas joined in, and we soon had ample room for a two-man tent for Nevison and Harrison and a four-man tent for the Sherpas. We carried on to level a large flat area for the big dome tent that would be coming up next day. From this camp we could see the route running up to the foot of the great ice *couloir*. I was astonished at the bare ice showing and the lack of snow. Early in the afternoon the camp preparations were completed, so we left Harrison, Nevison, Mingmatsering and Angtemba to spend the night here while we retreated to Camp II, chased down by a gathering storm. We were no sooner into our tents than they were swaying under an onslaught of driving snow.

THE WILD NIGHT WINDS

It was a wild night, very cold, with strong winds and more driving snow. And yet at 7 A.M. next morning it was clear again with only an odd vigorous gust of wind to remind us of the storm. On the daily radio schedule Pugh spoke from the Silver Hut and said he had decided not to come over and join us. This was disappointing news.

We were elated by the sight of four little figures high above us, moving across the snow traverse under Makalu II. Making good progress despite the soft snow, Harrison, Nevison, and their two Sherpas reached the great crevasse at the foot of the long steep slope leading up to the ice *couloir*. Then their pace dropped and we realized they had struck ice and were having to cut many steps.

There was wind and snow all day, but Harrison's party pushed on with determination. For five hours they hacked their way across the ice slope and hammered in five hundred feet of fixed rope—right to the entrance of the *couloir*. They weren't back in Camp III until 6:15 P.M. and then reported they had struck some small areas of possibly dangerous snow and recommended caution in the *couloir* itself. Meanwhile our strength at Camp II had been greatly increased by the arrival of the five wintering-party men who had been holidaying down the Barun Valley. I was pleased by their obvious fitness and high morale.

On May 1 I moved up from Camp II to III with a large group of sahibs and Sherpas. All day our eyes were on the slopes above, for Ortenburger, Mulgrew, and Annullu were carrying on with the route. We saw them climb up the established steps to the end of the fixed rope, scrape the powder snow off the ice underneath, and whack a line of steps in solid ice across into the *couloir*. This was a place for great care. Not only was the *couloir* very steep, but it drained out over a thousand feet of ice bluffs. They were lucky to find that the snow on top of the ice was in good condition and they made excellent progress—although from below they looked like black flies clinging to a great white wall. Two thirds of the way up the *couloir* they branched out to the right among some ice cliffs and zigzagged backward and forward to gain considerable height. Later in the afternoon they reached their highest point, 23,000 feet, and then worked their way down slowly, fixing a further five hundred feet of rope in the process, but leaving a wide unroped gap in the middle of the *couloir*. After nine hours of solid work they were back in Camp III, certainly tired, but well satisfied with their efforts.

My schedule required the establishing of Camp IV by May 3, so we had only one day left to finish the route up to it. In cloudy and snowy weather Romanes and I set off with Mingmatsering and Angtemba, determined to complete this task. We climbed slowly up the steep slope to the snow terrace with several halts to regain our breath. Then we moved steadily along in the poor visibility, feeling our way from flag to marker flag.

In a couple of hours we were passing the giant *sérac* at 22,000 feet where we had camped in 1954 (and from which I'd got down only with difficulty). Ten minutes later we were crossing the large crevasse and climbing up the fixed rope and the steps to the bottom of the *couloir*. It was now snowing heavily. Most of the steps had been filled up and required laborious excavation. To ensure the safety of the entrance into the *couloir* we drove in a dozen *pitons* and joined them with a hundred feet of rope. Romanes had born the brunt of the work to this stage, but now I took over and chipped steps up the first hundred feet of the *couloir* to join our rope with the end of the five-hundred-foot one put in by Mulgrew and Ortenburger. It was vital to have an assured anchor in this position, as any slip here would funnel the party out over the ice cliffs to a certain death. We hammered away at a crack in the rocky side of the *couloir* and were able to drive in several *pitons* to make a secure attachment for the rope.

We carried on up the fixed line—very conscious of the tremendous exposure—and then followed it to the right among the ice walls. In thick fog and snow we came to the end. We were at 23,000 feet and I was feeling very tired, but we still had to find a camp site.

Cursing our luck with the weather, I worked my way into the mist over to the right across a steepish traverse, looking carefully for a flatter spot. In the poor visibility it was hard to judge where we were or what we were coming to, and we moved very cautiously; we knew the slope sheered off abruptly beneath us. After an hour's fumbling progress I stumbled over a little ridge onto a flat piece of snow and realized we'd found a camp site at last—exposed a little, perhaps, to the odd chunk of ice and rock from above, but certainly better than anything we'd yet seen.

We dumped our extra gear here and then turned back into the fog and the snow. To make the route safer we ran a five-hundred-foot rope across the traverse and joined it to the top end of the Mulgrew-Ortenburger rope. We now had 1800 feet of fixed rope all the way from Camp IV down to the big crevasse—a comforting thought.

In thick visibility and steadily falling snow we shuffled our way down the *couloir*, kicking the fresh snow out of the steps. Soon we were crossing the ice steps down to the crevasse and dragging our weary legs back through the softness of the snow terrace, relying entirely for direction on the closely spaced flags. We arrived back at Camp III to find at least four inches of fresh snow lying on and around the tents, and nobody in camp had seen us all day. I was thankful to collapse into my sleeping bag. Tired though I was, I was glad to hear that the physiologists had rigged up one of the larger tents as a laboratory and had been carrying out experiments. It was good to see such enthusiasm. This warranted well for the success of the scientific work higher on the mountain.

All evening the snow kept falling and then the wind started blowing with great force and battered our tents. It was just like the Antarctic again, with drifting snow and high sastrugi (ridges of snow) building up everywhere. Morning finally came and I wasn't feeling at all well—generally off my feed and with a painful migraine-like headache on the left side of my face that even codeines didn't help much. It was a sad and glowering day. But I was determined that Camp IV must go in, even if it took some extra team work to get the party up there. I asked Milledge and Mulgrew to do the heavy job of going ahead to re-establish the route up the fixed ropes. They were followed by seven of our toughest Sherpas, each carrying forty pounds. Mike Ward and and Mike Gill came last.

As I expected, the leading pair found all the steps completely filled with snow and had a strenuous time making the route negotiable again. By midday the weather was thoroughly unpleasant, but despite these difficulties the party pushed on to reach the camp site and pitch the tents at 23,000 feet. Milledge and Mulgrew then returned to Camp III, leaving Ward and Gill in one tent, Urkien and Nima Dorje in the other. Snow fell steadily all evening, and then a tremendous wind sprang up and thrashed the tents unmercifully. With each powerful gust my thoughts kept turning to the little party on their exposed ledge at Camp IV, wondering if they were being blown off the mountain.

I have spent few windier nights than that one, and there was ample time to appreciate it for I managed to get very little sleep. As I tossed and turned with headache and backache and everything else, the tent billowed and cracked like a whip and shuddered and strained against the guy lines. Some of the gusts were so strong that it astonished me the tent didn't split in two. By morning we were still intact and the wind had retreated, to gather its strength for the next onslaught.

At 9 A.M. Nevison and Ortenburger set off for Camp IV with eight laden Sherpas. They had a strenuous and energetic day forcing a route up to the camp: the steps were all engulfed with new snow. It was some time before we saw any signs of life at Camp IV, but at 9:30 A.M. the four inhabitants appeared and started reconnoitering the way toward the Makalu Col. Although this meant we had all survived satisfactorily, I could only hope that the weather would improve a little and give us a reasonable try at the mountain. Every rock up to the Makalu Col was well plastered with snow and ice, and the continuously vigorous weather was making it hard to keep the route open.

OUT OF ACTION

All morning I watched the Camp IV party moving slowly across steep slopes to the foot of the rocks below the col. I knew they must be cutting steps and fixing ropes, a slow and laborious business. Well short of what appeared to be the obvious route, they turned right and shot up into the rocks. Somewhat puzzled, we watched them gain a little height, scramble around for a while, and then come down again. About 2 P.M. we saw them returning slowly toward Camp IV. Over the radio they told us they had been led astray by some remnants of fixed rope on the rocks. Apparently the French had tried this diversion without success.

For a change we had a night without any wind—the first I

could remember on the mountain. Ward's party left Camp IV
before 8:30 this time and made much faster speed across the
shelf where they had established the steps the previous day. Instead of going up the abortive route they kept along the shelf
and then struck up a subsidiary *couloir* toward the rock rib on
the right-hand side of a giant gut draining from the Makalu
Col. By 11 A.M. they were at the top of the subsidiary *couloir*
and cutting steps steadily upward on almost continuous patches
of snow.

At the same time Harrison and Romanes, taking advantage
of the fine weather, were climbing up to Camp IV with fifteen
laden Sherpas. They found the route in better condition, and
we could watch them most of the way as they zigzagged up
easily and traversed across toward the camp. But our main interest was on the high party. We followed their progress with
excitement. They scrambled up the rock at great speed and
then commenced chipping steps up the final snow dome toward the col. Just before noon we saw one figure, which even
at that distance I recognized as Michael Gill, cross over the
crest onto the col and then disappear from sight. The others
soon followed him. They weren't away long but reappeared and
started back down the ridge.

Gill reached Camp III by 3 P.M., tired but still with a little
energy in reserve. He gave us details of the route and explained
that much remained to be done with the establishment of fixed
ropes. Ward arrived over an hour later, exhausted and barely
able to drag one leg after the other. But it had been a good day.
And now the route to the col was open.

On May 6 I gave the Sherpas a rest. There was no carry to
Camp IV. But a very strong foursome (Romanes, Harrison,
Mingmatsering, and Pember Tenzing) spent the day on the
slopes up to the Makalu Col and put in many hundreds of feet
of fixed rope down the rock spur and the subsidiary *couloir*.
I talked to them on the radio at the end of a long day and
they confirmed that there were no major difficulties in the route
to the col, although they were getting short of rope. I arranged
for them to use two spare 120-foot nylon climbing ropes and to
remove the five-hundred-foot line from below Camp IV, trans-
ferring it to the rocks above.

I was still feeling rather miserable with pains on the left side
of my forehead and face so decided to go down to Camp II

for a short rest. Ward and Gill, after two days above 23,000 feet were also due for a change, so they came down with me. I didn't enjoy the trip. Feeling groggy, it was a relief to crawl into the tent at Camp II.

The reduction in height must have been beneficial. I had quite a good night's sleep, although I still felt miserable in the morning. It was an unpleasant day with heavy snow falling most of the time and fierce gusts of wind. I almost gave the word for everyone to have a rest day but then decided we couldn't afford to waste any time unless there was some urgent reason. Mulgrew and Ortenburger plowed their way with twenty-three Sherpas from Camp III up the ice *couloir* to Camp IV and established a crowded camp there. These men had the vital task of carrying the major quantity of supplies to the Makalu Col; on their success depended all the future activities of the party. Harrison and Romanes spent another day working on the fixed ropes to the col under frightful conditions and completed the job before returning to Camp III late in the afternoon. They had proved a strong pair and had done magnificent work.

Up at Camp III one of our steadier Sherpas, Aila, had a sharp and sudden onset of pneumonia. He had to be evacuated as soon as possible. Aila could still walk, after a fashion, so two of the doctors, Jim Milledge and John West, came down with him in a heavy snowstorm. Even though they supported and helped him it was a long and tedious job, and finally he collapsed some hundred of feet above Camp II. Jim Milledge rushed down to camp to get a bottle of oxygen. Breathing oxygen, the sick man regained immediate strength and was able to get down to Camp II without too much difficulty. He was kept on oxygen for the rest of that day and the following night.

I had felt seedy all morning. During the afternoon I managed to get off to sleep and didn't know any more until I was wakened by a Sherpa with the evening meal. The pain in the side of my head and face had now intensified considerably. I couldn't get the Sherpa to understand that I didn't want any food. I felt helpless, divorced from my limbs and, although perfectly rational, when I tried to say something it just came out as gibberish—a most unpleasant sensation.

The Sherpa went away, puzzled, and as the pain was pretty grim I managed to shout out for Mike Ward, whose tent was

some distance away. Finally he heard me and came across with
Jim Milledge. They immediately realized my condition and
rushed off for oxygen equipment. They put me on oxygen for
the whole night and also drugged me, but it wasn't a period
I enjoyed too much. Whenever I awoke—which was quite
frequently—Jim Milledge or Mike Ward was sitting up watching
me in the light of a candle. I felt very appreciative of their care
and attention.

Early in the morning I dropped off into a deep sleep and when
I awoke I was human once again, although still rather fumbling in speech, with slightly impaired balance. The doctors
called it a cerebral vascular accident and there was a certain
amount of talk of altitude, blood clots, vascular spasms, and so
on. Mike Ward spoke severely to me: I simply must go down
below 15,000 feet immediately and not come up for some months
at least. He warned in no uncertain terms of the dire consequences of not following his advice. As I still wasn't feeling
particularly bright, I didn't put up too much of a struggle. In
the late morning I set off for Camp I with a couple of Sherpas
to assist me, but I didn't need any help. I was slightly wobbly at
times but still did the journey in a creditable two hours. I arrived so much in advance of my luggage that I became rather
cold and crawled into a Sherpa's sleeping bag for an afternoon's
rest. I certainly had my rest, although the sleeping bag left its
mark and I was scratching for a week afterward.

During the day I kept my eyes on the slopes up to the
Makalu Col. This was a vital stage in the expedition. The weather
in the morning wasn't too bad, but in their cramped quarters
at Camp IV the Sherpas had difficulty in getting their food
quickly and were reluctant to make an early start. Some energetic hurrying along by the sahibs finally got them under way
and the twenty-three Sherpas moved off, each carrying thirty
pounds of vital supplies. There were casualties quite early in the
piece: two of the Sherpas became violently altitude sick and
refused to go on. The twenty-one remaining were a strong and
vigorous group, and though the weather was rapidly deteriorating, Mulgrew and Ortenburger led them up the steep rock and
snow and over the crest of the Makalu Col—straight into the
teeth of a gale. Fighting to keep upright, they dumped their
loads a hundred feet up from the col toward Makalu at 24,400
feet and then hastily descended out of the worst of the wind

to head for Camp IV again. It was snowing heavily now, but the party was filled with vigorous satisfaction at their success and dashed enthusiastically down to reach Camp III the same afternoon. Their effort had been a fine one and put us now in position to strike for the top.

On the morning of May 9 I woke in Camp I after a good night's sleep. Already I was feeling very much better at this low altitude and found it depressing to think of leaving the job on the mountain half finished. But my doctors remained so dogmatic on the subject that I let their counsel prevail—but hastily put an end to efforts to have me flown out to Kathmandu by helicopter. Jim Milledge had generously agreed to forego his chances on the mountain and was staying instead as doctor to the invalids.

I asked Mike Ward, who had spent more time in the Himalayas than any remaining member, to take over the leadership of the assault. Peter Mulgrew and Mingmatsering arrived down at midday; it was very good to see them. They were both quite prepared to abandon the mountain and come around with me through the Barun Valley and the low route to Khumjung, but I wouldn't agree as I knew how keen both of them were to go really high—and with Bishop, Milledge, and myself out of the assault party it was getting too low in number already. At least I felt I was leaving things in fairly good condition. The camps and route were established to the Makalu Col; there were ample supplies up and down the mountain; the assault necessities and the majority of the scientific equipment were already on the col; and we had an excellent group of Sherpas obviously ready to go anywhere. With a bit of luck and a marked improvement in the weather I felt we could confidently hope for success.

On my return home I had a medical examination which showed no residual effects from my experience. But the doctors warned me against reproducing similar conditions of strain. I'll certainly be a little more careful next time.

On the afternoon of May 10 Jim Milledge and I, plus the sick Aila, were escorted by Sirdar Dawa Tenzing and four Sherpas down the very rough moraine of the Barun glacier to the old French base camp on the grass at 15,300 feet. Here we quickly regained our full strength. Then, after nearly a week of relaxation, we turned our backs on Makalu and in fifteen vigorous days over steep ridges, precipitous gorges, and foaming torrents reached our house at Chanmitang without having gone much above 15,000 feet. Meanwhile the grim story of Makalu was unfolding behind us.

15

THE ASSAULT

On the morning of May 11 the assault of Makalu commenced.

The first team was Romanes, Gill, and Ortenburger. Supported by Ward and West, they left Camp III with a strong group of Sherpas, bound for the higher camps. It was a lovely morning, one of the rare ones experienced on the mountain, but it was exhausting work plugging the steps up to Camp IV in almost a foot of new snow. As usual, the weather didn't last, and by midday it had clouded over and a brisk wind was blowing.

It seemed too good to be true when it was fine again next morning. They made a leisurely start from Camp IV up the fixed ropes toward the Makalu Col and in three hours of steady climbing had surmounted the rock and snow pitches and approached the crest of the col. There was a strong wind blowing here and it became decidedly unpleasant. One of the Sherpas suggested that the French had camped in an ice gully about a hundred feet below them, but it looked like a sheet of polished green ice and was completely devoid of shelter. Instead the tents of Camp V were pitched on a big plateau among a lot of huge mushroom-shaped sastrugi at a height of 24,400 feet. To the west they could look into Tibet and on the sky line was the great peak of Kangchenjunga. After a rest and a hot drink they spent the afternoon on physiological work—collecting alveolar air samples and doing psychological tests. Ward decided that when the assault party left in the morning he and West would set up the stationary bicycle and carry on with the full physiological program.

It was windy all night and still blowing hard when the first assault party made their preparations to leave Camp V. Everyone was reluctant to start up and the Sherpas were actually ready a quarter of an hour before the sahibs. Led by Pember Tenzing, who had been up here with the French, they started on ahead, but instead of traversing straight across the face as the French had done, they tried to climb up the right-hand side of the glacier. By the time the sahibs caught up to the Sherpas they were at 25,000 feet and had two alternatives in front of them: they could either carry on up the right-hand side of the glacier, hoping they would find a route which would lead them out to the left, or else they could get back onto the French route, but this would mean dropping about three or four hundred feet. After some discussion, influenced by an aversion to losing any hard-won height, they decided to carry on up, to try crossing the middle of the glacier among some ice pinnacles and towers (an unfortunate decision, as it turned out later).

Romanes and Ortenburger shared the lead at this stage while Gill tried to do some filming with his movie camera. He found the problem of climbing and filming at the same time at over 25,000 feet just too much of a burden and he was forced to abandon the camera for the rest of the assault. They chose a site for Camp VI at 25,800 feet in the shelter of a tall ice *sérac* and soon had the Sherpas at work, digging out a platform. Once the tents were pitched, they crawled inside and recovered quickly from their efforts in the warmth of their sleeping bags. Then, with admirable determination, they collected alveolar air samples for the physiologists and ran psychological tests. Despite the energy they had expended during the day they were not hungry. In fact, they felt quite nauseated when they tried to swallow any food.

With the aid of sleeping pills the three sahibs had a reasonable night's sleep. They awoke refreshed but found a full gale was blowing and were depressed to see snow being whipped off in sheets from the face above. The mountain looked a most unhealthy place. But the thoughts of turning back or even waiting didn't enter their minds—or at least nobody mentioned the subject. They crawled out of their tents into the wind, determined to find a way across the ice *séracs* onto the old French route.

Romanes and Gill were on the leading rope while Ortenburger was tied on with Urkien, Nima Dorje, and Pember Tenzing, who were carrying all the requirements for Camp VII. One other Sherpa—Phudorje—had stayed in Camp VI with them, but he had vomited and coughed up blood during the night and now refused to go any higher. Clad in every piece of clothing, they pushed off into the wind and began climbing up a steep polished ice slope which led them onto a ledge consisting of powder snow lying deeply over hard ice underneath. In places many steps had to be cut on particularly steep slopes. The climbers soon found this an exhausting process. They realized, too, that this could be a difficult pitch if they had to bring down a sick or injured man from above.

The weather grew worse as the day progressed, and about midday the cloud was well down on the mountain, giving them almost blizzard conditions. After a lot of strenuous effort they forced a route through the *séracs* and came out into the snow gully on the left-hand side of the Makalu glacier. Despite the shocking conditions they carried on up this for a few hundred feet, until at a height of about 26,300 feet they decided they simply could not go any further. Rather than establish a camp here, a mere five hundred feet above Camp VI, they agreed to make a depot of the supplies and to return to the overnight camp. Bitterly disappointed, they turned downward again, only to find the traveling even worse. Previously the wind had been at their backs, but now they were going straight into it and the ice-laden blast soon had their goggles completely frozen up. Blinded, they dragged off their goggles and struggled back against the wind without them—only finding their way with difficulty. Their faces were caked with ice; they felt terribly weak from the constant battering of the wind and the bitter struggle for breath in the thin cold air. On the last ice pitch just before camp the tired Gill slipped on the hard ice and dragged Romanes off his belay. They both tumbled down some fifty feet and ended up half buried in the snow below, but by then both were too exhausted to care much. They dragged themselves to their feet and covered the last few steps to Camp VI. Phudorje had the primus going, and over this they thawed off the deep layer of ice on their faces. Gill found that his nose was

70. *Construction gang assembling Silver Hut at 19,000 feet. Hillary in foreground, Mul-grew on left, Romanes beyond Hillary, and Milledge on right.*

71. (ABOVE) *Silver Hut sections made up into sixty-pound loads (at the start of the journey in Kathmandu).* 72. (RIGHT) *Sherpa Mingmatsering carrying hut parts up the Mingbo Glacier to 19,000 feet.* 73. (BELOW) *Laying out the foundations of the hut.*

74. (ABOVE) *Assembling the outer walls of the hut.* 75. (RIGHT) *Gill and Romanes preparing a meal in the Silver Hut.* 76. (BELOW) *The first of the eleven prefabricated rings being put in place on the hut foundations.*

77. *Silver Hut and large polar-type tent during blizzard in middle of winter.*

78. *Silver Hut with tent used for extra storage and cooking. The ice-fluted peak behind was climbed by Gill and Ward.*

ASSAULT ON MOUNT MAKALU

This 27,790-foot peak is, in the words of Desmond Doig, "hugely formidable
even in distance, its rock summit dark among the other glittering peaks, as somber and prophetic as a black veil at a white wedding." Shown here is the route
used from Camp II to the site of scientific studies, Camp III at 21,200 feet, and
then on to the ice-encrusted ridges and steep slopes attempted by Mulgrew and
Nevison at 27,400 feet. "From the top trailed a long plume of snow, fair indication of the strong wind that must be blowing up there and an ominous sight to
the mountaineer."

frozen solid and had quite a nip of frostbite. Luckily none of them had frostbite in fingers or toes, where it is usually most dangerous. They were all very tired and had taken a terrible beating.

After a restless night they awoke to find that the weather was as bad as ever. They agreed to retreat to Camp V to save any further deterioration. Gill found that coming down was a terrible effort, and Romanes and Ortenburger seemed in little better shape. The wind had blown much of the fresh snow off the plateau on the col, leaving bare polished ice, and on this even their crampons were insufficient to give them safe footing in the gale. One of the Sherpas was blown off his feet and slithered across the ice until the rope came tight. He scrambled to his feet and they struggled on into the wind. Over the last few hundred yards they were forced to have a rest every fifty yards or so. They tumbled into the flapping tents on the col with enormous relief. It was May 15, the day we had hoped this party might reach the summit, but here they were, battered and bewildered, down at Camp V again.

A CHANGE OF PLANS

Meanwhile, spaced a day apart, the other men to be involved in the later assaults were moving steadily up the mountain. Harrison and Mulgrew reached Camp IV on May 13. From this camp they had a magnificent view of Everest and Lhotse, but the clouds were gathering about them even as they watched and the wind was rising. They had been rather startled on arrival to find that a boulder the size of a four-gallon drum had come to rest three yards on the downhill side of a tent. Deep gouge marks brushed past the guy ropes. The boulder had probably been dislodged by the strong wind the night before. There was no evidence to suggest that this sort of thing happened regularly. Harrison commented, "Anyway, the boulder made a jolly good seat." It was very windy indeed in the morning as they climbed up the route to the Makalu Col, and Mulgrew had difficulty in keeping his hands warm and had to stop frequently to thaw them out. They arrived at Camp V to find Ward, West, and Nevison in residence and the scientific work in full swing—complete with bicycling. Visibility was poor when they arrived, but late in the evening Makalu shed her clouds and they were able to trace the route to the summit. And still the wind blew!

With the return of a rather shattered first assault party to Camp V the plans were reviewed. Michael Ward, one of our strongest and most experienced climbers, had already spent five days with West carrying out the physiological program on the col and was no longer fit enough to take part in the assault. He decided to remain in support on the col. The first assault party recommended that two further teams be mounted. The first, composed of Mulgrew and Nevison, should go ahead and establish Camp VII but not sleep there, merely leaving it intact and ready for the next assault. Then the fittest sahib, John Harrison, and the best Sherpa available, probably Urkien, should make a drive for the top. Everyone, of course, was anxious to have a crack at the summit. Later in the day this plan was changed. Mulgrew and Nevison were to become a full-scale second assault, while the determined Ortenburger, who had experienced a rather easier time of it on the first assault than his two companions, was now to join Harrison for the third assault. Gill was too tired to do anything else but go down to Camp III, and Romanes was having difficulty with his breathing—these two men were temporarily out of action. In fact, over the next couple of nights both Romanes and Ward found it necessary to have spells of oxygen to counteract their irregular breathing.

On the morning of May 16 the weather looked a little more promising. There was still a brisk wind blowing but considerably less than in the last few days. The second assault party, Nevison and Mulgrew with eight Sherpas, made their preparations and then set off for Camp VI. The wind was blowing quite hard at their backs, but they weren't too worried by it and had a fairly good trip. They found the camp located under a huge ice bulge near the edge of the glacier and had to chip a few steps to get up to it. They cleared a lot of surplus snow from around the tents, then crawled inside to get a brew of tea and prepare a meal. Two of the Sherpas went off back to Camp V, leaving six with the two sahibs.

They spent an uncomfortable night with little sleep, and early in the morning their hearts sank when the wind started to blow with some vigor. Rather hopelessly they commenced preparations for departure—and were greatly relieved at 8 A.M. when the wind eased considerably and they were able to make a start.

Learning a lesson from the first assault, when the two strongest
sahibs had exhausted themselves by doing the majority of the
work, Nevison and Mulgrew carried nothing at all and left the
arduous trail breaking to the Sherpas. The route across the
glacier had been marked by the first assault party, although
they hadn't been able to fix ropes or cut much in the way of
steps. Following these flags, the second assault party devoted
a good deal of time to enlarging the steps up several ice walls
and around a number of ice pinnacles, and they also established
fixed ropes across the more difficult portions. Traveling steadily
with frequent stops for breath, they cleared this broken ice area
and started climbing slowly up toward the depot of food and
equipment left by the first assault party at 26,300 feet.

Running down the center of the mountain was a huge broad
rib of ice, splitting the face in half. At the foot of this was the
depot, now well buried in snow. The French party had climbed
the left-hand side of this great rib up a little channel, but
Nevison and Mulgrew thought this looked rather a dangerous
route—especially as they lacked the reserves of strength of the
oxygen-breathing Frenchmen. Instead they decided to go up the
right-hand side which was a steep but open snow field.

SIX MEN ON A ROPE

A hundred yards ahead of the sahibs the six Sherpas climbed
up the last steep slope leading to the depot, and Annullu started
digging around at the base of the ice rib to locate the buried
food. The last Sherpa on the rope, Da Tenzing II, not paying
much attention, suddenly lost his balance and started to tumble
and slither down the slope. After a couple of seconds the rope
came taut with just enough pull in it to yank the next man off
—and then the next. Soon all six Sherpas were tumbling down
the hill. Mulgrew and Nevison could only watch in horror as
the men shot away at a rapidly accelerating pace without anyone
making much attempt to get an ice ax into the snow or any
other form of self-arrest. Sliding free, scattering ice axes and
equipment all over the slope, they surged over a bulge in the
ice, shot into the air for ten or fifteen feet, to come down with a
great wallop and slide on toward some great precipices further
down the mountain.

The petrified Mulgrew and Nevison were now quite convinced
that they had lost all six of their Sherpas. Hopelessly they
watched them shoot over a lightly bridged crevasse—and saw

two of the men drop out of sight as the bridge gave way. Then the rope snapped tight and the other four men were jerked to a halt. Pulling themselves together, the two sahibs climbed carefully down toward the silent bodies, gathering ice axes and pieces of equipment as they went. First one, then another Sherpa shook himself and sat up, and soon the whole six were sitting on the edge of the crevasse, examining themselves for wounds. Angtemba had hurt his leg and Nevison suspected it might be a break; Mingmatsering had been cut in the head with someone's crampons during the fall and he had quite a lot of minor cuts with blood streaming down his face; but the other Sherpas seemed in good shape, although their morale had been shaken a little.

Nevison suggested they all turn back and get the two injured men safely down, but both Angtemba and Mingma claimed they could get to Camp VI quite well on their own. In the end the sahibs agreed. It wasn't really very far; the route was now well roped through all the difficult pieces, and they were a capable and experienced pair. Traveling slowly, they started off down, and although Angtemba was having difficulty in moving, Mingma now seemed quite strong.

Mulgrew and Nevison, plus the four remaining Sherpas, clambered laboriously back up to the depot. Then the two sahibs discussed the problem of getting everything up to Camp VII. They were now short of carrying strength and realized they would have to break their resolution of saving their energies until the last day. They agreed that Nevison would lead from this point and do any making of steps or step cutting that might be required, while Peter Mulgrew would carry a Sherpa load of twenty-odd pounds. The other load was to be spread out among the remaining four Sherpas.

With every step something of an effort, they made slow but unhindered progress up the snow field on the right-hand side of the great ice rib and finally came out on a point looking directly across to the proposed Camp VII, near the foot of a rock ridge which ran up to join the summit ridge. They had two altimeters with them and were checking fairly constantly. Here they both gave a reading of 27,000 feet. They cut across the top of the snow field with difficulty—it was steep—and the Sherpas were keen to dump their loads and head back to Camp VI. The heavy snowfall of a couple of days before hadn't consolidated very well and it was still very soft, but the wind was at their backs and didn't trouble them unduly. As much as their labored breathing would let them they were able to enjoy the tremendous view across to Lhotse and Everest. They could now look down onto the south col and see far out into Tibet.

Finding a site for Camp VII wasn't easy. The area was extremely steep; the most promising position was directly under the rock ridge but endangered by falling rocks. They dropped down a few feet and chose a camp site on the edge of a crevasse in a precipitous and exposed position but safe from any rockfall. The Sherpas dropped their loads and were off for Camp VI as soon as they could, leaving Annullu, Tom Nevison, and Peter Mulgrew to clear a flat space and pitch the two tents. They found difficulty in digging out even a tiny platform as there was very little room and the slightest amount of physical effort made the men gasp for breath. The two tents were finally erected with the entrances facing into each other. On one side they had a deep crevasse and on the other the slope fell straight down toward Camp III—6000 feet below. From the upper lip of the crevasse little pieces of ice continued to rattle down onto the tents.

Once their camp was established and they had tea on the stove there was time to look around. They could see the summit of Makalu quite clearly not very far away—only eight hundred feet above—with the wind blowing snow in a long stream over into Tibet. And once again they had a wonderful view across onto the south col of Everest.

They were finding that any sort of activity was hard work. It had taken them a long time to get the camp ready and to get their gear off. Annullu got into the smaller tent and started the cooking, and although they originally intended to have a stew from their high-altitude ration, at this stage they didn't feel quite up to eating it. They drank a lot, mostly lemon drinks, and ate biscuits with jam, but this was all. It was bitterly cold outside, yet with most of their gear on and their double sleeping bags they were snug and warm. They had time now, too, to discover that Mulgrew's small red climbing pack with his Canon camera, expedition money, and spare socks and gloves had been lost in the Sherpa fall and that, worse still, Annullu had apparently hurt a rib at the same time. (It turned out later to be cracked.) However, they weren't too worried as they were all still going quite well and their camp was, after all, only a mere eight hundred feet from the summit.

The three men had a restful night's sleep and started early in their preparations for the summit attempt. Mulgrew was feeling nauseated and vomited a little, a fairly normal reaction at this altitude. There was no doubt in his mind about starting out. It took them a long time to get their boots on and to pull on their heavy outer clothing, and although they had commenced their preparations at 6:30 A.M., they weren't ready to go until about half-past nine. Even then it seemed to take a very long time to strap their crampons onto their boots. There was a fresh wind blowing from a southerly direction. Although it would be all right going up with the wind at their backs, coming down might be very hard work indeed. There was a lot of cloud around, but it was nearly all below them and they had a fine uninterrupted view of the surrounding peaks—dozens and dozens of them thrusting up through the cloud. Everest stood up quite clearly, with the clouds lapping the south col and clouds drifting around the Tibetan plateau. Above them on the summit of Makalu snow was blowing off in rather ominous fashion, and they knew they could expect difficulty when they reached the summit ridge.

Despite the wind up top they decided to make an attempt. They started slowly out toward the great rock ridge that ran up toward the final summit ridge, and spent about an hour getting to the base of it. Then, instead of climbing directly up it, they cut around to the right onto a long tongue of snow that went at least halfway up the ridge before it petered out into the rocks. By the time they reached the top of the slope they had been going for three or four hours, moving slowly and finding every step sheer punishment. They were now about four hundred feet above Camp VII. Annullu, who had been worried by the wind, suggested that they should turn back, as they had no hope of getting to the top with it blowing so strongly. It was certainly cold, and they were all having difficulty in keeping their fingers warm, even though they were wearing a good pair of woolen gloves underneath their down gloves. Earlier Annullu had complained about a sore chest, but none of them realized there was anything wrong with him at this stage except that he didn't like the wind.

Altimeter check: 27,400 feet. They felt they could almost

reach out and touch the summit from here, although they didn't like the way the snow was whipping off the ridge above. The tongue of snow had given them relatively easy climbing, but now they decided to cut across onto the crest of the ridge. They were determined to keep going and had changed positions on the rope before starting off again when Mulgrew's strength suddenly ran out and he doubled up and dropped to the snow. For a few moments he lay there, gasping for breath, but his strength didn't return and it was clear that something was terribly wrong with him. He realized with despair that he couldn't go on. His only thought was that the others must go on without him.

He asked to be left on the rocks while Nevison went on to the top with Annullu.

Nevison had a difficult decision to make. It was a bitter blow to have to throw in their hand while only four hundred feet from the summit, but not only was Mulgrew incapacitated; Annullu was also in difficulty.

They started back down, belaying Mulgrew from above and below. On four or five occasions he collapsed into the snow and had to wait there to recover before getting up and struggling down a few more feet. At times he would slide a little, checked by the others on the rope, then stagger to his feet and plunge on a little further. Part of the time he wasn't really conscious of what was happening. He'd come to his senses and find he was lying in the snow or just sitting there. By the time they reached camp Mulgrew was in a state of physical exhaustion and Annullu seemed to have suffered a mental collapse. A tremendous burden was thrown on Nevison. He put Mulgrew into his sleeping bags, found Annullu lying immobile in his tent, and had to manhandle him into his too. He got the cooker going and made tea and soup. Mulgrew took his without too much trouble. Annullu had to be shaken sharply before he would drink the life-giving fluid.

Mulgrew felt a little better once he was in his sleeping bag and with typical optimism was full of talk about another try the next day. Nevison didn't take this very seriously. He had the horrifying situation of two sick men on his hands at 27,000 feet. (Mulgrew was in much worse shape than either of them realized: he had experienced a pulmonary embolism in his right lung which probably should have killed him on the spot.) They did nothing for his periodic stabs of pain as they felt that morphine would restrict his breathing even further and the nearest emergency oxygen was 1200 feet below them at Camp VI. So they settled down to a long and grim night, and Nevison tossed and turned with the knowledge that their chances of getting Mulgrew down the mountain were pretty slim.

16

THE DESPERATE DAYS

Mulgrew's second night at Camp VII was a bad one. He coughed up quite a lot of blood. But in the morning he was feeling a little better and Annullu, too, was much more cheerful. They started down with Mulgrew staggering ahead, Nevison and Annullu belaying him from behind. They hadn't covered a hundred yards before the pain in his chest became so great that he collapsed again. He said he couldn't go on.

But, coaxed and cajoled by Nevison and Annullu, he crept downward, a few steps at a time, with belays from above and below. Sometimes he stumbled and sometimes he slid. After an eternity they reached the foot of the ice rib where there was a little depression with a constant stream of wind-driven snow whipping around the corner. This was about the only possible bivouac site between Camps VII and VI. Mulgrew just could not go any further. He was in severe pain and was blacking out, completely unaware of what he was doing. Nevison decided they would have to camp. He managed to get Mulgrew, still fully clothed, into two sleeping bags and then sent Annullu off to Camp VI for help. Their urgent need was for a tent, oxygen, and a stove.

Left with Mulgrew at 26,300 feet, Nevison kept worrying about what would happen if nobody was at Camp VI. Finally, as a precaution, he set to work to dig a snow cave.

It was a tremendous relief when late in the afternoon two Sherpas, Pember Tenzing and Pasang Tenzing, arrived up from Camp VI with a tent and food. They all worked hard pitching the tent, getting Mulgrew out of his sleeping bags, into the tent, and back into the sleeping bags again. The two Sherpas then rushed quickly down to Camp VI before dark. The night that followed was an absolute nightmare.

Nevison himself was now feeling rather ill and had great difficulty in breathing except when he was sitting up. There was no water and they were both critically dehydrated. Nevison used all of his remaining matches trying to light a candle and failed. He spent the night eating snow and achromycin. Next morning he found that his sputum was frothy and pink which, with his cough and shortness of breath, he diagnosed as pulmonary edema, a condition which has killed so many climbers. Mulgrew was even worse than the day before. Both had to get down at once. "What's *wrong* with them?" they asked each other. "Don't they know we're dying up here?"

Meanwhile, a couple of days earlier, down on the Makalu Col, the third assault party of Harrison and Ortenburger had been making preparations to move up to Camp VI. It had blown furiously the night before and they felt sure that the Mulgrew-Nevison assault party would not be able to attempt the summit that day but would wait at Camp VII in the hope of better weather the next day. But the wind persisted all morning. They decided to delay their departure as it would be madness to move up the mountain under these conditions. At 11 A.M. Sherpas struggled into camp to inform them of the accident below the ice rib. Angtemba had sprained or broken his ankle and could not walk beyond Camp VI. This was a serious blow to the third assault plans, and at first it was agreed that Harrison and Ortenburger and their Sherpas should head off immediately for Camp VI to carry Angtemba down. But Mike Ward, who was still on the col, although far from well, decided to ascend himself with the aid of oxygen to examine Angtemba, thus sparing the third assault party. By 4 P.M. Ward had reached Camp VI with Pember Tenzing. He reported over the radio that Angtemba probably had a badly fractured ankle and would have to be carried down by a strong group of Sherpas. This was obviously going to put an end to the hopes of the final assault party.

On the morning of May 19 the wind was at its usual strength. Ortenburger and Harrison, plus their Sherpas, made the long sidle and the stiff pull up to Camp VI to join Ward. Neither of

the sahibs were going particularly well that morning; Ortenburger felt much more tired than he had on his first trip up to
this camp. They duly reached Camp VI. Then the Sherpas commenced the descent with the injured Angtemba, being watched
over by Mike Ward who was himself looking very tottery. He
was, in fact, already suffering from pneumonia and profoundly
hypoxic, as the following conversation shows. On their arrival
in camp Ward has said to Ortenburger, "Why did you come all
the way up here? Do you want to go to all the effort required to
make a second ascent of the mountain?"

Ortenburger, somewhat puzzled, replied, "I don't understand.
Did Tom and Peter reach the top?"

Ward said, "I thought I heard a rumor that they had."

Ortenburger said he hadn't heard this rumor. So Ward replied,
"Maybe I'm mistaken . . . I thought I heard a rumor like that."

The rescue party disappeared out of sight and the two sahibs
were left at Camp VI with Pember Tenzing and Pasang Tenzing.
Drift snow was whirling about them, and while the Sherpas
busied themselves inside the Meade tent, the sahibs, with faces
frosted up, dug out the second tent which was almost completely
buried. It took them two hours of work to do this. Just as they
finished at 3 P.M. Annullu suddenly appeared with the news
about Peter Mulgrew. The work of digging out the tent had left
neither of the sahibs with enough energy to get higher that day,
so they asked Pember Tenzing and Pasang Tenzing to take the
smaller tent, a stove, and some food up to the ailing men. This
they agreed to do and they left at 4 P.M.

The two sahibs now started digging out the Meade tent which
would have to hold both the two Sherpas and themselves for the
night. Under the conditions it was a difficult job, very windy
and cold, and Harrison's feet froze up. Finally they crawled into
the tent, thoroughly exhausted. At 7 P.M. the two Sherpas returned, having made a remarkable effort in getting the emergency gear up to the two sick men. That evening they made
contact with Camp III on the radio but were unable to raise
Mike Ward at Camp V, which puzzled them immensely. This
was serious—they had to get more oxygen up for Mulgrew.

Harrison, Ortenburger, and the two Sherpas spent a cramped
night in the tent and woke to a clear but windy day. Despite
repeated tries they still failed to make radio contact with Ward

at V and so decided that while one of them went up to Mulgrew
with the Sherpas the other would have to go down to V for
more support and to get more oxygen sent up. To make the
decision they tossed a marked hibutane pill. Ortenburger won.
Harrison made up his load with his personal gear and sleeping
bags and set off alone down the long sidle into a biting wind. By
the time he had reached the col he'd had all he could take. He
pushed through the doorway of the large Blanchard tent and
was confronted with a prostrate Ward who cried in a shaky
voice, "Who are you?"

Harrison was staggered until he realized that Ward was delir-
ious. After giving him immediate attention and adjusting his
oxygen set (his breathing was feeble) he got busy on the radio
and contacted Camp III. Most of the Sherpas had been carrying
Angtemba down the mountain so Camp V was almost deserted,
but Harrison was now able to explain the full situation to Camp
III and get a major operation under way to rescue Ward and
Mulgrew.

High on the mountain life was still grim. After Harrison's
departure from Camp VI Ortenburger set off with Pember
Tenzing and Pasang Tenzing plus a bottle of oxygen and climbed
steadily up to the emergency camp—VI½. His first impression on
seeing the camp and its occupants was one of horror. The tent
was badly pitched with poles incorrectly assembled; it was partly
caved in by drifted snow, and there was almost as much snow
inside as out—it was the worst picture of misery he had ever
seen, yet the occupants were more or less of good cheer. They
discussed what to do and agreed that there was not enough
strength in the new party of three to help both of the sick men
down that day. It was decided that Nevison should take the
oxygen and go down with the two Sherpas. Ortenburger would
stay at VI½ with Mulgrew, awaiting the arrival of help. This
night was Mulgrew's fourth above 26,000 feet and his second in
a row without an air mattress. Ortenburger tried to dig the tent
out and pitch it a little better, but it was still a miserable night.

The morning of May 21 passed rather quickly while they were
waiting for the arrival of the Sherpas from Camp III. It was
close to 1 p.m. before they showed up—first Pembertarkay, then
Pangboche Tenzing and Siku. It was 2 p.m., possibly later, before they started down. The Sherpas had brought up an oxygen

bottle and climbing set, and this helped Mulgrew enormously. They tried moving with one Sherpa helping Mulgrew, the other two cutting steps ahead of him, and Ortenburger belaying from the rear. As soon as he started again Mulgrew felt the full pain return and could only make the slowest progress. The slope was too steep for him to be piggy-backed or even for men to help on either side—they could only help from in front or behind. Frequently Mulgrew dropped to the snow; at times he would get up and stagger only a few paces before dropping again.

During his rational moments Mulgrew kept worrying about crossing the glacier to Camp VI. This was technically quite difficult and he expected to have a lot of trouble in negotiating it. Slowly they worked their way across to the first of the fixed ropes. By this time the oxygen had run out so they threw the bottle away. It was getting colder and the wind was strong. Mulgrew was soon having trouble with his hands. At times he felt he couldn't go on; Ortenburger was very patient—but very determined. It became dark as they reached the last ice traverse.

Urkien, waiting at Camp VI with another Sherpa, now came out to help. First he installed a fixed rope on the last hundred feet down to the camp. Although this was not a difficult place in daylight it was decidedly tricky at night with a sick man.

Tired and frozen, they crawled into Camp VI in the dark, then fell into the tents. A little earlier Urkien had made a brew of tea, but this was cold now; there was no fuel left in the cooker, and they couldn't have anything hot. Also their sleeping bags were wet from condensation. That night in Camp VI was the worst Mulgrew had ever spent. He didn't remember sleeping at all, although he must have dozed now and again, and it was during this period he felt sure he received his worst frostbite. His hands were a mess by the time he arrived at Camp VI; he wasn't able to do anything about his feet—in fact he didn't even know they were frostbitten. He was having long periods of black-out. There was also the matter of sleeping bags and air mattresses. The Sherpas had expected, as had the sahibs, to reach V that night and had no sleeping bags and only one air mattress. Mulgrew slept in two damp bags, Ortenburger in his inner bag, two of the Sherpas in his outer bag, and Pembertarkay in Ortenburger's down pants.

Down to the Makalu Col

Ortenburger tells the story of the grim day down to Camp V. "In the morning all of us were in very poor shape. Although we were awake at a reasonable hour and there was no breakfast to prepare, we were unable to get started before 10 A.M.—it takes a long time to put on boots, and it took a long time to get Peter ready to go. The previous day he had done most of the work coming down, but it was clear that he was not as strong this day. Four of the Sherpas went down somewhat ahead of us, ostensibly to make steps for Peter. Urkien helped Peter and I belayed him.

"The four who went ahead soon got a significant distance away, since they were not making very good steps, and Peter was going very slowly. Peter had no oxygen at this point and repeatedly said that he would do much better with oxygen. Urkien also did not think much of this slow progress, so after only a hundred to two hundred feet from VI I told Urkien to go down to the four Sherpas who were ahead and send the strongest one down to V immediately to bring up a bottle of oxygen. He went down, talked with them awhile, and then set off himself downslope, leaving the other four behind. After I realized what had happened, I shouted to the other four to come back up and help. They either couldn't hear, didn't understand, or didn't want to understand, because in a little while they, too, went down hill to V."

(In actual fact the Sherpas were showing a good deal of common sense. After their rigorous night with no sleeping bags, no food or drink, they were dehydrated and weak. They decided to go down to V, get rid of their loads, have a big meal and plenty to drink, and then set off up again with food and hot drinks for Leigh and Peter.)

"This turn of events was extremely disappointing, to say the least, since Peter and I were now alone and the weather was beginning to deteriorate. We spent the next three hours or more in descending the long, moderately steep snow slope below VI. Peter was very weak by then and could make only three to fifteen steps at a time before he would lose his balance and more or less collapse in the snow. At this point I had no idea whether

Urkien would actually return with help. As the day wore on it appeared more and more as if he would not. Since I did not have the strength to carry him, it seemed that the only hope for Peter's life lay in this slow, unaided progress. A night out, I believed, would finish him and might well finish me. Hence, after allowing a reasonable amount of time for rest after each collapse, I would talk him into continuing the struggle.

"I gather from subsequent conversation with him that most of this time his mind was elsewhere—among the sun-blasted rocks of Aden, for example. In the late afternoon, 3 P.M. or after, we finally reached the rock rib which separates the slope we had been descending from a low-angled ice field across which very gusty winds blow, making it difficult to maintain one's balance. Peter sat on a rock and I crossed the rib and saw two Sherpas on the other side of the ice field. I brought back the good news to Peter that the oxygen was almost there and I, too, sat down.

"After we had been there something like half an hour I realized that the Sherpas had not shown up, yet it was not a half-hour climb across the ice field. I went back to the rib and found the two still standing around on the other side. I shouted and signaled for them to come—and after some time one of them started across. I assumed that he had the oxygen, but when he arrived all he had was the pair of down pants I had loaned to Pembertarkay. I was rather mad by this time. From the point where we were one must climb a hundred feet or so in order to get into the steps across the ice field. Summoning most of my remaining strength, I drove this fellow back across the ice field to where the other Sherpa was standing. He had the oxygen apparatus, and both he and Nima Gungi refused to cross the ice field. They both had crampons and really no excuse for not crossing. Thinking that these two represented all the assistance I was going to get that day, I became even madder and physically pushed them out onto the steps across the ice field and drove them across to the point where Peter was sitting alone.

"After dumping the oxygen set they turned around and were going to descend to V immediately. I physically restrained them and put the set on Peter, only to discover to my disappointment that there was barely enough oxygen in it for more than half an hour. With these two incompetent Sherpas helping I managed to get Peter about fifty feet over to the west side of the rock rib.

But during these proceedings it became clear that these two were no help at all. Then I noticed four or five Sherpas approaching at a good speed and immediately dismissed the other two. We only had to wait about ten minutes until the new and very good Sherpas arrived, led once again by Urkien. In no time at all they had Peter across the ice field and on the second rock rib that separates the ice field from the last snow slope above V. Using the oxygen, Peter was able to walk with considerable assistance during this portion, but his strength gave out at the rocks and it grew dark just about then.

"The weather was very bad by now, strong and gusty wind, driving snow and ice particles—in fact, worse than it was when the first assault team turned back on the fourteenth.

"As Peter had to be carried, one Sherpa went down to V to get a suitable headband for the job, but various carrying methods were used in the interim. These methods were not successful and it seemed to be a long time before the Sherpa returned. However, once we had the headband the Sherpas took turns with Peter, and we made rapid progress since the terrain was much easier and ultimately became flat snow.

"The difficulty now was in finding Camp V. I generally have a reasonable competence in route finding, but it was certainly not obvious to me where the camp was and my flashlight had been lost. After we had been traveling for about half an hour, all of us peering into the darkness, Urkien said he was going to look for camp and he disappeared for ten or fifteen minutes. He returned, saying that he had found camp and that it was only '20 millic' away. We actually reached it in about five minutes. It was completely dark and we would have passed it had not Urkien found it. In addition to this feat and his personally carrying Peter part of the way, probably the greatest thing that Urkien did was to realize that if Peter was ever to get down off the mountain it was his responsibility and not that of any sahib.

"We reached V at 8 P.M. Harrison and West were most helpful and kind. Peter was completely out of it by then and had to have his boots taken off and be put into his sleeping bag. Some assistance was given to me also, and I certainly appreciated the loan of a warm, dry sleeping bag, while John used the wet one that was brought down from VI. Warm drinks were given us and eagerly consumed."

Ortenburger had done a remarkable job in getting Mulgrew down to V, but Harrison and West were horrified at the sight of the sick man—his eyes were sunken and lifeless; his breath came in uneven shudders, and his color was dreadful. Nevertheless there was still life in him. They pumped him full of hot drinks and oxygen and even a little food and his improvement was immediate, but there were purple frostbite blotches all over his hands and feet and he was still coughing up quantities of blood.

On May 23 a strong group of Sherpas with oxygen and supplies moved up from Camp III but arrived at Camp V too late for them to start down again with Mulgrew. Ortenburger, who was showing some signs of wear after his experiences, descended down to IV and finally to lower altitudes. The others resigned themselves to still another night above 24,000 feet.

On May 24 the rescue swung into faster action. Altogether eighteen Sherpas arrived up at Camp V. Mulgrew didn't want to be moved and opposed every effort to get him ready, but by 10 A.M. he was dressed, complete with oxygen, crampons, and everything. With West under one shoulder and Harrison under the other, they staggered a few yards before collapsing in a heap, with Mulgrew again demanding to be left at V. They removed the oxygen set and tried again with no better luck. They knew that if they didn't get him down this day that they never would, so in desperation they tried to coax him into being piggy-backed, but once again he wouldn't have this either. The piggy-backing between VI and V had given his chest all the strain it could take, and now he was in continuous pain.

At this stage John West gave him a shot of morphine and Harrison decided to manufacture a stretcher. He collected pack frames from three protesting Sherpas, got twelve middle sections of Meade tent poles, and lashed them together into a rickety stretcher-*cum*-sledge, being watched all the while rather doubtfully by the Sherpas. West put Mulgrew (now almost out) into his sleeping bags and they lashed him securely into place. They attached a tangle of slings and ropes to the sledge and were under way finally at 1:30 P.M.

Had Mulgrew been conscious, the journey would have been a nightmare for him. The fixed ropes leading down from the col were a tremendous help—in many places the sledge was clipped to these with a karabiner and slid along in perfect security.

Though the day was better than most, it was still bitterly cold and everyone worked with a will. Romanes had come up with the last Sherpas and he took charge of the belaying and assured the safety of the descent.

At 5:30 P.M. they reached IV. Despite the lateness of the hour they decided to press on down to III, as Peter was still unconscious—in fact, every so often West had to check his pulse to see if he was still alive. Down the steep *couloir* they plunged and across the diagonal ice traverse, using the fixed rope all the way. Then, just as darkness fell, they crossed the bergschrund and started moving along the easy traverse. From here on it was straightforward going for the Sherpas and they easily left the sahibs behind. It was a very, very weary group that hobbled into Camp III at 8 P.M. By the time Harrison and Romanes reached the tents the now awake Mulgrew was already installed with a mug of his favorite lemon tea in his hand and looking much better despite his rough trip.

With the return to lower altitudes the majority of the party quickly improved in health, but Angtemba was still unable to walk on his ankle. Mike Ward had recovered from his pneumonia but was still weak and suffering from frostbite. And Peter Mulgrew was, of course, critically ill. The sooner these men could be got to hospital the better. From the Silver Hut Desmond Doig sent a message through to Kathmandu by radio, asking if it would be possible for a helicopter to try to get into the Barun Valley and evacute these sick men. We were fortunate that the high-performance Bell helicopter was still in Nepal. On May 29, despite cloudy conditions on the passes, it flew into the Barun Valley for the first time. It circled over Camp I at 18,000 feet while the men there waved vigorously down valley to indicate the sick men had been carried to a site at 15,500 feet. The helicopter swooped back and landed beside the hospital tents. Mulgrew and Ward were loaded aboard and the pilot set to work to get the aircraft off again. It took four or five attempts and much adjustment of the pitch of the rotor blade before they were able to lift off the surface and get away. Cloud was building up and the pilot doubted whether he would have time to get back to Kathmandu and then return for the next passengers, so he soared down valley between the great peaks above the grim Barun gorge and then out over the wide Arun River. At 4000 feet on the crest of a spur the pilot put the helicopter down beside the village of Num, to the considerable astonishment of the Nepalese inhabitants. Mulgrew and Ward were helped out of the plane and the pilot flew straight back into the Barun to pick up Angtemba and John West.

Mulgrew describes his sojourn at Num. "While we were waiting the villagers came down and gathered around us and they were very kind to me, realizing straightaway that I was sick. Several of them went and cut bushes down and made a sort of shield to save me from the sun, which was worrying me at the time, and another went off down to the river and brought back water for me. Although I couldn't speak to them or understand them, it was quite obvious they wanted to help. Also their witch doctor or medicine man arrived and had a good look at me and shook his head and looked a bit disturbed about the whole thing. After the helicopter arrived back I asked Angtemba, who was going out with us due to his damaged leg, what the witch doctor was saying, but Angtemba wasn't very keen on telling me. Finally he said that the witch doctor thought that the sahib would die. I wasn't too concerned about this as, although I wasn't feeling the best, I had no intention of dying."

West and Angtemba were to remain overnight at Num, and the helicopter took off again with Mulgrew and Ward on board. The flight was a decidedly difficult one. The clouds were now thick, and it seemed at times as if they wouldn't be able to get through. They edged their way down deep valleys and around heavily wooded spurs. On two occasions they just managed to get through passes when there was a little gap in the clouds. It required superb flying skill and the pilot had no time to talk—he was spending all his time watching the map and dodging around the cloud formations. Finally they came out in the clear over the Kathmandu Valley. An hour later the sick men were in bed in the Kathmandu Hospital, a sudden transition from the wind and storms of Makalu to the pre-monsoon warmth of Kathmandu.

17

FAREWELL TO
KHUMJUNG

In retrospect it is easy to point to things which cost us the summit of Makalu—the lack of positive leadership when first I, and then Ward, had succumbed to illness; shortage of manpower with Bishop, Milledge, and myself out of the assault teams; the poor choice of route above Camp V which forced Gill and Romanes to expend themselves; Gill and Romanes' fall; the long slide by the six Sherpas; the constant fierce winds with their sharp edges of frostbite; and Mulgrew's final illness. The turn of the tide was undoubtedly the Sherpa accident at 26,000 feet. Before this, despite weather and altitude, the party always had something in reserve. But now it was different—two of our best Sherpas had to descend, one being carried off the mountain; Annullu had a broken rib; Mulgrew had to carry a Sherpa load to 27,000 feet, and Nevison had to break trail—thus straining their reserves of strength to the utmost.

Pugh had always stressed the dangers of our non-oxygen assault, pointing out that all the organs of the body were working at the limit of their capacity at these heights and there was no margin of reserve. "This is certainly true of the brain, the heart, and the lungs as well as the muscles," he said, "and the danger of sudden illness or death from cerebro-vascular accident, acute heart failure, thrombosis, or pneumonia cannot be ignored. Another danger is the peripheral vasoconstriction associated with shock or illness. This virtually cuts off the supply of warmth to the hands and feet and frostbite is an inevitable consequence, for no clothing, however perfect, can protect the extremities once their supply of warming blood from the central organs is cut off."

Mulgrew's collapse put the end to any hope of a successful assault, and the strong reserves in Harrison and Ortenburger had to be devoted to the grim task of getting Mulgrew down the mountain. Only some remarkable efforts—notably by Ortenburger and by the Sherpas—had brought everyone out alive. Our reserves of medical and rescue oxygen on the col and below had proved invaluable, as had the pioneer helicopter flight into the Barun Valley to pick up the sick men.

I had always expected Makalu to be the final testing ground of my acclimatization theories and believed that the long periods my men had spent at 19,000 feet and above would make them so adjusted to living in rare atmospheres that Makalu would not be too formidable an objective for them even without the use of oxygen. And then, perhaps, Everest without oxygen might be the next step? But now I realize that my theories were a little too optimistic and these long periods at high altitudes were possibly our undoing. Despite the superficial adjustments made to 19,000 feet and the excellent physical and mental work done at this height, there is much evidence to indicate that resistance to disease was greatly reduced. It was almost impossible to gain sufficient daily exercise at 19,000 feet, so the party lacked the hard physical condition to enable them to be battered by the bitter winds above 24,000 feet and yet come back for more. Only Harrison and Ortenburger, the two newcomers to the team, showed the expected reserves of strength, and they had not been subjected to the slow and insidious sapping of weight and vitality experienced by the rest of the party over the previous six months.

None of us have any doubts that the summit of Makalu can be reached without oxygen, but my feelings have undergone a considerable change in this matter. I doubt if the risks involved in working at this height without oxygen make the effort worth while. With perfect weather and a fit party Makalu would undoubtedly fall, for it is not too difficult a mountain, but harsh weather can transform the picture and sap reserves of strength —bringing a party, as with us, within a whisker of disaster.

With the return to lower altitudes all of us quickly regained our full health again—except for Peter Mulgrew. His life was saved, but nothing could preserve his frostbitten feet and they ultimately required amputation. The explorer in any field knows that his health and indeed even his life may be prejudiced. But this is the risk we all take, and perhaps it even adds something to the challenge and makes it more worth while. Peter Mulgrew has shown the same fierce courage and spirit in this new problem as he did at 27,000 feet. With typical jaunty determination he has set as his objective the mastery of his artificial limbs so that he can return to the mountains again—and knowing his capabilities, I have no doubt that he will succeed.

DISMANTLING THE SILVER HUT

On May 29 Milledge and I arrived at Thyangboche after our energetic fifteen days' walk from the Barun Valley. We were just in time to commence the final evacuation of the assault parties. Over the next few days Romanes, Gill, Nevison, Ortenburger, and Harrison arrived at the house at Chanmitang and were able to tell me the full story of the previous fortnight.

I had sent a large group of Sherpas into the Mingbo Valley to strip the various camps of all their worth-while equipment and bring it back to Chanmitang. In particular we had felt some reluctance to abandon the Silver Hut to its fate on the glacier; it had proved such a successful home. I was therefore very happy to receive the news from Mr. Dayal, the Indian ambassador in Kathmandu, that the Himalayan Mountaineering Institute in Darjeeling would be very pleased to have the use of the hut for a physiological program they planned to start in the near future. We agreed that the expedition would pull the hut to pieces, carry it down to Chanmitang, and store it there. The chief instructor from the Institute, my old friend and climbing companion from Everest, Tenzing Norgay, would come in from Darjeeling and organize the carry of the hut parts back to civilization.

I was still chafing under the 15,000-foot height restriction, so Jim Milledge agreed to take on the job of dismantling the Silver Hut. With a handful of competent Sherpas under the leadership of Mingmatsering he camped under the Amadablam Col, and they tackled the task with speed and determination—for speed was essential if they were to save the hut from tumbling down into the crevasses which had opened up all around during the course of the summer. Ring after ring of the hut sections was stripped down until only one remained. Mingmatsering had become very casual about the whole procedure and was perched comfortably on top of the final ring, pulling out the attaching clips, when it collapsed abruptly into its seven sections and precipitated the flailing Mingma toward the gaping crevasse next door. Only by sheer good fortune was he able to grasp an icy outcrop and arrest his descent into the depths—and emerge to join in the typically hearty Sherpa laughter at his narrow escape.

In the evening of the same day Jim Milledge was lying comfortably in his tent beside the scattered remnants of our once-proud hut. The last group of men carrying loads over the Amadablam Col from the Hongu was expected any moment. Milledge poked his head out of the sleeve entrance and looked up at the col above him. He was just in time to see a small figure plummeting down the ice-fluted slopes. With a gasp of horror he watched the body and its rucksack fly apart, shoot over a low rock precipice, and then carry on at colossal speed down the ice. The slope eased a little four hundred feet down but was then cut by a gaping maw. Without seemingly a moment's hesitation the figure shot down the last slope and then dropped out of sight into the depths of this crevasse.

Shocked by what he had seen and quite convinced that the man had fallen to his death, Milledge dressed quickly and then joined his group of Sherpas and climbed slowly up to the bergschrund to do what they could. They were only a hundred feet away when they were startled by a sudden apparition—a tottering snow-covered figure, battered but undoubtedly alive. They rushed up to greet him and Milledge carried out a thorough medical examination only to find nothing broken and no major injury—merely shock and bruises. How this man survived such an experience is a mystery to all of us. Milledge was glad to see the last of the men off the col slopes and know that the mountain difficulties were now completely behind the expedition. Makalu was releasing its hold with reluctance.

With our departure for Kathmandu fast approaching we were invited to a number of farewells in the Sherpas' homes. One of these was with our sirdar, Dawa Tenzing, in his comfortable house at Thyangboche. After the formal drinking of tea and *rakshi* we had a sumptuous repast of boiled potatoes, rice, and curried stew, followed by a dessert of curds, *tsampa*, and sugar. It was a convivial occasion and, mellowed by the *rakshi* and food plus the pleasure of having us in his home, Dawa Tenzing

gave us an answer to a question that had been puzzling me for
some time.

It had all started in the Barun when Dawa had come down
to my rest camp at 15,000 feet. Soon after our arrival one of the
Sherpas, searching the rocky slopes above us for firewood, discovered a cave hidden behind a huge rock. Investigation of this
cave uncovered a store of Tibetan rugs, blankets, furs, and most
important of all, a sacred Tibetan book. Who had left this here
we didn't know, but our Sherpas considered that it must belong
to a lama escaping by this difficult route from Chinese oppression
in Tibet.

Dawa Tenzing, a competent Tibetan scholar for a lay Buddhist, commenced reading the book and became terribly excited
and engrossed by it. So much so that he set to work to copy its
Tibetan characters laboriously into an exercise book. For three
whole days he sat cross-legged in camp, writing. To our inquiries
as to the nature of this work he would only say that it was
sacred and that he wished first to show it to the head lama of
Thyangboche for his judgment and advice. On our departure
from this Barun Camp the Sherpas returned all their findings to
the secret cave and left it as before. Only Dawa Tenzing's
greatly treasured notebook traveled on with us to Thyangboche.

And now Dawa told us the story of the Sacred Village of Guru
Rimpoche—for this is what the book was about.

Guru Rimpoche was the great sage who brought Buddhism
to much of eastern Nepal and Tibet. A tremendous and hardy
traveler, he covered these countries when tracks were almost
nonexistent, sustained, the Sherpas believe, by the warmth and
fire of his great spirituality. One of the legends surrounding his
life was that he had created a spiritual Shangri-La, a Sacred
Village where those who had been closest to him could live in
peace for all eternity. Our Sherpas believed that the Sacred
Village was somewhere in the direction of the Barun Valley but
was invisible to the eyes of the ordinary man. Only a very holy
lama could hope to see it or, under a few rare circumstances, a
good man in the company of a holy lama. Even Dawa himself,
a man who had given all his considerable possessions to endow
the monastery, did not believe that he would be qualified for
such a vision. "I have sinned too much in my life! Perhaps in
another thousand lives I will be given a glimpse."

Dawa Tenzing went on to tell us that the book described the

79. *Ice pinnacle on way to Camp II on Makalu.*

80. *View from near Makalu Col at 24,000 feet. The tents of Camp IV (23,000 feet) can be seen in middle of picture.*